FAILURES IN PSYCHOANALYTIC TREATMENT

FAILURES IN PSYCHOANALYTIC TREATMENT

Editors

Joseph Reppen, Ph.D.

Martin A. Schulman, Ph.D.

IPBOOKS.net
International Psychoanalytic Books

International Psychoanalytic Books (IPBooks)
New York • http://www.IPBooks.net

Table of Contents

For Marty Schulman,
my late coeditor who, for 15 years,
edited the brilliant and successful
Psychoanalytic Review
and was good friend to me.

Table of Contents

Contributors

Emanuel Berman, Ph.D., Member, Israel Psychoanalytic Society; Associate Professor of Psychology, University of Haifa; International Editor, *Psychoanalytic Dialogues*; Clinical Professor, New York University Post-Doctoral Program in Psychoanalysis and Psychology.

Augusto Escribens, Ph.D., Professor of Linguistics, San Marcos University, Lima; Member and Scientific Secretary, Peru Psychoanalytic Society.

R. D. Hinshelwood, M.D., Member, British Psycho-Analytical Society; Professor, Centre for Psychoanalytic Studies, University of Essex; Former Clinical Director, Cassel Hospital; author of *Clinical Klein: From Theory to Practice* and *A Dictionary of Kleinian Thought*.

Marvin Hyman, Ph.D., Past President, Division of Psychoanalysis, American Psychological Association; coauthor of *Resolution of Inner Conflict: An Introduction to Psychoanalytic Therapy*.

José Américo Junqueira de Mattos, M.D., Member, Brazilian Psychoanalytic Society of Sao Paulo; President, Ribeirao Preto Study Group of Psychoanalysis.

W. W. Meissner, S.J., M.D., University Professor of Psychoanalysis, Boston College; member, Boston Psychoanalytic Society; former Clinical Professor of Psychiatry, Harvard

Medical School; author of twenty-four books including *Psychoanalytic and Religious Experience, Psychotherapy and the Paranoid Process, Ignatius of Loyola: The Psychology of a Saint.*

Cecilio Paniagua, M.D., Sc.D., Member, Madrid Psychoanalytical Association and American Psychoanalytic Association; former Clinical Assistant Professor, Department of Psychiatry, Georgetown University, Washington, D.C.

Ann-Louise S. Silver, M.D., was a member of the medical staff of Chestnut Lodge and Chestnut Lodge/CPC for twenty-five years. She is an Adjunct Professor of Psychiatry at the Uniformed Services University of the Health Sciences, and on the faculties of the Washington Psychoanalytic Institute, the Washington School of Psychiatry, and the Walter Reed Army Medical Center. She is a past president of the American Academy of Psychoanalysis and leads the United States Chapter of the International Society for the Psychological Treatments of the Schizophrenias and Other Psychoses. She is in private practice of psychiatry and psychoanalysis in Rockville, Maryland and in Columbia, Maryland where she heads the Columbia Academy of Psychodynamics.

Alan Z. Skolnikoff, M.D., Member, San Francisco Psychoanalytic Society; Associate Clinical Professor, Department of Psychiatry, University of California–San Francisco; coauthor of *Does Psychoanalysis Work?*

Johanna Krout Tabin, Ph.D., Member, Chicago Center for Psychoanalysis and Division of Psychoanalysis, American Psychological Association; author of *On the Way to Self: Ego and Early Oedipal Development.*

Stuart W. Twemlow, M.D., Member, Topeka Psychoanalytic Society; Clinical Professor of Psychiatry, University of Kansas School of Medicine; coeditor of *Journal of Applied Psychoanalytic Studies.*

Judith E. Vida, M.D., Member, Institute of Contemporary Psychoanalysis; member, American Psychoanalytic Association; member, Sándor Ferenczi Society; Professor of Psychiatry, University of Southern California.

Robert S. Wallerstein, M.D., Emeritus Professor of Psychiatry and Former Chair, Department of Psychiatry, University of California, San Francisco School of Medicine; member, San

Francisco Psychoanalytic Society; former President, American Psychoanalytic Association and the International Psychoanalytical Association; author, coauthor, or editor of eighteen books including *Forty-Two Lives in Treatment: A Study of Psychoanalysis and Psychotherapy* and *The Talking Cures: Psychoanalyses and the Psychotherapies.*

Introduction

JOSEPH REPPEN, PH.D.
MARTIN A. SCHULMAN, PH.D.

> *Instead of an enquiry into how a cure by analysis comes about (a matter which I think has been sufficiently elucidated) the question should be asked of what are the obstacles that stand in the way of such a cure [Freud, 1937, p. 221].*

Analysts frequently discuss but rarely write about their clinical failures, even though all analysts have experienced failures. Oberndorf (1948) stated, "the goal which the patient aims to attain through treatment does not always coincide with that which the psychoanalyst hopes to achieve and neither of these estimates may correspond to that which the patient's family or friends would consider a desirable outcome" (p. 14). We must add a caveat to Oberndorf's statement. The term *psychoanalyst* has always reflected individual differences among practitioners. It is not, however, a unitary concept, either theoretically or therapeutically. What holds for each and every one of the perspectives and models that define contemporary psychoanalysis is a dialectical unity of opposites. We cannot discuss "failure" without also defining "success." The evolving history of how psychoanalysis views success or failure would require a book-length treatise. We shall, therefore, present a cursory overview of historical trends, necessarily omitting many important contributions.

Ferenczi (1927) posited two factors as prerequisite for a successful analysis. The first was the necessity for a patient to distinguish reality from fantasy; that is, the ability to resolve the transference neurosis and to shift transference wishes from the analyst as a source of gratification to the world at large.

Ferenczi stated a second necessity: "Every male patient must attain a feeling of equality in relation to the physician as a sign that he has overcome his fear of castration; every female patient, if her neurosis is to be regarded as fully disposed of, must have got rid of her masculinity complex, and must emotionally accept without a trace of resentment the implications of her female role" (p. 84). This requirement meant the resolution of the oedipal conflict with the pain and freedom inherent in this ubiquitous human drama.

Freud's conceptualizations of "success" were closely tied to "models of the mind" (Sandler, Holder, Dare, and Dreher, 1997), prevalent during the theoretically diverse phases of his writing and thus evolved over time. During the earliest phase of trauma theory, he envisioned success as the synthesis of the ideational components of forgotten events with their affective core. During the topographic phase of theory formation the therapeutic aim was to make the unconscious conscious through interpretation and (re)construction. The structural/ego phase of Freud's theorizing, a model still prevalent today, views successful treatment with the dictum: "The business of analysis is to secure the best possible psychological conditions for the functioning of the ego; when this has been done, analysis has accomplished its task" (Freud, 1937, p. 250).

Contemporary American psychoanalysts have extended Freud's idea to include "the elimination of symptoms and inhibitions, modifications in character structure, improvement in capability to initiate and sustain fruitful object relationships, increased ability to work productively and creatively. Further goals are increased self-knowledge and self-acceptance, including the realization that perfection is illusory and unattainable" (Moore and Fine, 1990, pp. 185–186).

Kleinians view success not so much in ego terms and functions but, more globally, as a movement from the paranoid–schizoid to the depressive position. Concomitant with this advance is the diminution of the use of primitive defenses, such as projective identification, and the development of the mourning process and the attempt at reparation.

For Winnicott (1960), success can be evidenced by the ascendancy of the "true self" as opposed to the "false self," and the development of play as evinced in the transitional space that characterizes the psychoanalytic encounter (1971). For Balint (1968), success is the establishment of a "new beginning," a rebirth with the joy and exuberance that accompanies it.

Kohut (1977) sees success as the continuation of the unfolding of the process of self-structuralization that is attained through the development of idealizing transferences and the activation of unfulfilled mirroring or idealized selfobject needs—a deficit rather than a conflict model.

This brief overview should make clear that the aims, and thus the definitions, of success are related to the views of the nature of the therapeutic process and the nature of human development posited by different schools within psychoanalysis. The concept of "failure" is directly linked to the baseline criteria of success. Ferenczi (1927), predating and inclusive of many of the views to follow, stated the two factors lead to failure: absence of competence and patience on the part of analysts, that is, a problem of technique; and failure by analysts to deal with the weak points of their own personality, that is, a problem of countertransference.

Freud (1937), particularly in "Analysis Terminable and Interminable," highlights a multiplicity of factors that can lead to a failed analysis. Most of these variables are derivative of the biological bedrock that underlies psychological structures. Freud specifically mentioned the age of the analysand (50 being the cutoff point), adhesiveness as well as hypermotility of the libido, the negative therapeutic reaction, congenital weakness of the ego, intense early trauma, unconscious guilt, the female's unwillingness to resolve penis envy, the male's inability to confront his passivity toward another male, and, perhaps most important, the existence of the death instinct. Analysts' contributions to failure come from unresolved countertransference problems. In this seminal paper, Freud suggested a reanalysis by practitioners every five years.

Anna Freud (1969), extending the framework of ego psychology, noted that a contributory factor to failure and, simultaneously, a veiled allusion to Kleinian treatment, is the desire
to reconstruct the earliest preverbal phases of development
for which evidence is mere speculation. Anna Freud stated: "I
myself cannot help feeling doubtful about trying to advance
into the area of primary repression, i.e., to deal with processes
which, by nature, are totally different from the results of the
ego's defensive maneuvers with which we are familiar" (p.
147).

Object relations theory and self psychology shift the focus
for failure from the patient's resistances to the role of the
analyst in the therapeutic process. Along with problems of specific countertransferences unique to the history and personality of each analyst, Kohut saw as problematic the inability of
analysts to remain attuned to their patients' inner world
through the use of introspection and empathy. In other words,
empathic failures are seen as the main source of therapeutic
failure.

Contemporary relational theorists, intersubjectivists, post-
modernists, social constructivists, as well as some self psychologists and object relations theorists view failure as grounded in
a statement by Racker (1968): Analysis is "an interaction between two personalities, in both of which the ego is under
pressure from the id, the superego, and the external world;
each personality has its internal and external dependencies,
anxieties, and pathological defenses; each is also a child with
his internal parents; and each of these whole personalities—that of the analysand and that of the analyst—responds
to every event of the psychoanalytic situation" (p. 132). Analysis is, therefore, not only a dyadic process; for success or failure,
the "fit" between analyst and analysand is paramount.

When we asked the contributors to this volume to be forthcoming and courageous in discussing examples of what they
perceive as failed cases, we requested that they not write about
cases that might have come to a less than desirable end as a
result of ethical failures or external events, such as death, organic incapacitation, or physical relocations related to job or
career. Our contributors represent a wide range of views within

contemporary psychoanalysis and they view failure from many different vantage points. In most cases what is emphasized is the analytic ego ideal, a component of our work ego. Their contributions lead us to conclude that our contributors are often too critical of themselves. Reflecting a contemporary spirit of openness, they seem too willing to blame themselves, and at times downplay the difficulty of working with the patients they write about. Their concepts of failure are highly individualized, which seems fitting for a discipline that is noted for its ambiguity and subjectivity.

Marvin Hyuman, at one end of a spectrum, questions the concept of failure. For him, the term is a residue of the medical model and obfuscates the fact that psychoanalysis is a form of self-exploration and self-inquiry, independent of so-called "scientific" criteria. Judith Vida also sees failure as a limited concept since growth does occur in the case presented, even if, by some analytic standards, it might be viewed as a failure. The adage, "the operation was a success but the patient died," is turned on its head—"the patient succeeded but the analysis failed"—leads us to repeat Oberndorf's (1948) observation as to whether our standards or the patient's should be paramount.

The other end of the spectrum is highlighted by Ann-Louise Silver's chapter on the failure of the institutional treatment of schizophrenics by psychoanalysis, which was a frustrating yet poignant experience for those involved. The views of our other contributors reside somewhere in between these extremes. Stuart W. Twemlow and Cecilio Paniagua discuss narcissistic elements as crucial to failure. Johanna Krout Tabin explores deeper level pathology that appears in serial or repeated failures, and Robert S. Wallerstein reconsiders a case from early in his career in a new light, that of failure. W. W. Meissner's chapter emphasizes the inability of his patient to truly engage and the patient's sexual panic that underlay that resistance. Alan Z. Skolnikoff demonstrates how the use of reality can become a resistance to the deepening of the analytic process.

Focusing on the analyst's contribution to the process, R. D. Hinshelwood, from a contemporary Kleinian perspective, discusses countertransference issues as directly related to failure.

In a similar vein, José Américo Junqueira de Mattos, presenting
a frame derived from Bion's ideas, elucidates how the analyst's
inability to follow the dictum of "neither memory nor desire"
becomes a problem for treatment. Augusto Escribens intro-
duces the concept of subjective theories of pathogenesis and
of cure. He demonstrates how discordance, and at times consonance between analyst and patient can short circuit the analytic
process. Emanuel Berman, from a relational–intersubjective
position, discusses the concept of "fit" between analyst and
patient and the need to understand the transference–countertransference dynamic. For Berman, this is the one constant in
the unfolding of every analysis.

The contributors leave no doubt that psychoanalysis is happily inhabited by thoughtful, caring, and open practitioners
who, regardless of societal and cultural emphases on immedi-
acy and externalization, see the challenge and the need to
understand self and others. Psychoanalysis is alive and well in
their hands.

References

Balint, M. (1968), *The Basic Fault: Therapeutic Aspects of Regression*.
London: Tavistock.
Ferenczi, S. (1927), The problem of termination in analysis. In: *Final
Contribution to the Problems and Methods of Psychoanalysis*. London:
Hogarth Press, 1955, pp. 77–86.
Freud, A. (1969), Difficulties in the path of psychoanalysis. In: *Writ-
ings of Anna Freud*, Vol. 7. New York: International Universities
Press, 1971, pp. 124–156.
Freud, S. (1937), Analysis terminable and interminable. *Standard Edi-
tion*, 23:209–253. London: Hogarth Press, 1964.
Kohut, H. (1977), *Restoration of the Self*. New York: International Uni-
versities Press.
Moore, B. E., & Fine, B. D., Eds. (1990), *Psychoanalytic Terms and
Concepts*. New Haven, CT: Yale University Press.
Obendorf, C. P. (1948), Failures with psychoanalytic therapy. In: *Fail-
ures in Psychiatric Treatment*, ed. P. Hoch. New York: Grune &
Stratton, pp. 10–21.
Racker, H. (1968), *Transference and Countertransference*. London:
Maresfield Library.

Sandler, J., Holder, A., Dare, C., & Dreher, A. U. (1997), *Freud's Models of the Mind*. Madison, CT: International Universities Press.

Winnicott, D. W. (1960), Ego distortion in terms of true and false self. In: *The Maturational Processes and the Facilitating Environment*. New York: International Universities Press, 1965, pp. 140–152.

———— (1971), *Playing and Reality*. New York: Basic Books.

Failures in Psychoanalytic Treatment: An Oxymoron

Marvin Hyman, Ph.D.

Over the past century, psychoanalysis has evolved into many different theoretical and technical forms. Indeed, it would be more accurate to speak of many different psychoanalyses rather than assume psychoanalysis is a single, uniform movement. Any discussion of an aspect of psychoanalysis, such as "failures in psychoanalytic treatment," must begin, therefore, with a specification of the psychoanalytic viewpoint from which the aspect is being considered. As is usually the case, in this discussion the term *psychoanalysis* will refer only to the viewpoint described and held here.

Psychoanalytic Treatment and Psychic Reality

Psychoanalytic treatment can only take place within a context of psychic reality. In order to be able to listen to the associations of the analysand as associations rather than as descriptions of life events and experiences, the analyst must believe that the analysand is attempting to communicate his or her psychic reality through the linguistic forms of the associative language. For example, the analyst listening to an analysand say repeatedly, "I do not hate my mother," would hear that, in that analysand's psychic reality, just the opposite is true. Also, for the purposes of the analysis, the analyst does not have to assume that the analysand does or does not have a mother, only that the analysand is attempting to report a psychical experience involving the concept of mother. The statements of the analysand, therefore, have to be heard as though they are another language; one which has continuously to be translated into the language of the unconscious.

The psychic reality of the analyst is also continually present in psychoanalytic therapy. It is a given of the method that the analyst "hears" communications from the analysand's unconscious through both his or her conscious and unconscious perceptions. Since there is no way of proving that what the analyst hears is what the analysand said, it is crucial to recognize that the analyst's conscious and unconscious subjectivity needs always to be monitored, particularly when the analyst experiences an untoward or unexpected reaction in the situation. Such experiences as boredom, anger, arousal, need to be recognized as signaling that the analyst's psychic reality is interacting with the analysand's, and can thus be an important source of information in the analytic work.

Psychoanalytic treatment takes place in an atmosphere of artificiality. Only in the most superficial sense does it resemble a conversation or other social reality. From the outset, the analyst and analysand agree that this artificial situation will obtain in the analytic process. The analysand agrees in the interest of the work, which has to be done, and which requires the assistance of the adopted synthetic situation. So, for example, the participants understand why the analysand lies on a couch, why the analyst does not answer questions, why the analyst engages in only a minimum of social interaction and conversation, and why the analyst tries to minimize the occurrence of social interactions outside of the analysis. They both recognize that the artificiality exists in the service of the psychoanalytic method and for the purpose of enabling the participants to recognize as clearly as possible the psychic reality of the partners in the endeavor.

Success and failure in psychoanalytic treatment are specific aspects of the psychic reality of the psychoanalytic situation. What is success in the psychic reality of the analyst may be failure in the psychic reality of the analysand, and vice versa. Moreover, the psychic reality of an observer or discussant of a therapy might well differ from that of one or both the participants in the analysis. In sum, the perception of success or failure in psychoanalytic therapy is so subjective that one might doubt whether such phenomena can logically be discussed as a part of or relevant to the undertaking. However, if one decides to consider success or failure, then one has to address as many as possible of the factors that enter into the subjective perceptions of those involved.

The *Oxford English Dictionary* (1933) defines the word *failure* as "a failure to occur, be performed or be produced; an omitting to perform something due or required." An alternative definition is given as "the fact of failing to effect one's purpose; want of success." From these definitions, and others like them, it is clear that success and failure have everything to do with expectations and with the nonfulfillment of those expectations. Any discussion of failure in psychoanalytic therapy, then, must begin with a consideration of the expectations of those involved and those expectations that are conceived to be part of the enterprise.

Psychoanalytic Therapy and the Medical Model

For most analysts, so-called failures in psychoanalytic therapy have had to do with their expectations of the outcome of the analysis (e.g, Powell, 1994; Bloom, 1997; Bergmann, 1997). Originally and continuously defined as a medical procedure, psychoanalysis has shared the epistemological and definitional heritage of medicine. In addition to borrowing the terminology of medicine (e.g., diagnosis, treatment, pathology, cure), psychoanalysis has adopted the conceptual schema of medicine.

A crucial and defining element in this schema is the linear thinking that characterizes the relationships between diagnosis and treatment, treatment and cure, process and outcome, symptom and pathology, pathology and etiology, and, most importantly, between cause and effect. Those who see psychoanalysis as a medical or health-care procedure consider it, therefore, as a treatment that is expected to lead to a cure of an illness.

Psychoanalysis has long been a captive of this linear, medicalized way of thinking, despite the fact that one of the essential foci of the analytic method has been just the opposite; that is, the *discontinuities* between effect and cause, which are the focus of the analyzing process, regardless of the name or label that may be applied to any one of them.

When an analysand provides a slip of the tongue while associating (e.g., saying "him" instead of "her" or "father" instead of "husband"), most analysts do not view this as a psychopathological manifestation or as a product of a disease process. Rather, an analyst would note that there is a discontinuity in that the conscious intention (cause) of the analysand to say "her" or "husband" was seemingly opposite to the word that was vocalized (effect). Applying the principle of "If one said it one meant it," the analyst would then recognize that the discontinuity was a product of *unconscious* motivation and that by reasoning from effect to cause (rather than from cause to effect) one could discern that what was said was unconsciously intended. In this fashion, the analyst and analysand could discover the unconscious motivation and, equally important, the verbalization could be recognized as unconsciously produced by the analysand as a contribution to the work of the analysis (i.e., doing what is necessary to learn about that motivation). The acquisition of such knowledge of unconscious motivation is the goal of the psychoanalytic work with the justifiable expectation that such learning will take place. In no way, however, can this be considered the equivalent of cure or even the amelioration of a pathological condition. Further, it does not follow that learning and sharing knowledge of unconscious manifestations lead to behavioral change or that they should be expected to. To be sure, the analytic work includes continuing curiosity about whatever "consequences" do or do not accompany the analytic process; but curiosity is distinctly different from expectations of specific consequences.

From the psychoanalytic point of view, such everyday phenomena as slips of the tongue are identical to the more dramatic manifestations of neuroses and psychoses, which have been given the label *symptoms* (e.g., hysterical paralyses, obsessions, hallucinations, and delusions). In the analyzing process, however, symptoms have to be viewed as the discontinuities reflective of unconscious motivation that can be discovered and understood by the participants in the process. Viewing "symptoms" as the linear effect caused by a disease process (e.g., a disorder of brain chemistry) is antithetical to the alternative conceptualization of the psychoanalytic enterprise. Yet, as a result of its medical heritage, psychoanalysis is expected, by society and by some of its practitioners, to be a *treatment* for various *pathologies*, including slips of the pen, of the tongue, of the memory, dreams, as well as the symptoms of the so-called neuroses and psychoses. And, if psychoanalysis chooses to continue to try to be a part of the medical domain, then it has to recognize that it will be expected to demonstrate *cures* for these pathologies, an expectation that it cannot fulfill. Carried to its absurd conclusion, psychoanalysts will be and are expected to cure dreaming and slips as well as delusions and obsessions.

The understanding of the phenomena produced by unconscious motives constitutes a unique contribution of psychoanalysis to the knowledge of the human condition; it does not, however, further in any way the curative expectations of the society and those members of the professional community who believe it should do so. Moreover, knowledge of the psychoanalytic method does not endow the practitioner with the wherewithal to effect change, behavioral or otherwise, or compel it from the analysand.

When an analysand consults an analyst, he or she often brings to the consultation statements of complaint or distress. For example, such statements might include reports of suicidal ideation or reports of intentions to act upon such thoughts. Upon hearing such statements, and within his or her psychic reality, the analyst might choose to consider them as veridical reports of experiences of the person or intentions to act. Alternatively, the analyst might choose to consider them as thoughts that have come to the mind of the individual for the purpose of conveying the person's unconscious motivations, which is an entirely different psychic reality.

Should the analyst choose to adopt the first listening stance, then the analyst will have to go beyond the analyzing effort with multiple, nonanalytic consequences. Included in those consequences could be informing others of the individual's status as a danger to himself or herself; arranging to have the intervention of a third party who would exercise managerial control over the analysand's life; taking steps to introduce extra-analytic interventions into the situation, such as prescribing medications or escorting the person to the hospital. In all of these actions, the analyst is no longer acting as an analyst since she would not be analyzing; she would be curing the patient, saving a life, or ameliorating a self-destructive tendency. Certainly, these actions will have an effect upon the way in which the analysand perceives the analyst and the analysis.

If, on the other hand, the analyst chooses to adopt the second listening stance, then the analyst would analyze the reports of the person by listening to them in the context of the other associations, formulating the psychodynamic and transference significance of both the content of the statements and of their appearance at this moment in the analytic enterprise, and communicating that formulation for the consideration of the analysand. Nothing more is required by the analytic method. Further, if the analyst felt inclined to do something other than analyze, it would be an indication of the empathic responding on the analyst's part; something to be examined rather than acted upon. What the analysand does with the observations made within the analysis, as these consequences are perceived individually by the participants, can only be the responsibility of the analysand.

When psychoanalysts are functioning as analysts, they subscribe, implicitly or explicitly, to the ethical position that the analysand is a competent individual, capable of assuming responsibility for his or her life, notwithstanding the experiences that have led that person to seek analysis. It is demeaning of the analysand, therefore, for the analyst to do anything other than analyze, however humane that anything may be. The analytic enterprise requires the analyst to adopt the position and the psychic reality that analysands are capable of living their lives the way they consciously want to, and, if they are not doing so, it is a matter to be explored in the analysis as an unconsciously motivated intention. If individuals are perceived as incapable of so living their lives, then the analyst has to conclude they need a guardian rather than an analyst. If the analyst chooses at that point to function as a guardian, the fact that he or she is an analyst does not make the activity into an analysis.

From a medical point of view, a patient is considered not to be responsible for the illness or for its amelioration (other than by following doctor's orders and prescriptions). The diagnosis and treatment are, ethically and pragmatically, the responsibility of the health-care provider. Accordingly, the practitioner assumes responsibility if the diagnosis is in error or if the treatment does not succeed, that is, conform to the practitioner's expectations. In the psychoanalytic situation, in contrast, the only responsibility the practitioner can assume is for his or her portion of the analyzing work. Whatever consequences ensue for the analysand from the analytic work is, and has to be, the responsibility of the analysand.

For those who perceive psychoanalysis to be a health-care or medical procedure, including many of those who consult a psychoanalyst as well as most of the public who do not consult one, the psychic expectation, consciously and unconsciously (via transferences), is that the analyst will assume responsibility for the individual who seeks the consultation as well as for that individual's life. All that the consultee has to do is remain passive and enjoy the relief from subjective distress and other benefits that the benevolent health-care provider will bestow. Thus, while the psychic reality of the analysand may require this transference-determined perception of the analyst as omnipotent and omniscient (as well as maternally and paternally benevolent), it is always a manifestation to be analyzed rather than acted upon, even by analysts whose psychic reality is in agreement with the analysand's.

The characterization of psychoanalysis as a medical treatment leads to the ultimate and unhappy conclusion that, as such, it is endless, subjective, without standards or criteria of success, and inadequate as a treatment. One rarely hears it argued that, because these conclusions are correct, it would justify recognizing that psychoanalysis is not a medical procedure and therefore not subject to the epistemological constraints of medical conceptualization. Psychoanalytic treatment is not a medical procedure whose lack of value has been demonstrated; it is a procedure outside of medicine and, therefore, has to be judged by other criteria.

Psychoanalytic Treatment and Change

Most analysts and analysands expect that psychoanalytic treatment, even if not viewed as a medical procedure that will cure symptoms and pathological conditions, will result in noteworthy changes in the analysand. The specific expectations are as varied in number and form as those who hold them. These so-called positive expectations include relief from subjective distress, psychically and behaviorally altered functioning, improvement in interpersonal relations, disappearance of symptoms, correction of undesirable character traits, and greater happiness with oneself and with one's life. The list is, of course, endless, but those expectations noted here illustrate that expectations for changes ensuing from psychoanalytic treatment include manifestations that need not be viewed in the linear, cause-and-effect mode utilized by medicine. Therefore, if such changes are perceived, it is inconsistent and illogical to consider them as improvements, except in the psychic reality of the one making the judgment. The alternative is to consider them only as changes perceived by one or both of the participants without any requirement that the perceived changes be judged as real. Logical considerations notwithstanding, the expectation of positive change requires that the psychoanalytic treatment be considered a failure if such change is not perceived or experienced.

How should these expected changes be evaluated—and by whom? An analyst might perceive an analysand as significantly different during and after the analysis. Can this perception be "validated"? Does the analysand have to agree with the analyst's perceptions of change? Can "outside" observers validly judge whether changes have occurred and what they are? Can psychoanalytic treatment be empirically validated, and how?

A substantial segment of the professional community believes that questions such as these can and need to be answered, and that it has been a failure of psychoanalysis that this has not already taken place. In contrast to that position, it is argued here that the study of such questions, and the epistemological base from which they derive, illustrates that they cannot be answered because of the very nature of the psychoanalytic process and the purposes for which it is undertaken. Questions such as these are inapplicable because they posit a set of assumptions that are antithetical to those inherent in the psychoanalytic treatment being considered here.

Negative Therapeutic Reactions

Psychoanalytic therapists have labeled changes in an unexpected and undesired direction as negative therapeutic reactions. Eidelberg (1968) defines the phenomenon in this way: "Negative therapeutic reactions denotes an increase in neurotic behavior after an improvement has been derived from analytic treatment" (p. 253). Again, the emphasis is upon judgments that derive from the expectations and perceptions of the evaluator. Thus, the terminology explicit in the definition of negative therapeutic reaction, such as "increase," "neurotic behavior," and "improvement," all reflect a particular value system, and implicitly, the psychic reality of whomever uses the concepts and makes the judgment of their presence in an analysis. Further, they reflect the belief that what is perceived is what exists within the analysand, a stance that contradicts the neutrality of judgment that is necessary for listening analytically to the associations of the analysand.

It is an interesting paradox that negative therapeutic reactions are approached in most psychoanalytic discussions as the product of the psychodynamics of the analysand. Suggestions

that have been offered for the phenomenon when it is perceived include: masochistic character traits requiring the analysand to suffer; guilt that is alleviated by torment; anxiety at the
possibility of separation from the analyst, which can be as-
suaged by the fantasy that feeling worse will insure the continued involvement of the analyst. The paradox lies in viewing
negative therapeutic reactions as akin to failure while at the
same time attributing them to the essential psychodynamics of
unconscious mental life.

Success and Failure in Psychoanalytic Treatment

When psychoanalysis was in its adolescence, its adherents held
rather grandiose views of its potential as a treatment. It was
lauded as a replacement for the limited and somewhat mecha-
nistic approaches of those who previously sought to alleviate
the so-called disturbances of emotional life. Periodically during
the past hundred years, it has been declared dead and bur-
ied—and yet it continued to survive and even thrive. Now,
however, the psychoanalytic enterprise seems in great danger.
Regardless of which of the many forms of psychoanalysis one
considers, it is in essence a procedure which emphasizes the
exploration of the inner life of people as a means of addressing
whatever conscious (and unconscious) issues are a part of their
lives. The procedure has fallen out of favor, however, a result
in large part of ignorance about what it is and the many criticisms that have been made of it. Among those criticisms are
accusations that it shows no results, it is expensive and time
consuming, and it is based upon an invalid theory. It seems
ironic that any discussion of failures in psychoanalytic treatment must include a discussion of the impending failure of
the psychoanalytic enterprise.

It would be fair to say that psychoanalysis has not lived up
to the expectations that people had of it. The primary expectation has been that it would be curative. Psychoanalysis, however, has never cured anybody. Those who have experienced
being cured by psychoanalysis have, lurking in the back of their

(conscious) minds, the uncomfortable feeling that they have cured themselves. For many others who have participated in psychoanalytic treatment, the experience has been that they feel they are different, even though they may be hard put to describe how they are different or how it came about. Frequently, they are convinced that in whatever way they are different, the analyst and the analysis had nothing to do with it. And for still others, the experience has been that they have learned a good deal about their unconscious motives, but they are still waiting for that experience to make them better in whatever way they define that outcome.

Notwithstanding the impossibility of demonstrating that analysis is curative, the analytic community continues to support, if not promulgate, the idea that it is. That idea, a product of a way of thinking rather than the result of empirical proof, seems to have a life of its own. One reason that this may be so entails the discomfort that accompanies an encounter with the startling world of psychic reality. Most people label such encounters as "crazy," and, if they are of any duration, seek out some means of making the experience go away. In other words, many people come to psychoanalysis in order to be cured of their unconscious mental life. Parenthetically, it is a bonus that the analysis, for many, enables them to live comfortably with their unconscious mental function and to enjoy and even be amused by its cleverness and ingenuity. We all know about jokes and their relation to the unconscious; in analysis the analysand and analyst can come to appreciate that relation.

Success in psychoanalytic treatment does not result in the expunging of the unconscious. After analysis, people still dream, still make slips, still have so-called symptoms and character traits. Those who are seen as sows' ears are not changed into silk purses in the eyes of those who interact with them. For those who enter analysis or think about the endeavor with the grandiose expectation that they will emerge as paragons of mental health (whatever that is), will be disappointed and may conclude that the analysis has been a failure. They are the victims of their own unfilled expectations, and therefore unable to appreciate whatever the analytic situation has been for them.

Analysts have impossible expectations of analytic treatment just as analysands do. Because they think in terms of cause and effect, because they are optimistic, because they have analytic ambitions, and because they have unconscious motives for being in the field, analysts think in terms of success and failure. They writer papers describing what they believe have been successful and unsuccessful analyses. They develop criteria for evaluating the outcome of the analyses in which they participate; they ponder the factors which they believe influence such outcomes; they write chapters in books on the subject of failures in psychoanalytic treatment. Often, the psychodynamics of the analysand (as the analyst conceives them; not as they "exist" in the analysand's unconscious) are described elaborately as causal to the perceived outcome of the analysis. Incidentally, psychodynamic explanations are offered most frequently in cases that have been labeled failures; they rarely play a part in discussions of "successful" analytic treatments.

Expectations of success and failure in psychoanalytic treatment are the products of the unconscious psychodynamics of those who have such expectations. Indeed, one might say that just as hysterics "suffer" from reminiscences, psychoanalysts suffer from expectations. The rationalizations mustered to justify such expectations require that one subscribe consciously to a philosophy and way of thinking that is essentially antipsychoanalytic.

Assessing Psychoanalytic Treatment

Oberndorf (1948) cites a statement of Ernest Jones regarding the definition of psychoanalysis. "As Ernest Jones says in his recent Valedictory Address (1946): 'We cannot do better than follow Freud's own definition. Psychoanalysis is simply the study of mental process of which we are unaware, of what, for the sake of brevity, we call the unconscious, by the free association technique of analyzing the unobservable phenomena of transference and resistance'" (p. 14). This statement is noteworthy as much for what it does not say as for what it does—nowhere is there mention of cure, improvement, amelioration, or outcome. All that defines psychoanalysis in the

statement is the *process* that is described. In assessing psychoanalytic treatment, all that has to be considered is the process;
outcome has to do only with the subjective fantasies of those
who need such fantasies to fulfill the unconscious motives in
that part of their psychic reality they call psychoanalysis.

The only purpose of analysis is analyzing (i.e., studying the
mental process of which the analysand is unaware), but about
which the analysand informs us through the free associations
he or she produces. If analyzing, as just defined, takes place,
then the analysis cannot be a failure. The analyst need not
expect a particular outcome of the effort because that is the
responsibility only of the analysand. Even in the matter of the
psychoanalytic process itself, the analyst need not have expectations, for analyzing includes discovering anew in each analysis
the defining elements of the psychoanalytic theory and
process.

In order to function effectively in the analytic situation, the
analyst has to enter it without memory or desire. To expect
that the analysand will improve or change or to expect that
one will encounter transference or resistance in the analytic
hour or in the overall treatment, is to bring into play those
elements of desire that are likely to distort the listening and
formulating process. In the purely technical sense, the analyst
has only to be concerned with the analysis and not with the
analysand. The analysand, as an always capable individual, will
look out for him- or herself.

As a partner in the analytic treatment process, the analysand
is free to have all sorts of expectations in and about the process
and outcome. It is helpful if the analysand understands that
those expectations, when voiced, will be treated as associations,
as thoughts that have come to mind in order to communicate
in an analytic fashion whatever unconscious content and process is currently available and seeking expression. It is also helpful if the analysis is recommended to the prospective analysand
after there has been some demonstration of the operation of
unconscious process, for then it would be understandable that
the analyst suggests that it might be advantageous for the analysand to know and understand the hidden (i.e., unconscious)

motives and processes. This principle entails the value judgment that it is advantageous to know one's hidden motives so that one is not taken unawares when those motives make their appearance as discontinuities in one's life. At the very least, that knowledge provides the analysand with the choice of recognizing such discontinuities as a part of psychic life rather than some mysterious, powerful, malignant force taking control of it.

On Redefining Psychoanalytic Treatment

If an individual attends a university for four years, majoring in ancient history, and then, after graduation makes a career of being a ski instructor, we do not consider that his education has been a failure. In an identical fashion, if an individual spends a number of years in analysis and yet appears to have chosen not to make use of the insights thus obtained, we cannot consider the analysis a failure. If the individual evaluating that analysis experiences disappointment at that outcome then the appropriate course is to analyze the unconscious factors in the choice made by the analysand and the disappointment experienced by the evaluator. To take other judgmental actions beyond those is irrational in that it is oxymoronic to link the subjective character of psychoanalysis with the objective nature of linear, cause-and-effect judgments.

Since psychoanalysis devotes itself to the study of unconscious content and process, and to the psychic reality in which they are encountered, it is radically different from medicine and other of the domains of science. Rather than continuing to struggle to be accepted as a medical discipline for the dubious benefits thus conveyed, psychoanalysis would be better served by considering itself one of the intellectual disciplines devoted to the study of the human condition (e.g., the arts, history, and the humanities). By changing to this orientation, analysis could better accommodate, theoretically and clinically, to its subjective, relativistic, postmodern character. After all, Freud, by developing the concept of psychic reality and by depicting the unconscious as a sphere in which there is unlimited motility of cathexes, contributed substantially to a nonlinear view of the world. If, in the unconscious, anything can be represented by anything else to which it is cathectically linked, then within that psychic reality there can be no truth, no absolute certainty, no unanimity of meaning. In addition, if unconscious processes are ubiquitous in human existence and more pervasive than we let ourselves believe, then the absolute truth of conscious mental life is merely a comforting illusion that we use to mitigate the anxiety aroused when we let ourselves realize how tenuous is the certainty about ourselves, others, and the world as we would like it to be. Analysands develop a significant and essential appreciation that they alone are the source of their experiences and that others and the reactions of others are only figments of the analysand's perception. The one certainty that can come with analytic treatment is that one is one's own determiner of one's reality, certainly of one's psychic reality, and probably of the rest of the reality that one perceives. It is a significant way, this can be a substantial blessing, for if one is unhappy or distressed by the perceived actions of others, one can always change one's perceptions. Psychically, it is most helpful to be aware that one can change how and what one perceives in others and that one does not have to have others change in order for one to be content.

Psychically, change is omnipresent since we are continually changing our psychic reality in accordance with changes in our psychic motivation. We do this in our dreams and we do this in our life discontinuities by changing the unconscious cathectic representations as motivational demands require. To the extent that analysis enables us to accept change in ourselves, it should also enable us to accept change in our analysands, but on their terms rather than ours. Freed of the need to have our analysands change for the better, get well, improve, we can observe appreciatively the skill with which they resolve psychic conflict within themselves. We can conclude that while such resolutions of conflict may not be to our taste, it is important to keep our values out of the analyses in which we participate. If the resolutions of psychic conflict are too psychically expensive for an individual, that person is always free to explore alternatives in the analysis. As we all know, the "problems" that people bring to analysis are better viewed as solutions to psychic conflict that have become too costly in terms of their impact upon the person's life.

Human beings are always doing the best that they can for themselves psychically; in analysis they come to know that; as analysts, we ought also to know that; and when we do, we can stop going to work every day to stamp out mental disease. Instead, we can indulge ourselves in the joy of psychoanalyzing as we observe and appreciate the expertise with which our analysands live their psychic lives.

References

Bergmann, M. (1997), The Achilles heel of psychoanalytic technique. *Psychoanal. Psychol.*, 14:163–174.

Bloom, V. (1997), Interminable analysis? *J. Amer. Acad. Psychoanal.*, 25:313–316.

Eidelberg, L. (1968), *Encyclopedia of Psychoanalysis*. New York: Free Press.

Oberndorf, C. (1948), Failures with psychoanalytic therapy. In: *Failures in Psychiatric Treatment*, ed. P. Hoch. New York: Grune & Stratton, pp. 10–21.

Oxford English Dictionary (1933), "Failure" c.v.

Powell, A. (1994), Ending is for life. *Group Anal.*, 27:25–36.

2

The Indispensable "Difficult Event"

JUDITH E. VIDA, M.D.

> *It is as if the mind were a squeamish organ which refused to entertain difficult truths unless encouraged to do so by difficult events [Alain de Botton, 1998].*

To Gershon Molad (1999) we owe the valuable notion of "the effect of the door frame," the metaphorical door frame of thinking that "clinical space" is separate from "conference space"—a distinction between what happens in the privacy of the consulting room and what we allow ourselves to say to our colleagues. Molad holds that such a door frame is nothing but an illusion, "an illusional-mark, part of a packing box, which bounds the arrested development of the analyst" (p. 5). In the notion of the door frame I include the peculiar boundary with

Author's acknowledgment: Without the essential conversation of Gershon Molad, this could not have been written. As ever, the comments of G. W. Pigman III and Ernst Falzeder gave clarity.

which we tend to separate life in the consulting room from "real" life outside it. I will use what I say here about failure to place myself forever *outside* that door frame, which, though an illusion, is a harmful illusion (Barish and Vida, 1998). In any current condition of life and practice, I aspire to reach a state in which the part of myself that mediates "internal–clinical reality" and the part that mediates "external–social reality" become increasingly congruent (Molad, 1999). What I will take up in these pages is the contribution of clinical failures to the genesis of that aspiration.

The Analyst's Experience of Failure

What is "failure"? It is a part of all the analyst's relationships, not only clinical ones (remember: no door frame). Failure is failing to love, failing to hate, or failing to notice the difference. It is failing to go deep, and failing to take things at face value. There is failing to say enough and failing to keep quiet, as well as failing to wait and failing to jump in. In a purely internal context, we fail ourselves by failing to notice, failing to feel, failing to forget or to remember who we are and have been. Failure is what stops relating from being smooth, seamless, and unremarkable (not an exhaustive list).

In the analyst's closed-off private space, it can be that to fail is the most despicable of outcomes. To fail is excruciating. Either to reflect on having failed or to anticipate failure makes on the victim of a sadistic torturer. In the grip of the torturer, life is reduced to a limitless succession of failures. On the level of consciousness, it can feel like a battlefield in a war without end. Each day's survival is a miracle, an accident of fate. Each morning brings afresh the prospect of annihilation. How does one go on? The apt comparison is to the circumstance of a conscripted soldier: simply stated, there are no alternatives. Unconsciously, at every turn, there is the risk of discovery. When failure is a capital crime in the unconscious, execution awaits.

In our previous collaborative work, Samoan Barish and I described the dawning of our understanding, mediated by the above-mentioned despicable failures, that it is the operation of idealization, specifically an idealization of theory, that makes failure so venomous an experience in which to be caught. From Ferenzi (1932), we drew the astonishing, useful notion that ego indebtedness, the neglect of one's own requirements, can be every bit as much a source of guilt as neglect of responsibility for others. (A delayed clinical appreciation of this second source of guilt in both transference and countertransference is the subject of our continuing work.)

Ironically, idealization is often what draws us to the practice of psychoanalysis in the first place, a utopian longing (Berman, 2000). Idealization of theories, and of charismatic and powerful others, is the Sisyphean boulder that we carry out of our training and into our autonomous practices. Each "failure" threatens to increase the gap between ourselves and the idealized other(s) and creates a crisis to which we will respond in one of several ways. We could change ourselves internally, to resemble more and more completely those whom we have idealized, either crudely (by rote) or more elegantly (by discipleship); this is what constitutes *identification*. Or, we could dismantle the idealization. The most reliable means of doing this is through becoming more wholly, more trustingly ourselves, and in that form having an impact on the other, whom we will then see differently. This does not mean that nothing from the other is taken in; it is rather that what is taken in is transformed in a process of absorption and metabolism by the entire personality. This is also what Ferenczi (1909) and Abraham and Torok later (1972) referred to as *introjection*. I am regarding introjection as the process of authentic growth, as distinct from identification (and incorporation, for that matter). This application of the concept of introjection bears a striking resemblance to Symington's Inventory Model (1996). "Invention Model" is Symington's name for a radical personal pedagogy in which a psychotherapist creates an "intellectual structure" that uniquely fits his own "emotional shape" (p. 17).

The operation of a process recognizable as introjection in the development of the analyst was always referred to vaguely, if at all. Early on, Freud (1912) said that technique would have to suit the individuality of the analyst. Klauber's (1983) description of his personalized transformation as an analyst was a later rare exception. On the other hand, Heinz Kohut thought that it was identification with the internal contents of Freud's personality as purveyed in *The Interpretation of Dreams* (1900) that was the element of analytic training responsible for the creation of an analytic ego ideal and was also the essential basis of psychoanalytic group affiliations (1976).

Not until the long-delayed publication of Sandor Ferenczi's *Clinical Diary* (1988) was there an introjective model of substance. The *Diary* chronicles the gradual process of Ferenczi's internal emancipation from his discipleship of Freud, a discipleship that Ferenczi himself had done much to promote, subsuming his own creative strivings to serve Freud's program in the (ultimately vain) hope that Freud would reciprocate with not applause so much as deep understanding of Ferenczi's discoveries (Vida, 1999b). Ferenczi never did "mind being wrong" (Vida, 1999a). He disturbed his colleagues when he made the parapraxis of encouraging all analysts to "commit errors" when he had meant to say "confess errors." Ferenczi knew that analysts didn't need encouragement to commit errors because they all did, all the time—*And we still do.*

"Why do we tend to think that technique then was not so developed as it is today," ask Haynal and Falzeder, "as if today we had access to a definite and undoubted technique. . . . [O]ne can just as well say that analysts then were *aware* that all this is always a matter of *experimentation*" (1991, p. 11). "All in all still no universally applicable rules," wrote Ferenczi in the *Clinical Diary* (p. 157). Psychoanalysis as practiced today is still mediated by the personality (and what Molad calls "the autobiography") of the analyst, an *art*. The practice of that art will vary according to whether it has been achieved by *identification* or by *introjection*. The experience of "failure" similarly will vary according to whether it is an identificatory psychoanalyst or an introjective one who has failed. The identificatory psychoanalyst will either suffer greatly and scramble to "improve" to avoid failure next time, or use identifications to defend against his awareness of failure. The introjective psychoanalyst will take the failure deeply within to make changes in what he had thought he knew about others and about himself; the quality of the pain will relate to the nature of the change that is required. Without failure, there is megalomania, omnipotence, smugness, certainty, contempt for the difficulties of others. There is no growth because there is nothing to be learned.

Some Emblematic Vignettes

The following material about my patients is substantially disguised and sketchy where details would be especially revealing. I hope thereby to accommodate some of the knotty issues of confidentiality that are inevitable when analyst and analysand live cheek by jowl in the same interlocked community. However, I will speak of my own internal situation quite frankly. If this appears unseemly, it is because I have lost my taste for an analytic anonymity that all too often seduces the partners on both sides of the couch into idealization and complicity. I will describe my first analytic case (I.N.), in which many facets of failure embedded in a "successful" treatment were premonitory of my subsequent development as an analyst. Then I will take up a case that failed in the first session and had to be unilaterally terminated ten years later (F.P.). I will briefly take up the matter of other analysts' failures and conclude with some thoughts about the worst failure of all: failing to fail.

The First Analytic Case (Mr. I.N.)

I.N. was an earnest young married professional in his late twenties who was referred to me for analysis twenty-three years ago when I was a candidate. He would be my first analytic patient. The referral came from a faculty member of the Institute who had treated Mr. N.'s older sister in analysis for many years; in fact the request had been initiated by her in response to her brother's increasing distress. The referring analyst said, "I must tell you, theirs is the coldest mother I have ever heard of."

Mr. N. was just beginning to practice his profession after a lengthy period of graduate work and postgraduate specialization. The background anxiety that had beset him during graduate studies had escalated to reach crippling proportions. Only the regular use of benzodiazepines, from a supply obtained surreptitiously by his father from a pharmacist friend, enabled him to go to work every day. In addition, he was intimidated by the beauty of his wife, of whom he felt undeserving, and feared that if he failed at his profession, she would leave him. He brought a dream to the first consultation, which I thought of as an indicator of analyzability, and he was so eager to accept my recommendation for a four-times-a-week analysis that he appeared to leap onto the couch. That was possibly the only time we seemed to be in agreement. During the ensuing four and a half years, Mr. N. tried innumerable ways to wriggle out of the analytic situation, from moving his office out of town to failing to clear conflicts from his schedule that prevented him from coming on time. We disagreed about the fee, which was modified a number of times as his income improved along with his ability to work, about the scheduling of sessions, about vacations. With each disagreement, his anxiety would flare up, and he would push me to settle things quickly with him in order to calm down. It took all my novice resolve to stand firm and to resist premature closure, so alarming were his symptom exacerbations.

The chief transference configurations had to do with a mother who was not only emotionally cold, as with the sister, but was peculiarly yielding to all his requests, which we came to realize he used as substitutes for real maternal care. So long as he was a "good little boy," which meant no crying and no protest, he was rewarded with any food he liked, relieved of chores, and of the need to do anything difficult. He became the confidante for his mother's constant belittling of his father, a hapless soul who worked seven days a week at his retail business, fearful of thwarting any of his customers' requests, and taking no pleasure in the family or in any recreation. In fact, working all the time was the sole characteristic that escaped mother's contempt and earned his son's respect.

Mr. N. moved rather readily into the analytic process, despite his regular comments that it seemed silly. He had some spooky dreams, which elegantly captured the horrors of his anxious states, and as we worked steadily along through his associations to day residues and both manifest and latent content, he was amazed to the point of disequilibrium to recover so much affect in childhood memories which he had long assumed were flat and unremarkable. Following the ambiguous outcome of a health crisis, Mr. N. was startled by my sympathetic acknowledgment of the terror and shock he had experienced when undergoing some invasive diagnostic procedures during my vacation; it created quite a contrast with what he characterized as my usual hard and mean stance.

Eventually, there was significant improvement in all Mr. N.'s circumstances. His anxiety virtually disappeared leaving in its wake a disquieting awareness that he really disliked the profession he had studied so diligently to pursue. Nevertheless, his expertise grew and his services were in demand. He was respected by colleagues and in the community. In becoming less intimidated by his wife, he warmed to her, despite discovering that she remained emotionally distant toward him. After my maternity leave, which Mr. N. professed to welcome, he returned with reinvigorated protests about the hours we were attempting to negotiate. For most of a year he held out against compliance, much longer than I would have thought possible. Then he named a date several months in the future when all conflicts would be resolved. When that week arrived, he announced his firm decision to terminate the analysis, that very day. Although I was taken aback, I accepted this but made a plea that he allow at least some time for us to reflect on this action together. He agreed to come for one more week of sessions but only on the proviso that I acknowledge that this was not for his need but for mine. It had been a frequent complaint of his throughout that the treatment was for me, not for him. As I wrote in my final report to the training committee, in that one week was compressed as full a process of termination reflection and review as could be wished, complete with symptom flaring and resolution. At the end, we were both quite moved to consider how much had been accomplished.

Despite the apparent success of the treatment, there was a subtext of failure throughout that merits fuller explanation. I was receiving my training in a traditional Freudian institute, and my supervisor upheld the classical model. During the course of Mr. N.'s analysis I had been introduced in my seminars to new ideas under development by Bernard Brandchaft, who, in parallel with Heinz Kohut, was questioning the validity of the concept of primary aggression. I presented to my supervisor the ideas that seemed particularly applicable and took them up in my case reports. My supervisor tolerated hearing this without much comment. She was pleased but perplexed at how rapidly Mr. N. was responding to treatment, and seemed accepting of the unusual circumstances of termination. In her final report to the training committee, however, she realized that there had been serious deficiencies in the analysis, principally my failure to interpret Mr. N.'s primary aggression. (In retrospect, this was a passive refusal because by then I didn't believe in it.) To her this suggested I had a problem of such magnitude that I would need significant self-analytic work, if not more full-scale personal analysis, and I would certainly need to demonstrate satisfactory analytic work with another male patient before I could be permitted to graduate.

Where did this leave me but up the creek? There were a number of aspects of this case about which I already felt quite uncomfortable. I had quickly become extremely fond of Mr. N., looking forward as eagerly to his sessions as he seemed to. This remained true even when the sessions were contentious (which they often were), and even though he was remarkably resistant to developing the classical hallmarks of transference dependency, and despite my feeling frequently quite deficient in conducting the treatment. I thought that perhaps my enjoyment of Mr. N. was a countertransference response to his "good little boyness." This was regarded in supervision as an undesirable problem, possibly a symptom. Even worse, I myself experienced a powerful somatic phenomenon that Mr. N. reported having had repeatedly as a child: at times of great isolation from his mother, he would be eating his special dinner alone in front of the television set and have flashes of feeling quite close to the screen, even pressed up against it. Some three months before his actual termination, when I had just returned from maternity leave, and we were struggling to negotiate our new hours, I had a sudden flash of feeling quite close to the wall of my office at Mr. N.'s feet. My immediate response was to feel ashamed, though my supervisor made no comment, critical or otherwise. When Mr. N. eventually announced his intention to terminate, my first private thought was to wonder if that "close to the wall" experience had been my response to an unconscious communication of his plan to leave. But in general I had no way to make sense of these experiences. Much later, I heard Ernest Wolf describe such a phenomenon as a "brief countertransference regression." (In those years, the mid- to late-1970s, a substantial part of the early appeal of self psychology was its ability to describe in relatively normative terms experiences that in classical thinking were described as significantly pathological.)

Even more troubling was my growing posttermination awareness of the operation of coercion throughout the treatment. Mr. N. was my first analytic case; of course the treatment was at least as much for me as for him. A compliance born of helplessness was his principal problem, of which the analysis took wholesale advantage. It actually felt better to consider how (and that) he had ultimately freed himself from the coercion. But at the same time, it had now been made clear to me that my aberrant views of the treatment disqualified me for consideration as a legitimate analyst. I was a failure either way, to my patient or to my profession. This awareness lent a certain poignancy to the eventual completion of my training. However, it is also true that I felt less tortured during this case than subsequent ones, which I think is because I started out with a greater sense of certainty about the background of psychoanalytic theory. That certainty was definitely challenged by the course of the treatment and at some point became "it or me." Either I was an illegitimate fraud, or the theory was.

There is a postscript to this. Five or six years later, Mr. N. called me up to say thank you, that he felt that the treatment had helped him greatly. Then, about five years after that, full eleven years after termination, I had another call from Mr. N. who asked to return, though only on his terms: once a week, face to face, and if Prozac would help him, he wanted to take it. If I wouldn't do it, perhaps I'd refer him to someone who could. He was again experiencing crippling anxiety and a disturbance in the concentration he needed to work, as a result of an overwhelming financial reversal that had come to light for an investment group in which he participated with several colleagues. The financial reversal at first had seemed to be the not surprising (and not uncommon) result of overleverage when the boom of the 1980s was followed by the bust of the early 1990s.

With a private sense of gratitude, I welcomed him back. In the course of the next three and a half years, I worked with him, I saw him together with his wife, and I saw his wife separately. The financial crisis had reawakened many of Mr. N.'s fears for the marriage, which proved to be justified. I could see how the analysis had papered over many of the difficulties between the two, creating a distance that each found tolerable enough until the financial crisis overturned the materialistic adaptation they had made to one another. It helped Mrs. N. to become less mad at Mr. N. when it was discovered that the investment group's financial manager had been indulging in shady dealing that was only detectable when things fell apart. I could see that the analysis had indeed given Mr. N. the means to identify his feelings and to express them, but that had given him an unfair advantage in the marriage, since his wife had always been a silent accommodator (during Mr. N.'s analysis, Mrs. N. had been in treatment briefly, but it didn't "catch"). Now I was able to introduce Mr. N. to the myriad beneficial, nonfinancial contributions of Mrs. N. to the marriage. The financial situation proved to be quite dire, but Mr. N.'s nimble negotiating skills allowed them to emerge intact, though reduced in circumstances. They were not without the possibility of recovery, but now Mr. N. was willing to face how much he really did dislike his work. At the time they stopped treatment, they had a plan for retirement and they were drawing some real satisfaction from the marriage. I later heard that Mrs. N. had (so far) successfully undergone treatment for breast cancer, which their new closeness was allowing them to weather.

As for the old subtext of failure with Mr. N., this was a transformational experience. I could see how the analysis had both healed and harmed Mr. N. (and harmed Mrs. N.), but I could use what I had learned about Mr. N. now to help them both, and I could use this modified experience with both of them to confirm and expand what I was learning about how I was willing to use psychoanalysis. A coercive treatment is always wrong. Following the initial phase of this case, the coercion emerged only gradually into consciousness, and in a later phase circumstances fortuitously allowed it to be redressed. But the battle lines were drawn for me with this first case, and each side was problematic. As an identificatory psychoanalyst, I was destined to be a dud; as an introjective psychoanalyst, I was unacceptable to the system that trained me.

A Case That Failed in the First Session—and Didn't Leave (Ms. F.P.)

This was a gruesome, ten-year treatment from which I extricated myself only with difficulty, after excoriating self-scrutiny. It was one of the cases to which Samoan Barish and I referred circumspectly in our 1998 article, "As Far as Possible: Discovering Our Limits and Finding Ourselves." Extrication required the supportive participation of multiple colleagues, and even now I cringe a little to bring it up more explicitly. This case fits the criteria of Richard Chessick's definition of "impasse," which is not the same as a simple failure or interruption.

> An impasse occurring even in one single case is very serious for the conscientious psychoanalyst because it forces the analyst to review his or her entire professional choice, theoretical orientation, and discipline. . . . The impasse . . . involves a very subtle interaction between the analyst and the patient so that it may go on for months or even years before the analyst realizes what has happened. In fact, the patient who is suffering the impasse not only often does not mention it, but will resolutely deny it if it is suggested by the analyst. It is complex and multidetermined and the countertransference is always deeply and subtly involved. In my clinical experience, when the analyst realizes that an impasse has occurred, it may be a shocking and humiliating experience and requires serious self-analytic study . . . [Chessick, 1993, pp. 170–171].

Ms. F.P. was a young unmarried professional completing her graduate studies when she sought analytic treatment. She was in a disgruntled state following several years of a dodgy situation in which she attended both group and individual treatment with the same therapist, and in which there was a certain amount of "boundary crossing" going on, outside socializing among the group members, which the therapist seemed to encourage. Ms. P. was adept at psychotherapeutic lingo; in fact, a psychologist friend had given her a substantial earful about self psychology, which seemed to be just what Ms. P. wanted: empathy (it was never more specific than that). She was referred to me since I was thought of as an early proponent of self psychology. Ms. P. recounted a history that placed her in an intact family blighted by an emotionally abusive style of relating. Her education was self-supported by a succession of grueling jobs, and so far romantic relationships had proved disappointing. It was, all in all, an unremarkable presentation, except that she specifically wanted a four-times-a-week treatment.

Ms. P. would later inform me that so far as she was concerned our initial session was terrible. My responses to her were as trite and stupid as those of her previous therapist, and she wanted to walk out and forget the whole thing. But she was desperate, and when she spied a copy of Kohut's *The Psychology of the Self* beside my chair, she took it as a sign that somehow I would be okay. But I would not know this for years. What did begin to become apparent was that there was going to be no room for me in this analysis. Only a week or two into the treatment, before she had begun to use the couch, there was a dispute about my policy regarding patients' vacations, which at that time was quite classical, namely that she was financially responsible for sessions unless I was away or was able to fill vacancies. I was no stranger to disputes about the arrangements for analysis (recall Mr. N. above), and I was even prepared to be flexible in some circumstances, but there was an unusual degree of venom in Ms. P.'s assertions that did not elicit my generosity. I said to her that I had been practicing in this fashion for quite a few years, but that she was not required to find it acceptable. Since we had barely begun, it was possible that what had surfaced represented a real impediment to the treatment for her, that I might not be the right analyst for her.

I can scarely describe the firepower of her outrage at hearing this: "How dare you? What kind of an analyst are you? I'm the patient. It's your job to take care of me. You're saying this is my fault. I trusted you and now you do this to me."

This diatribe fell squarely in the gap that had opened up between my classical training and my limited progress in absorbing newer clinical ideas into my practice; there was another gap as well, the mistrust between my psychoanalytic persona (viz. Berman's "false analytic self") and my, for lack of a better phrase, "private self" that had opened up during the treatment of Mr. N. These gaps, along with what had been my mantra during medical, psychiatric, and psychoanalytic training and practice, namely to privilege the patient's perceptions ahead of my own preconceptions, made me vulnerable to being taken over by Ms. P.'s pressure, and that is exactly what happened *for the next ten years.* Perhaps the most benign result was that I changed my vacation policy to permit each year two weeks of sessions for which the patient is not financially responsible, not just for Ms. P. but for all and subsequent patients (this I have retained to the present day, and do not regret).

But beyond that, Ms. P.'s exquisite sensitivity to any impingement of my person upon her began slowly to take its toll. The impingements ranged from my makeup, my cologne, my clothes, the layout of my office, and of course included everything I said. It is not just that she was disrupted by such impingements and they would be talked through to the point of repair, as was the case with other patients. Her disruptions were of terrifying magnitude, which she insisted could only be managed by my accommodation, thus there was never a deepened understanding nor a stretching of her tolerance. At one point, when she had completed her studies and was working within the correctional system, she had confiscated some guns and had quite improperly taken them home "for safekeeping." With each disruption, she would tell of soothing herself by keeping the loaded pistols under her pillow while she slept, and on some occasions, sucking on the barrel in order to fall asleep. She finally made it clear to me that she conceived of the treatment as her being in a boat in which she held the rudder and I was the (mute) passenger. She insisted that I arrange backup treatment for her to use if she wished during my vacations, but the therapist and I were not to communicate about her. Upon my return she would be full of praise for the backup therapist and scorn for me and my pitiful therapeutic capacities. What I would hear, illicitly of course, from the backup therapist would be an account of Ms. P.'s misery and disequilibrium at my absence, which I could never make use of.

Eventually, I found myself becoming progressively constricted by Ms. P., and in a way that seeped into my everyday life. I said less and less, and eventually became unable to free associate or even to think during her sessions. From time to time she would break her own rule of requiring my silence and instruct me when I was to be empathic, admiring, or to take her side in a dispute (of which there were many). I stopped wearing eyeshadow and cologne, and began to dress in looser, more shapeless clothing. From time to time I would dream of Ms. P. installed on an analytic couch in the living room of my house.

This is a necessarily abbreviated account of a most distressed and disturbing treatment in which I made many mistakes, all of which Ms. P. demonstrated to be irretrievable and by which ultimately I felt held hostage. Conventional consultation was ineffective in dealing with the situation (Barish and Vida, 1998). It is strange to recall now that most other patients whom I treated during this period seemed to do all right and that there were good and successful experiences in other parts of my life. The catalytic event that led to my eventual disengagement from Ms. P. was her request for a therapist that she and her unsatisfactory boyfriend could consult (with whom, again, I was required to have no contact). However, that therapist, Dr. X., appalled by the monstrous controlling presence of Ms. P. to whom her boyfriend was abjectly submissive, initiated unauthorized communication with me. From the time of that first contact something began to shift in me. This unsolicited confirmation of the nature of Ms. P.'s personality broke the spell. For the next year and a half, I found myself regaining little by little some power of thought during Ms. P.'s sessions.

Occasionally, I even ventured to say something, which no matter how innocuous would elicit Ms. P.'s scorn and rage. I began to wonder if "escape" was possible. Finally came a session during which I commented that the incident Ms. P. was describing must have been disappointing. Ms. P. erupted savagely that my remark was unwarranted (no one but she was allowed to name her affect). I repeated it. Ms. P. attacked me for not obeying her command. I repeated it once more. This time, Ms. P. got up from the couch screaming that if I couldn't control myself she would have to leave. Which she did. She called me several times, to say that she would not return to her sessions that week, and that when she did come back, to the first session of the following week, we would have to get a few things straight, because my behavior was having a terrible effect on her.

Ms. P. returned with many pages of yellow foolscap on which were written my crimes, including once again the infamous first session, which she patiently but with barely concealed rage read to me. I replied that she had made me very aware on numerous occasions of all those failures, but that however many times we went over them, there never seemed to be any resolution or any improvement; she didn't feel any better about me or the treatment than she ever had. Since, during our years together she had had many complaints about unsatisfactory situations and relationships that she never seemed able to leave, perhaps ours was the first one about which she could take a different stand. My message, which I had to repeat several times in the final few sessions, which occurred once a week and face to face, at her request, was that we had tried for ten years to develop something workable, and since I was as unable to satisfy her as ever, it would be *wrong* for her to continue with me.

This phrasing was suggested in fact by Dr. X. who was correct that Ms. P. would not be able to object to such a proposal. It had to be couched, as everything else in the "analysis," exclusively from her perspective. Anything "wrong" was in me, or in each of her other persecutors. And so, as Ms. P. summoned herself to make an exit speech, she concluded that what I was saying was that I had lost hope for myself in working with her (which was partially correct). She somehow had been prepared to go on, once I apologized to her for my inappropriate intrusions (think of Chessick's patient in the impasse who refuses to believe it exists). She finally asked if I had anything to say, to which I eventually replied that I thought she underestimated the impact of her anger on others. She airily dismissed such an idea, but did offer that she had appreciated both my not overreacting to the guns (by that time I was nearly mute, *but actually that incident evoked little feeling in me*) and my allowing her to have control over the fee, which she knew was substantially less than my regular fee, finishing, "I probably should have paid you more." She had been quite able to pay my full fee for some time, as she was handsomely remunerated for her more recent work in the private sector, but I simply didn't have the energy for the horrendous assault that merely discussing a fee increase would have meant.

And so it finished. Alongside unspeakable relief, there was a tremendous internal turmoil, which subsided very slowly. I have already intimated the aspect of my vulnerability conferred by efforts to assimilate the principles of self psychology. But as Chessick said, there was indeed a deeper and subtler component contributed by countertransference, if you will, although Molad's term *autobiography* is a much better word. I became aware of a crucial aspect of my history, not retrievable by any analytic means, only during the end-phase of Ms. P.'s treatment. I was in Budapest for the first time, for a Ferenczi conference, when I suddenly knew from a strange buzzing in my mind that I had spoken Hungarian as a baby. This meant definitively that certain elements of the family story told of my earliest years were incorrect. As a child I had been shamed and criticized harshly for having feelings incongruous with the story told, but with no independent memories, I had nothing with which to defend or even understand myself. I can easily see now that this state of affairs had made me quite vulnerable to regressive intimidation by Ms. P.'s malignant externalizing. My gradual internal transformation joined forces with the collegial support of Dr. X. to make possible my escape. It is impossible to imagine what it might have been like to meet Ms. P. in that first session without such vulnerability, and what might have tran-spired. My biggest regret is that her successful intimidation of me made Ms. P. less amenable to learning from the experience of having her grandiosity thwarted by others; the analytic situation made her more of a monster. Dr. X., who has intermittently followed Ms. P. and her boyfriend since their marriage, reports that the extent of Ms. P.'s contempt defies comprehension and that refusal to engage is the only way to deal with her.

Other Analysts' Failures

As a result of these and myriad other experiences with failure, I take a stance of humility with regard to the clinical work of others, not presuming to know how they "should" have done it. For me, this is an important component of the striven-for congruence of "internal–clinical" and "external–social" reali-ties (Molad, 1999). Whole analyses that "fail" generate enor-mous suffering, no doubt, yet they can be the very "difficult events" that encourage one to know the "difficult truths" (de Botton, 1998, p. 73). I have developed a maxim: Analysts are qualified to treat another analyst's failure only after a case of their own has defected to find superior treatment at the hands of a subsequent analyst. In treating another analyst's failure, there are actually two patients: the corporeal analysand on the couch, and the ghost analysand, the analyst who failed. It is necessary to know that oneself is a ghost, too.

Failing to Fail

I wish to propose as an apt metaphor for the psychoanalytic endeavor the ultimate importance of a certain kind of failure described by Alain de Botton in *How Proust Can Change Your Life*. De Botton describes Proust dealing with a period of de-spondency with an intense study of the work of the English art critic, John Ruskin, who "expressed things which Proust might have felt himself but could not have articulated on his own" (p., 191). But after an immensely valuable six years' immersion, Proust was ready to move on, having discovered that:

> [B]ooks could not make us aware enough of the things we felt. They might open our eyes, sensitize us, enhance our powers of perception, but at a certain point they would stop, not by coincidence, not occasionally, not out of bad luck, but inevitably, by definition, for the stark and simple reason that *the author wasn't us.* There would come a moment with every book when we would feel that something was incongruous, misunderstood or constraining, and it would give us a responsibility to leave our guide behind and continue our thoughts alone [p. 196].

De Botton recommends our conferring upon Proust the same judgment Proust passed on Ruskin, "namely, that for all its qualities, his work must eventually also prove silly, maniacal, constraining, false and ridiculous to those who spend too long on it" (p. 215). I suggest that in a similar vein an analysis that aspires never to fail, or that goes on too long in an attempt to substitute analysis for life, robs the analysand of the necessity to be, *to discover,* his own person. After all, "[e]ven the finest books deserve to be thrown aside" (p. 215).

Conclusion

The paradox at the heart of this essay is my aim to succeed in saying something about failure. To succeed is to risk muting the sting of failure, yet the sting of failure is precisely what announces its presence and also makes it useful. However, if what I have written is of assistance is considering failures that are unique to your "autobiography," we would call it not "success" but "company."

References

Abraham, N., & Torok, M. (1972), Mourning *or* melancholia: Introduction *versus* incorporation. In: *The Shell and the Kernel: Renewals of Psychoanalysis,* ed. & tr. N. T. Rand. Chicago: University of Chicago Press, 1994, pp. 125–138.

Barish, S., & Vida, J. E. (1998), "As far as possible": Discovering our limits and finding ourselves. *Amer. J. Psychoanal.*, 58:83–97.

Berman, E. (2000), The utopian fantasy of a new person and the danger of a false analytic self. *Psychoanal. Psychol.*, 17:38–60.

de Botton, A. (1998), *How Proust Can Change Your Life*. London: Picador.

Chessick, R. (1993), *A Dictionary for Psychotherapists: Dynamic Concepts in Psychotherapy*. Northvale, NJ: Jason Aronson, pp. 170–171.

Ferenczi, S. (1909), On introjection and transference. In: *Selected Writings: Sandor Ferenczi*, ed. & tr. J. Borossa. Harmondsworth, U.K.: Penguin Books, 1999, pp. 31–66.

——— (1932), The three main principles, Biarritz, 14/9/1932. Notes and Fragments. In: *Final Contributions to the Problems and Methods of Psycho-Analysis*, ed. M. Balint. London: Maresfield Reprints, 1955, pp. 252–253.

——— (1988), *The Clinical Diary of Sandor Ferenczi*, ed. J. Dupont; tr. M. Balint & N. Z. Jackson. Cambridge, MA: Harvard University Press.

Freud, S. (1912), Recommendations to physicians practicing psychoanalysis. *Standard Edition*, 12:109–120. London: Hogarth Press, 1958.

Haynal, A., & Falzeder, E. (1991), "Healing through love"? A unique dialogue in the history of psychoanalysis. *Free Assn.*, 2:1–20.

Klauber, J. (1983), The identity of the psychoanalyst. In: *The Identity of the Psychoanalyst*, ed. E. D. Joseph & D. Widlocher. New York: International Universities Press, pp. 41–50.

Kohut, H. (1976), Creativeness, charisma, group psychology: Reflections on the self-analysis of Freud. In: *Freud: The Fusion of Science and Humanism*, ed. J. E. Gedo & G. H. Pollock. New York: International Universities Press, pp. 379–425.

Molad, G. J. (1999), On presenting one's case: Embraced trauma and the dialogue between analysts. Revision of a presentation to the Israel Psychotherapy Association's 23rd Annual Conference, "Sándor Ferenczi, The 'Mother' of Modern Psychoanalysis and Psychotherapy," the Fifth International Sándor Ferenczi Conference, Tel Aviv, May 8.

Symington, N. (1996), *The Making of a Psychotherapist*. Madison, CT: International Universities Press.

Vida, J. E. (1999a), Which Ferenczi is it? Discussion of Panel "Contemporary applications of Ferenczi." Presented to the Israel Psychotherapy Association's 23rd Annual Conference, "Sándor

Ferenczi, The 'Mother' of Modern Psychoanalysis and Psychotherapy," the Fifth International Sándor Ferenczi Conference, Tel Aviv, May 8.

———— (1999b), Not "filed away as finally dealt with." In: *In Memoriam Sandor Ferenczi,* ed. J. Meszaros. Budapest: Osiris Press.

3

Thorns in the Rose Garden: Failures at Chestnut Lodge

ANN-LOUISE S. SILVER, M.D.

> *You need not see what someone is doing*
> *to know if it is his vocation,*
>
> *you have only to watch his eyes:*
> *a cook mixing a sauce, a surgeon*
>
> *making a primary incision.*
> *a clerk completing a bill of lading,*
>
> *wear the same rapt expression,*
> *forgetting themselves in a function.*
>
> *How beautiful it is,*
> *That eye-on-the-object look*
> *[W. H. Auden, 1954, pp. 629–630].*

Introduction

This chapter addresses long shadows and ultimate nightfall. It explores the sense shared currently by many mental health professionals that somehow we have failed in our mission. Using Chestnut Lodge as a case study, and some examples from my own work with patients, I have devoted these pages to an unflinching look at celebration's opposite.

The time is right for a book on failures during the mental health profession's current epidemic of disappointment. We can only fail at something attempted, or at something we sensed we had mastered. We decide to try for something, then commit time, energy, and usually money, hoping to acquire the skills needed to reach a goal that only gradually defines itself. We become "professionals," and find a professional home. At some point, we acknowledge, "I can't do it. I don't have what it takes," or alternatively, "I have to get out of here; it's got to be better somewhere else." Whether we fail in isolation or as part of a group dedicated to a particular cause or at a given institution, we endure loneliness when we perceive we are failing. Voicing a negative assessment seems deeply disloyal, even unprofessional. We mourn the loss of our questing origins. Even if we choose a new quest, we have still abandoned the first. We find little comfort in calling the humbling diminution of our narcissism "maturing," or in recognizing that aging inexorably leads to failing life, whatever the external situation.

The *Oxford English Dictionary* (OED) as usual provides a dependable linguistic foundation, informing us that at one time, to fail meant simply "to die." The OED's creation (Winchester, 1998) is itself a fascinating story of a quest that probably would have failed were it not for an insane physician-murderer. This surgeon volunteered to serve in the Civil War, but found himself forced to brand a soldier apprehended for desertion. The deserter had been Irish. The physician developed the delusion that the Irish were seeking revenge. He killed an Irishman who was hurrying to work and then lived for decades in a hospital for the criminally insane near London, sending many erudite entries to the OED editor.

"Fail" now means: to become exhausted, come to an end, run short; to become extinct, to die out, to lose vitality, pass away; to grow dim; to cease to speak of; to fall short in performance or attainment. Every instance of a definable mental illness or difficulty is, by the nature of the act of diagnosis, a definition of some variety of failure. We mental health clinicians make our livelihoods delineating the failings in those who pay our way in life. In agreeing to provide service, we imply that through teamwork with us, we foresee the possibility of improvement. Yet essentially everyone in the mental health field has endured or witnessed profound personal failure during this era of deinstitutionalization, the national push for a balanced budget, and the disruptions caused by the managed care experiment. Psychiatry's public and private hospital and community programs have shrunk, merged, or disappeared. Those still surviving lack money for repairs or to replace ragged furnishings. Dynamic psychotherapists seem disconnected from the emerging psychosocial rehabilitation programs. Psychiatric training programs minimize or neglect to teach psychodynamics. Medical students now rarely choose psychiatry. Many of our mental health journals struggle to stay afloat. Few people quest after the right psychoanalyst. In the past, we worked with patients who failed to respond to our efforts. Books then had titles such as *The Treatment-Resistant Patient* or *The Chronically Mentally Ill.* We rarely studied our own dysfunction, a notable exception being Richard Chessick's 1971 *Why Psychotherapists Fail.*

Now we psychodynamic clinicians claim failure as our own issue. Take, as just one example, our relationship to money—a crude capitalist measure of success or failure. We move our offices or residences to more modest settings, downscale vacation plans, attend fewer professional meetings, and wonder about continuing to pay yearly dues to professional organizations. Or we decide to retire to eliminate the expense of office, malpractice insurance, and other fees. A decade ago, retirement seemed an option we would not choose unless our health failed us first. We expected to teach the next generation of practitioners, never dreaming that academic centers would exclude those not on the full-time faculty from continuing their usually volunteer roles. Those accommodating to the managed care pressures and joining a panel of preferred providers often fall behind on required paperwork and lose reimbursement of already reduced fees. To add to our tensions, we hear of federal agencies and managed care firms auditing practitioners' records, demanding return of money if sessions are not adequately charted. The cacophony of howling grows raucous as we blame our bosses or the leaders of professional organizations for failing to protect us.

In 1956, Dr. Frieda Fromm-Reichmann, the psychoanalyst most associated with psychoanalytic applications in schizophrenia, was interviewed about her years in Europe. Discussing her first impressions of America when she arrived here in 1935 at the age of 46, she said:

> I feel so very strongly that the Americans are different from Europeans in that there is no tragedy and no fate. You *are* a success and you *are* a failure, and it's your fault if you are a failure, and if you try hard, you can be a success, including being the President of the United States. And there isn't such a thing as fate or energies outside yourself. Therefore, Americans say, "I *am* a success" and "I *am* a failure." There are two British men whom I asked, and they said no, the British would also not say, "I am a success." They may say, "I am successful," but they wouldn't say, "I am a success." This, from the very beginning, when I came to this country, I experienced as the greatest difference [Silver, 1989, p. 481].

Perhaps a similar dichotomy will emerge among the contibutors to this book. Joanne Greenberg, author of *I Never Promised You a Rose Garden*, received the Frieda Fromm-Reichmann award at the American Academy of Psychoanalysis in 1967. In her acceptance speech, she quoted Fromm-Reichmann as adding, " 'The risks of failure are so much higher in English, it's a wonder you people try anything' " (Greenberg, 1967, p. 75).

If one *is* a failure, and then feels sad, does this account for our country's massive consumption of antidepressant medications? We have grown up in a culture in which we await the birth of perfect babies, expect all our children to be above average, and dread anyone in the family bringing home an F. Children and teens call each other "losers," "failures." We professionals, growing up in this culture, have denied ourselves much leisure as we have striven both to be successes and to avoid being failures. I am hearing increasingly of psychiatrists self-medicating for depression. Are they too ashamed to acknowledge patienthood, or are they perhaps too cynical or too anxious to finance psychodynamic treatment? And who among us can still afford hospitalization? Where are the hospitals that could treat us in the style to which we had become accustomed? Are these newer medications safe enough that one day they will be sold over the counter?

Chestnut Lodge closed its doors on April 27, 2001, exactly forty-four years after Fromm-Reichmann's death. Having enjoyed the advantages conferred on professionals working within our institution, we now feel disadvantaged. But even a passing thought of the plight of those we treat compounds our outrage with intense guilt. I sit on my screened-in front porch writing at my laptop computer, gazing at the sprinkler watering my neighbor's freshly mown grass. Her daughter drives up, returning home with her toddlers. They are the ages our children were when we moved into this then-new development twenty-five years ago, about the time when I adopted Chestnut Lodge as my professional home. The neighborhood trees, sapling whips at first, now arch over the street. At the Lodge, now the grounds of the Waldorf School, many of the trees top a hundred feet. My Chestnut Lodge patients found stability within the hospital community. As they grew stronger, they moved gradually from the hospital to supported living and then independent living nearby. Now, a rapid and arbitrary treadmill pace is set for our patients and for us.

During these decades of decline, probably hardest hit have been the sickest patients and those who work with them. The newer antipsychotic medications are clearly better than the phenothiazines, which universally caused parkinsonian difficulties and the risk of tardive dyskinesia. Often patients are dramatically freed of psychotic thought disorder and sometimes can resume sophisticated college and graduate school programs. At the same time, almost universally, they have been deprived of insight-oriented therapy and the assurance of having a particular mental health professional dependably present in times of crisis. Their housing situations are uncertain at best. In the Scandinavian countries, efforts are made to locate children at risk and to treat them and their families intensively, thus lowering the national incidence of schizophrenia (Johannessen, Larsen, McGlashan, and Vaglum, 2000). In the United States, by contrast, there seems to be little money or support allocated for preventive medicine of any sort, least of all for mental illness.

As Michael Winerip writes (1999), "[T]he state of the nation's shattered mental-health system [has] all but assured . . . calamities" (p. 42). "In 15 years of reporting on mental health, I have never seen the system in such disarray" (p. 48). When a long-time colleague resigned, a new medical administrator at Chestnut Lodge told me he was surprised by the anger in the terse resignation letter. "I'm angry, too," I said. "You? You're angry? You shouldn't come to work if you're angry. You should stay at home in Columbia [Maryland]. You should be a grandmother. Spend time with your grandchildren. You would be much happier. You should not come to work if you're angry." Not only was his outburst absurdly rejecting, it illustrated his lack of understanding of the requirements for dynamic work with chronically ill patients. Anger and its management through self-reflection fuels our work. As I recount this anecdote, I recall the movie *Network,* in which, on the urgings of the broadcaster, people around the city all open their windows, lean out, and yell, "I'm mad as hell and I'm not going to take it anymore."

The reader might presume that I despair about the future, but I have two hopes. The first is that public outrage will build, and that our mental health institutions will receive support approaching what they deserve. As president of the newly formed United States chapter of the International Society for the Psychological Treatment of the Schizophrenias and Other Psychoses (ISPS), I hope to help encourage debate with those who would see these disorders as simply brain dysfunctions needing medication and support.

My second hope is that we will see places of sanctuary and unpressured treatment emerge in new, smaller contexts. Perhaps we will see a return of the sanatoria run by individual practitioners, the norm at the start of the twentieth century. Perhaps such places will develop outside of the medical establishment, which seems currently to overemphasize prescribing the right combination of drugs to quell symptoms. We need retreats—sanctuaries—health spas in the mountains or by the shore, with a regimen of relaxation, physical exertion, contemplation, education, and discussion. We need settings and relationships that foster both trust and insight. I am encouraged by the return of the health spas of a century ago. Both our patients and mental health professionals could benefit from aspects of the old "water cure" spas, including cold wet-sheet packs, group support, and intimate informed conversation. We have been pulled into an age of efficiency, pressured to believe we can stamp out symptoms like brushfires. The doctors working in the clinics of CPC (the local nonprofit organization which purchased Chestnut Lodge) had been asked by a new medical director to see four patients per hour and to evaluate and prescribe for a new patient in half an hour. They declined, reminding him of our mission statement to provide quality care, and having voted some months earlier to join a union.

Chestnut Lodge and Its Evolution

When I arrived at Chestnut Lodge in 1976, I would never have predicted a medical union. What happened to our rose garden, now choked with weeds? Both patients and staff contended with chronic anxiety. We worried about the very survival of the place. So many staff members left, voluntarily or under duress or facing fatal illness, that we too often failed to organize a good-bye party or did not hear in time about a funeral. We blamed managed care, the overbiologizing of psychosis, the inability of the new hospital administration to manage a complex billing system or to see the hospital staff as its best resource. However, the difficulties began earlier. Few of us were left who remembered when patients and staff knew each other by name and personality. The patient I presented in "Chestnut Lodge: Then and Now" (Silver, 1997) has moved to a residential treatment center far away. I will discuss our parting later in this paper. Most of my long-time colleagues often alluded to the *Titanic*, while others called for a new study of Chestnut Lodge, a follow-up of the Stanton and Schwartz study, depicted in their classic text, *The Mental Hospital* (1954).

The Bullard family sold the hospital in 1994, the front twenty acres going to CPC Health, the back forty going to a local building contractor. The actual construction of townhouses finally began in mid-June, 1999. Bulldozers tore through the sod of the open fields, as we knew they would. But I was horrified by the huge pile of felled trees, their green leaves drooping in the sun, and on hearing the screams of disrupted birds. Next, some of the Lodge's buildings (Hilltop, the Clinical Center, the Research Center, and the buildings constructed in the mid-1970s to house adolescent patients) became heaps of rubble. The programs housed in these buildings were relocated. I avoided seeing the Lodge's only chestnut trees felled. They had lined the road leading to these buildings as did tall pine trees that once had been Christmas trees on the inpatient units.

Analyst Harold F. Searles (1960) said:

> [T]he nonhuman environment, far from being of little or no account to human personality development, constitutes one of the most basically important ingredients of human psychological existence. It is my conviction that there is within the human individual a sense, whether at a conscious or unconscious level, of *relatedness to his nonhuman environment*, that this relatedness is one of the transcendentally important facts of human living, that—as with other very important circumstances in human existence—it is a source of ambivalent feelings to him, and that, finally, if he tries to ignore its importance to himself, he does so at peril to his psychological well-being [pp. 5–6].

Must I then acknowledge some satisfaction at seeing Chestnut Lodge lose its chestnut trees, shrink in area, then disappear? The Lodge work described by Fromm-Reichmann (1950, 1956, 1959), Searles (1960, 1967), Farber (1966), Pao (1979), Feinsilver (1986), McGlashan and Keats (1989), myself (1989, 1997) and others required the strong container of a secure institutional home. While the earlier writings often assumed that the patient's early family life and social environment set the stage for psychosis, we finally found our own hospital family dysfunctional. As we tried to keep our ship afloat, our shared attention was diverted from the nuances of treatment processes.

The OED's cluster of definitions of failure summarizes aspects of Lodge existence. Beginning in the late 1970s, we began losing our grip on a shared creativity. We talked about the spotlight of attention no longer shining on us. Why write? Who reads anyhow? Even before the managed care era, our clinical conferences were often uninspired ritualized exercises. I had given a paper on the Lodge's Wednesday Conferences at the 1988 International Symposium on the Psychotherapy of Schizophrenia, in Turin, Italy (Silver, 1993). A few years later, an Italian psychiatrist came to the United States and included a Lodge conference in his itinerary based on my enthusiastic report. Disappointingly, the discussion focused on the patient's medication history. "Boring," the visitor concluded. I agreed.

I believe that the great pharmacologic advances have diminished the possibility of fundamental treatment of psychosis. With medication, inner conflicts and turmoils become artificially muted, chemically disconnected. While collaboration *seems* improved, I have felt that it lacks the genuine connection established when patient and therapist reached mutual trust uninfluenced by drugs, after a long phase of intense mutual ambivalence. In my early years, three of my patients made such progress that two required no medication for years afterwards, and all three entered into enduring marriages. Since the medication era, my patients and I have enjoyed no such sweeping victories. And while one would assume that patients committed suicide more frequently when enduring unmedicated psychosis, intriguingly, the rate of suicide seems unchanged.

Fromm-Reichmann and Her Legacy

I have developed a peculiar career quest, to keep alive the spirit and philosophy of Freida Fromm-Reichmann, a person whom I never met, who died at age 67 at a time when I was studying for finals in my sophomore year of high school. Fromm-Reichmann's message (1950, 1956, 1959, 1990; Hornstein, 2000) is as important now as when she taught and wrote in the 1940s and 1950s (McAfee, 1989; Silver and Feuer, 1989). She emphasized that psychotic communication contains meaning, that

within every seemingly hopelessly deranged person there is a
beleaguered ego, and that as the therapist persists in reaching
out, and respects the patients and their struggles, gradually
more becomes clear to the therapist. Therapists must be open
to their own psychotic aspects as elucidated by their personal
psychotherapy and psychoanalysis. The process of self-scrutiny
must continue throughout one's career as we struggle with
our personal demons. Anxiety in the therapist and defensive
projection and denial are the biggest obstacles. Fromm-Reichmann saw psychotic process as an extreme amplification of the
human conflict between dependency needs and self-sufficiency, the patient's envy fueling a fabricated grandiosity that
develops into a grandiose sense of his or her magical destructiveness. When the therapist fears the patient, and especially
when the therapist doesn't acknowledge the fear or explore its
roots, both therapist and patient contribute to obstructing the
therapeutic process. She stressed the importance of bringing
in a third person, a supervisor or colleague to help the therapist clarify countertransferential processes.

I had an altogether too typical interaction when someone
stopped me on a path at the Lodge, and asked, "Where is the
FFR cottage? I have no idea why they call it that." I pointed
out the weathered clapboard little house, and said it had been
the home of Frieda Fromm-Richmann, the one who had put
this place on the map, and who worked here from 1935 until
her death in that cottage in April of 1957. "That's important
to know," she said, "I just started working here. I just completed my orientation course, and they didn't say anything
about her. I had no idea. That would have been important
to know."

Failure in the Holding Environment

For Chestnut Lodge, the staff mission was to treat severe mental
illness through intensive analytically oriented therapy and scrutiny of countertransference. Outspokenness was considered a
requirement for intrastaff discussion. We joked that when a

therapist's case presentation expressed confidence of progress, open discussion would be critical, but if the therapist felt things were stuck, the audience would find evidence of fundamental change. We defeated feelings of either success or failure, looking for equilibrium, all of this taking place in a rather dependable environment.

Over the years, we made specific accommodations to outside pressures. Each accommodation modified our mission. These modifications included backing away from the dynamic model that considered extreme tensions in one or both parents during the patient's early years as crucial to the later psychotic breakdown. Schizophrenia was increasingly viewed as a biologic disorder with some genetic loading. We became far more cautious in exploring family dynamics than we had been a generation earlier. The Lodge must "live down" Fromm-Reichmann's phrase, "the schizophrenogenic mother" (Hartwell, 1996; Silver, 1996). To my regret, we no longer refrained from the use of psychotropic medications—a practice outside the increasingly regimented standards of the psychiatric community. Use of cold wet-sheet packs was deemed unnecessarily restrictive.

I consistently advocated for a corner of the hospital in which the old methods could still be practiced, for those patients and families committed to this approach. I have quoted Joanne Greenberg repeatedly, as she described her first cold wet-sheet pack.

I was on Main IV, having a very tough time. A doctor, whom I don't remember—since I subscribed to the theory that if you've seen one person, you've seen them all—said, "I think you need to be in one of these." So he put me in one. I think it would be a bad idea for anyone who was claustrophobic to be in a cold pack, but for me it was the first time that I was ever able to look down into my mind, to get clear, to be clear. Once that happened to someone who had never had that, I think he would do anything on earth to get it again. That kind of stillness had a clarity, all of that yelling that went on all of the time inside me, wasn't there and I was at the end of it. You're not going anywhere. You are not going to hurt you or it or anything. That's all; that is it. You can fight and fight and fight. I knew that the ability to stop dead and look inside myself was what well people have. And I knew that that high feeling in the pack

was coming from me, not a drug. I learned for the first time
that there's a difference between inside and outside and that
inside then became available to me. Once I saw that, once I
learned that, I would do anything to promote it [McAfee, 1989,
pp. 520–521].

I ruminated about founding my own sanatorium, but got no
further than the talking and proposal-writing stage, and locating a site that got away from us. I have considered myself a
failure in this regard for almost two decades. My anger is more
complicated since I had led a failed attempt to place a bid for
purchase of the Lodge. I proposed this venture, located and
then raised the money for legal backing, and headed a campaign that enlisted the support of most of the Lodge's employees. We filed for nonprofit organization status with the IRS. To
place our bid, we needed to team up with a building contractor,
who would buy the back forty acres, while we would purchase
the twenty acres that formed the hospital in the 1930s and
1940s. After meeting with one contractor, the organizing group
balked, refusing to meet with another. I could not persuade
the group that we would not be risking personal capital, and
that our lawyer had said that while banks would not lend us
money to buy the entire sixty acres, they would have supported
us in this partnered venture. We had come close to cobbling
together a proposal identical to that of CPC. The Bullards
would probably have preferred selling to Lodge employees
than to an outside, even if related, agency. Indeed, had we
found ourselves in the same dire straits as the current owners,
we would have been Noah rather than the animals. When CPC
filed for Chapter 11 bankruptcy in October 2000, they declared
$11 million in debts.

The plan failed because I could not convince the representa-
tives of the various hospital departments of my own or the
plan's credibility. They viewed me as just a therapist. My foray
into business leadership seemed unbelievable, ungrounded,
and crazy. They misunderstood our lawyer's report that he had
failed to find a bank willing to fund purchase of the entire
sixty-acre campus. They did not hear his statements that were
we to agree to go into partnership with building contractors,
the much smaller sum was available.

Additionally, I believe that other group dynamics operated. The days of my "perpetual residency," the first decade or so of my Lodge tenure, placed the therapist at center stage. The Wednesday Conferences gave the therapist forty-five minutes of speaking time, while the psychologist who performed psychological testing was given only ten minutes, as was the social worker who was charged with presenting a detailed family history and a report of her weekly telephone sessions with the family. For a while, these conferences were limited to the medical staff and those other department members directly involved in working with the patient being presented. Only the therapist presented formally, while others on the team could contribute during general discussion. The patients were invited to attend only late in this phase, and then only occasionally. The medical doctors were the elite group on the plantation and the other department members greatly resented our status. I was the only M.D. on the organizing group. I would add that interpersonal and interdepartmental tensions were not some new development at the Lodge. Their occurrence and their effects on patients' functioning and regressions were amply illustrated in Stanton and Schwartz (1954).

I also wonder whether I would have wielded sufficient authority had I been male. I had wanted to be a unit administrator early in my time at the Lodge and had been passed over on three occasions. I resented this, since prior to coming to the Lodge I had been a ward administrator for three years at the Clifton T. Perkins Hospital Center, Maryland's state forensic hospital. Of my thirty patients, almost all suffered from severe psychoses and character disorders and had, often repeatedly, done very horrifying things. But at the Lodge, men would be assigned to run much smaller and simpler wards. I was told that the then clinical director refused to have a woman administrator trying to work with a woman head nurse. He felt it couldn't be done. I later thought that my reluctance to rely on antipsychotic medications was more at issue, as Dr. Bullard, Jr., found the denial of medications to psychotic patients cruel. "How can you *do* this?" he once asked me. The final effect of the administration's decision to deny me an opportunity to develop my own unit was that the Lodge staff did not know me as someone with authority, but only as someone who treated patients individually, chaired some committees, and organized symposia.

Chestnut Lodge, when I had arrived there in 1976, was well established in the minds of mental health professionals as the place to send their "failures," assuming that the patient came from a financially comfortable family or one with a generous insurance policy. We still told families to expect an inpatient stay of two years or so, and said that if treatment were progressing well, we would be working together for years. Intensive insight-oriented therapy formed the center of our treatment programs; everything else was "ancillary." When the patient's symptoms flared, staff immediately called the therapist, asking, "What happened in the most recent session? What clues do you have; what is the patient reacting to?"

Even then, we referred wistfully to "the golden years," when there was a two-year waiting list both for patients seeking treatment and doctors seeking employment and continuing training. It was the place for psychoanalytically oriented treatment of the psychoses. Fromm-Reichmann attracted an extremely ambitious staff, who published voluminously and were influential in developing family, group, and milieu therapies.

While I happily referred to my "perpetual residency," senior staff mourned the time when the Lodge was the world's beacon for such work. My job brought me a resident's salary, but with ongoing supervision on most of my cases, two-hour weekly grand rounds where a treatment was presented and reviewed in depth, and two "small-group meetings," one held for an hour after lunch on Tuesdays, and the other for ninety minutes each Friday. The same group of seven doctors met to discuss clinical issues. Then, everyone on the staff was in supervision. Steve Rosenthal, M.D., who began at the Lodge the same year I did and who is a psychiatrist-philosopher, supervised Dexter Bullard, Sr., for example. I attended Ping-Nie Pao's psychotherapy seminar and participated in or organized study groups. Each week, not counting my personal analysis and my psychoanalytic institute work, I spent nine hours studying aspects of the work with other staff members. Lunchtime conversations were usually work related, and always interesting. In the

Lodge's final years, supervisions were far from universal; small-group meetings were gone; the Wednesday conferences were shorter, and not so clinically focused. Few on the staff ate lunch in the dining room. We too often heard the word *productivity*. We saw the millennium as having closed out a century in which we took asylums for granted.

Back in the 1970s and 1980s, patients earned their privileges, gaining increased freedom around the hospital grounds, then in Rockville and beyond, moving very gradually into outpatient status. They lost privileges if regressive symptoms reemerged. We worked at minimizing anxiety through slow titration of change. The frequency of conferences and the intensity of the review process and the freedom expected of the staff in revealing their own turmoils, gave us a sense of being part of a big, messy, interestingly contentious professional family. We all knew a great deal about each other and each other's patients and they knew a lot about us. The units developed their own ambiance under the leadership of particular administrative psychiatrists and head nurses, many of whom received Lodge financial backing for their personal psychoanalyses.

During these years, Thomas McGlashan (1984, 1986a,b; McGlashan and Keats, 1989) directed a mammoth follow-up study of the Lodge patients between 1950 and 1975, funded by the Lodge. He presented aspects of the research at our yearly October symposia. He horrified us, announcing, "Dexter, Sr. and Frieda embarked on a grand experiment. The results of the experiment are now in. The experiment failed." Later, we realized that he and our boss agreed. He went on to show that only 9 percent of the schizophrenic patients were either markedly improved or recovered. His review did support schizophrenia as the appropriate diagnosis for Joanne Greenberg, and he did assess her as among the recovered. He later reported, too, that 80 percent of those with borderline disorders were markedly improved or recovered. Dexter Bullard, Jr., McGlashan, and a few others then interviewed each of the members of the medical staff, assessing our views on whether to continue the no-medications policy. I was informed that I had been the most "conservative" person interviewed.

The medical staff agreed to discontinue the practice of stopping medications on admission, and soon after agreed to discontinue use of cold wet-sheet packs; this preceded the famous Osheroff case in which Osheroff claimed the Lodge had damaged him by withholding medications (Hornstein, 2000, pp. 383–390).

As soon as medications became part of the regular treatment approach, it seemed as if the therapists had been set adrift on an ice floe. I thought often of my childhood Golden Book, *Pablo the Warm-Blooded Penguin*, who drifts toward the equator on an ever-shrinking block of ice. Finally, he floats along in his bathtub. Most of the therapists readily took on the task of prescribing medications, and the therapist–administrator split in functions essentially disappeared. With these changes, I believe, the Lodge had lost its identity and its center.

During the Bullard family's creation and ownership of the place, we were part of a dysfunctional family. The topic of suicide became temporarily forbidden and discussion of family dynamics became muted with the death by suicide of our medical director's 17-year-old son in 1976 as he was about to set off for college and while in treatment with a senior analyst. We shared the added horror that the event had been reported on the evening news, cameras focused on the family home. Years later it was recalled in the *Washington Post* article about the Lodge (Boodman, 1989). The arguments of the spokespersons for the National Alliance for the Mentally Ill found a resonance with our boss's anguish. Even now, since his death, I feel terribly gauche about mentioning these events and my ideas about them. But many of us thought that our boss believed his son would have lived had he been medicated. He began pushing for use of meds, moving us in this direction long before the Osheroff case in 1982 gave him the final impetus to discontinue the initial evaluative nonmedication phase.

The primacy of an analytic approach was replaced by our joining the "modern" era of eclecticism, emphasizing the "bio" of biopsychosocial. Likewise, the use of cold wet-sheet packs stopped in a seemingly proactive avoidance of a confrontation with the Maryland Disability Law Center. Unruly behavior was met with increased medication levels, and the therapists, once at the center of the treatment team, were less likely to hear about the outburst, while earlier the assumption would be that the outburst followed upon something in the most recent therapy session.

In my opinion, the therapeutic regression carried with it the loss of transference psychosis, and thus a lost opportunity to establish that primitive bond between infant and parent, which carries uniquely fundamental connection. Ambivalent symbiosis requires intense interdependency. I have worked with continually medicated patients for over a decade, still with a sense that we have never really met.

When Chestnut Lodge became part of Community Psychiatric Clinic (CPC), a local nonprofit business enterprise, the new director's management style was one of distance from the staff (he had no prior connection with the Lodge's approach). He was responsive primarily to the corporate board of directors and kept himself remote from personal contact with employees. He avoided clinically oriented meetings. Younger staff members, an impressive, articulate, and intuitive bunch, relied far more on patterns of work acquired in their residency or other postgraduate training, asking for and receiving far less orientation than was the case when I began at the Lodge a generation ago.

Treatment Failures

Having reviewed failings in the holding environment, I turn now to dyadic work undertaken in an institution that specialized in treating others' failed cases. The following examples represent a range of experience. I worked with a patient who had come to us at age 15 from another hospital where she had nearly amputated her left hand with a buzz saw. We worked together for two years, when she abruptly fired me. I said I felt she was cutting off her helping hand. She stubbornly refused to discuss her sudden and startling decision. She told me not to take this personally; it was time to move on. She worked with another therapist for three years, abruptly firing her as well. During work with the next therapist, she killed herself by overdosing.

Another patient, whose father killed himself, probably accidentally, by overdosing on illicit drugs, manifested an intense multiple personality during our work together. She repeatedly told me I was not treating her properly, since I was not following the protocols for working with multiples, and that she would look for a better therapist. I had been horrified when one of these multiples placed a down payment on a pistol. She brought the receipt asking what this could mean. I blocked her ability to purchase a gun in Maryland. She then "forgot" about the incident and took offense whenever I referred to it. About a year later, she decided to move across the country and patch up a broken relationship with her mother. On her return, two years later, she called asking if I would work with her, and I reminded her that while I felt better able to work with multiple personality disorder, I still didn't think I would structure the sessions as she had wanted. She found a different therapist, but suicided by overdose a few months later.

A man, who became psychotically depressed while serving at the Arlington Cemetery as a member of the honor guard during the Vietnamese War, was a Lodge patient until diminished resources required his transfer to a veteran's hospital. He was mute when we parted, staring fixedly ahead, denying me even eye contact. I realized only many months later he was dealing with the death of our relationship as if he were standing at attention, still in the honor guard officiating at a military funeral.

I endured intense feelings of failure in the final sessions with my patient Jody, whose treatment I have written about in "Chestnut Lodge: Then and Now" (1997). She had told me some months earlier that she was fed up with the Lodge point of view. She had given it enough of a chance. She was tired of psychoanalysis. Besides, she had been in a program in her home state that had gone bankrupt in the early 1970s, and it was horrible. Everyone got so mean. She would never go through that again, and she was seeing signs of it at the Lodge. She would force us to transfer her elsewhere. She would give us no choice. On the unit and grounds, she launched her campaign loudly and repeatedly. She trashed her room twice, fell down claiming paralysis and loudly threatening to resume her earlier symptom of incontinence. Her escalations occupied almost all the resources of the domiciliary care program, necessitating readmission to the more costly hospital unit. She knew her lifetime resources were dwindling. She comes from a very long-lived family.

However, in our final session, neither Jody nor I would call our work a "failure." She said she had stayed this long (over fifteen years) because of me, but she still doubted she would ever contact me. She listed former Lodge patients, friends who had written to her but whose letters she never answered. She said she hoped I would understand that she liked me and appreciated our work together, adding "I'll miss you," and I said, "Likewise." We both were teary-eyed. She enumerated her gains: "I don't say my parents are perfect anymore. I can talk about my disagreements with them. I don't have to interrupt everyone all the time. I don't use the 's' word (suicide) when I don't get what I want. I don't call my parents four times a day. I like people here, and I can say good-bye to them." As I was walking back to my office from the building where we met for the final session, she called after me. "I'll send you an announcement if I get married." "I'll want to come to the wedding," I called back. "You'll have to stay locked in the bathroom until the ceremony is over," she responded, alluding to the disastrous outburst she made at her sister's graduation, and to the family decision that she would not be allowed to attend her parents' funerals. I said, "I'll deal."

I had thought Jody and I would be working together for years and that she would succeed in living in her own place. Early in our work, however, I had horrified those attending a Wednesday Conference when I shared the following fantasy: my patient had left the Lodge, and would be expelled from a series of group homes. She would be a bag lady in Washington. I would be driving by, would notice her as I stopped at a traffic light. I would ambivalently consider greeting her and taking her to some place safe, either back to the Lodge or to my home. In my fantasy, the light changed and I drove off. Now, she has left me feeling a bit like a bag lady, carrying around my tattered possessions—clipboard, pen, my dog-eared copy of

Principles of Intensive Psychotherapy, mumbling, "I can't do it. I just can't do it."

However, my most intense professional anguish, an ongoing sense of failing, is in relation to work with a patient from the premedication era. Fran was one of my first patients at the Lodge, arriving there at age 16 having been ill since age 9. Psychological testing documented her psychosis and her high risk of suicide. Staff called her the sickest schizophrenic patient admitted to the adolescent hospital, which had opened three years earlier. Over the course of our seven years of work, Fran's visual, auditory, and olfactory hallucinations, her self-mutilation by cutting and burning, her impulsive acts such as setting fire to her bed, her running away, all stopped. She graduated from the Lodge high school, attended the community college, and then state university, held jobs and had friends, had her own apartment, all this without receiving psychotropic medications. I felt we had succeeded in working through and diminishing her extraordinarily intense ambivalence toward those she needed—her parents and parent substitutes. Fran had become simply human and had left a hallucinated world where she was tortured by a mad queen and where she spoke a private language.

Fran returned home, across the country, graduated from college, enrolled in a graduate program, and fell in love with a fellow grad student, whom she married. They had four children, living in a tiny and remote college town in the south. She received no psychotherapy and was symptom-free for almost fifteen years. I heard from her occasionally, and felt extremely proud of our work, the individual treatment, and the work of the hospital community. We had conquered her schizophrenia, had won the war.

Disaster struck with the birth of Fran's fourth child. She called me, and we began weekly conversations which have continued for years, and for which I do not charge her. She told me that each baby was larger than its predecessor was. Delivery of this one had cracked her pelvis. She had felt it happen, and since then had felt her body tilt and come apart with every step. One year later, her doctors diagnosed a dislocated sacroiliac joint, something apparently not surgically treatable, previously having said that her body was fine and that she was

imagining this pain. She could not work or care for her ener-
getic brood. She was beset by flashbacks to chronic sexual
abuse perpetrated by a man who had lived with the family from
the time she was 8. He had begun abusing her almost as soon
as he arrived. What? At first I dissociated, actually forgetting
her revelation. Next, I simultaneously believed and didn't believe her, and kept tuning out during our telephone conversations. There had been so much that was unbelievable in her
earlier flamboyant hallucinations and complex delusions. This
might just be another one, borne of the media's attention on
sexual abuse, which erupted after we had concluded our seven
years of work together.

How could I, seeing this patient four times weekly, and how
could the staff, working with her daily, or the so erudite psychologist, how could all of us have missed this? I suspect none
of us ever asked her whether she'd been sexually abused. We
seemed to have succeeded in overcoming her psychosis until
a painful complication of delivery catapulted her back. Only
after she began a partial reintegration did she disclose chronic
sexual abuse. But revealing this to me and to her current clinicians has not sufficed in permitting her to fully resume her
professional or family responsibilities.

Even though we have long and regular telephone conversations, which support Fran's ongoing psychotherapy and impressive pharmacological regimen, we have yet to recover that
sense of humor, joy, and optimism that carried her forward for
fifteen years after she left the Lodge. For all of our analytic
orientation and intensity, we had not considered it. She in turn
had many rationalizations for not telling us: Her parents would
kill her; her abusing relative would come to rescue her from
the hospital when his marriage, which had ushered in her psychosis, finally ended. But we would be alert to his significance
and would not let him visit; her unit administrator would hu-
miliate her in the unit meetings. I had been diagnosed with
cancer; she and my other patients were informed about this
(Silver, 1990). She feared I would not be able to withstand
hearing about the horror she had endured. But I had never
guessed. She had talked about being raped at knifepoint in a
park. Her parents said no such thing could have happened,

since she was never left unsupervised. One Thanksgiving, she screamed in agony, as she hallucinated delivering a baby. I certainly recognized the sexual nature of her distress, but did not consider the possibility of sexual abuse beginning during latency.

Conclusion

Chronically ill patients and the therapists who treat them have much in common. I suspect that from our earliest years, we all, therapists and patients alike, dedicated ourselves to making one or both parents really integrated, predictable, confident, happy people. Thus, we are no strangers to chronic frustration and feelings of doom. "Only insofar as the therapist becomes able to see, and respond to, the patient's genuinely therapeutic striving toward him, and earlier toward the parents, will the patient be himself receptive to therapy" (Searles, 1967, p. 75).

I speculate that those of us who became therapists had parents who rejected our efforts to heal them while praising our efforts and accomplishments in related areas—academic, athletic, or social. Lodge therapists who stayed at this work seemed to identify more with the patient than with the patient's parent, while inevitably taking a parental role in the patient's life. Somewhere in our development and our paradoxical personality adaptations may lie an explanation for our much higher than usual incidence of malignancies. While we acknowledge our therapeutic despair, we securely acknowledge that we need more help than we can get. While I often joked that I was not ready for outpatiency, inpatient work became increasingly taxing. The hospital's mission, working with people who cannot get by in less intensive treatment settings, defined itself as a specialized community, attending to the needs of patients and staff *alike*. The needs of both groups grew greater as pressures mounted to produce more with less.

Searles assumes a psychodynamic basis for schizophrenia. Without explicitly stating it, he implies a need for a careful prospective study of parents and infants, with emphasis on mothers who because of depression, paranoia, psychosis, or other inner stress, are not able to admire and revel in the miracle of the new soul to whom they have given birth. We now have supporting data from two sources: infant observation and national demographic studies. The research efforts of Beebe, Lachmann, and Jaffe (1997; Beebe, Jaffe, Beebe, Feldstein, Crown, and Jasnow, 2001) are producing powerful data confirming the currently unpopular notion that when the primary caretaker cannot focus positively on the baby, the baby suffers enormous developmental disruption. Likewise, the Finnish studies of very young children unable to socialize have shown that early family intervention leads ten years later to a significant decline in the incidence of schizophrenic break-down (Alanen, Lehtinen, Lehtinen, Aaltonen, and Räkkö-läinen, 2000).

Using the data collected and studied by McGlashan (1986a), Bert Nayfack has studied the crucial questions: What happened in those treatments that worked? What differentiated the effec-tive from the ineffective or even destructive therapists? I hope this study will find its way to publication as a working guide to those case managers and other clinicians who are still meeting regularly and intensively with patients suffering from schizo-phrenia. To summarize, those therapists who bullied and con-fronted their patients, who prodded them into improved functioning, who insulted their patients, failed. Those with re-spect for them, who recognized the damaging power of insults and sarcasm, who had a generally tender but not diminishing style, supported the patients' growth and recovery.

We have been humbled by the fiscal and professional limita-tions imposed on our working conditions. In the proud days of Chestnut Lodge and of psychoanalysis, Harold Searles warned of the gloomier times to come:

> Psychoanalysts are essentially the only group of therapists who, by reason of their commitment to a courageous and unceasing exploration of their own inner lives in the service of their treat-ing of their patients, are equipped to discern, explore, and rescue the components of common humanity in the patient who is overwhelmed by schizophrenic illness which, to less in-formed eyes, marks him as essentially nonhuman. . . . If the psy-choanalytic movement itself takes refuge in what I regard

essentially as a phenothiazine-and-genetics flight from this problem, then the long dark night of the soul will have been ushered in, not only for these vast numbers of schizophrenic patients—for the current ones who are already largely lost, and for the multitude who will follow them in the future—but also for those relatively few psychoanalysts who are particularly interested in this field. . . . For once we give up our heretofore unremitting, open-mindedly observational effort to discern, through an empathic exploration of our own so-called countertransference responses to our patient, the human essence in him which is struggling against the psychopathology which besets his humanness, there is no end to this flight on our part [Searles, 1975, pp. 227–228].

I was a part of the Lodge system to the end. I mourn the family feeling that held the place together during the Bullard years. Staff members and patients who left were leaving their newfound home, each of them having formed their own transferences to the place, its trees, its buildings, and its people. Whether such an institutional transference is necessary for the recovery of patients and their therapists remains an open question.

References

Alanen, Y., Lehtinen, V., Lehtinen, K., Aaltonen, J. & Räkköläinen, V. (2000), The Finnish integrated model for early treatment of schizophrenia and related psychoses. In: *Psychosis: Psychological Approaches and Their Effectiveness*, ed. B. Martindale, A. Bateman, M. Crowe, & F. Margison. London: Gaskell International Society for the Psychological Treatments of the Schizophrenias and Other Psychoses (ISPS), pp. 235–236)

Auden, W. H. (1954), Horae Canonicae. In: *Collected Poems*, ed. E. Mendelson. New York: Vintage, 1991, pp. 627–642.

Beebe, B., Lachmann, F., & Jaffe, J. (1997), Mother–infant interaction structures and presymbolic self and object representations. *Psychoanal. Dial.*, 7:133–182.

Boodman, S. (1989), The mystery of Chestnut Lodge: A horrible place and a wonderful place. *Washington Post Mag.*, October 8:18–24, 38–43.

Chessick, R. (1971), *Why Psychotherapists Fail.* New York: Science House.

Farber, L. (1966), Schizophrenia and the mad psychotherapists. In: *The Ways of the Will: Essays toward a Psychology and Psychopathology of Will.* New York: Basic Books, pp. 184–208.

Feinsilver, D. (1986), *Towards a Comprehensive Model for Schizophrenic Disorders: Psychoanalytic Essays in Memory of Ping-Nie Pao, M.D.* Hillsdale, NJ: Basic Books, pp. 184–208.

Fromm-Reichmann, F. (1950), *Principles of Intensive Psychotherapy.* Chicago: University of Chicago Press.

——— (1956), Reminiscences of Europe. In: *Psychoanalysis and Psychosis*, ed. A.-L. Silver. Madison, CT: International Universities Press, 1989, pp. 469–481.

——— (1959), *Psychoanalysis and Psychotherapy: Selected Papers of Frieda Fromm-Reichmann*, ed. D. M. Bullard, Sr. Chicago: University of Chicago Press.

——— (1990), The assets of the mentally handicapped: The interplay of mental illness and creativity, ed. & intro. A.-L. Silver. *J. Amer. Acad. Psychoanal.*, 18:47–72.

Greenberg, J. (Hannah Green) (1964), *I Never Promised You a Rose Garden.* New York: Holt, Rinehart & Winston.

——— (1967), In praise of my doctor—Frieda Fromm-Reichmann. *Contemp. Psychoanal.*, 4:73–75.

Hartwell, C. (1996), The schizophrenogenic mother concept in American psychiatry. *Psychiatry*, 59:274–297.

Hornstein, G. (2000), *To Redeem One Person Is to Redeem the World: The Life of Frieda Fromm-Reichmann.* New York: Free Press.

Jaffe, J., Beebe, B., Feldstein, S., Crown, C. L., & Jasnow, M. (2001), *Rhythms of Dialogue in Infancy.* Monograph series of the Society for Research in Child Development, Vol. 66, No. 2.

Johannessen, J., Larsen, T., McGlashan, T., & Vaglum, P. (2000), Early intervention in psychosis: The TIPS Project, a multi-centre study in Scandinavia. In: *Psychosis: Psychological Approaches and Their Effectiveness*, ed. B. Martindale, A. Bateman, M. Crowe, & F. Margison. London: Gaskell International Society for the Psychological Treatments of the Schizophrenias and Other Psychoses (ISPS), pp. 210–234.

McAfee, L. (1989), Interview with Joanne Greenberg: With three poems by Joanne Greenberg. In: *Psychoanalysis and Psychosis*, ed. A.-L. Silver. Madison, CT: International Universities Press.

McGlashan, T. (1984), The Chestnut Lodge follow-up study: I & II. *Arch. Gen. Psychiatry*, 41:573–601.

——— (1986a), The Chestnut Lodge follow-up study: III & IV. *Arch. Gen. Psychiatry*, 43:20–30, 167–176.

——— (1986b), Predictors of shorter-, medium-, and longer-term outcome in schizophrenia. *Amer. J. Psychiatry*, 143:50–55.

——— Keats, C. (1989), *Schizophrenia: Treatment Process and Outcome.* Washington, DC: American Psychiatric Press.

Nayfack, B. *The Comforting Presence: Narratives on Therapist Outcomes with Schizophrenia-labeled Patients in the Chestnut Lodge Follow-up Study.* Typescript.

Oxford English Dictionary (1933), "Fail." c.v.

Pao, P.-N. (1979), *Schizophrenic Disorders: Theory and Treatment from a Psychodynamic Point of View.* New York: International Universities Press.

Searles, H. F. (1960), *The Nonhuman Environment: In Normal Development and in Schizophrenia.* New York: International Universities Press.

———— (1967), The "dedicated physician." In the field of psychotherapy and psychoanalysis. In: *Countertransfernce and Related Subjects: Selected Papers.* New York: International Universities Press, 1979, pp. 71–88.

———— (1975), Countertransference and theoretical model. In: *Psychotherapy of Schizophrenia,* ed. J. Gunderson & P. Mosher. New York: Jason Aronson, pp. 223–228.

Silver, A.-L. (1989), Introduction. In: *Psychoanalysis and Psychosis,* ed. A.-L. Silver. Madison, CT: International Universities Press.

———— (1990), Resuming the work with a life-threatening illness—And further reflections. In: Schwartz, H. & Silver, A.-L. (eds.) *Illness in the Analyst: Implications for the Treatment Relationship.* Madison, CT: International Universities Press, pp. 151–176.

———— (1993), The Chestnut Lodge Wednesday Case Conference: The One-to-One Laboratory in its Psychosocial Setting. In: *The Psychotherapy of Schizophrenia: Effective Clinical Approaches—Controversies, Critiques and Recommendations,* ed. G. Benedetti & P. Furlan, Seattle, WA: Hogrefe & Huber Publishers, pp. 195–198.

———— (1996), Women who lead. *Amer. J. Psychoanal.,* 56:3–16.

———— (1997), Chestnut Lodge, then and now. *Contemp. Psychoanal.,* 33:227–249.

———— (2000), The current relevance of Fromm-Reichmann's works: The 2000 Frieda Fromm-Reichmann Lecture. *Psychiatry,* 63:308–322.

———— P. C. Feuer (1989), Fromm-Reichmann's contributions at staff conferences. In: *Psychoanalysis and Psychosis,* ed. A.-L. Silver. Madison, CT: International Universities Press, pp. 23–45.

Stanton, A. H., & Schwartz, M. S. (1954), *The Mental Hospital.* New York: Basic Books.

Winchester, S. (1998), *The Professor and the Madman: A Tale of Murder, Insanity, and the Making of the Oxford English Dictionary.* New York: HarperCollins.

Winerip, M. (1999), Bedlam on the streets. *NY Times Mag.,* May 23:42–70.

4

Hidden Influences on Success or Failure in Clinical Psychoanalysis

STUART W. TWEMLOW, M.D.

> *It would be far easier if we could avoid the patient as*
> *we explore the realm of psychopathology; it would be*
> *far simpler if we could limit ourselves to examining*
> *the chemistry and physiology of his brain, and to treat-*
> *ing mental events as objects alien to our immediate*
> *experience, or as mere variables in impersonal statisti-*
> *cal formulae. Important as these approaches are for*
> *the understanding of human behavior, they cannot*
> *alone uncover or explain all the relevant facts. To see*
> *into the mind of another, we must repeatedly immerse*
> *ourselves in the flood of his associations and feelings;*
> *we must be ourselves the instrument that sounds him*
> *[Nemiah, 1961, p. 4].*

John Nemiah's comment forty years ago preempted the American revolution in psychiatric treatment of the mentally ill in
the 1980s. Psychoanalysts reading this chapter might well ask
why such a quote would be included here. In my opinion one

of the main problems facing contemporary psychoanalysis is the failure of some of the old guard to accept the importance of the integration of psychoanalysis into the mainstream of modern psychiatry. This is equally so for the mainstream of modern psychiatry, which has failed to give a prominent place to psychoanalytic approaches to psychiatry.

Although it is well known that Freud not only predicted, but also hoped that analysts would lead research into the biological basis of mental illness, one wonders whether he would today not turn in his grave at the current childish territorial antagonism between the biological and psychoanalytic camps.

Our profession of psychiatry is undergoing some major shifts in its identity. Whereas this chapter is not the place to review these shifts in gory political detail, it is important to outline some of the implications of the various choices available to make sense of the material that will follow, which addresses some of the potential causes of failures in psychoanalytic treatment.

In contrast with most developed countries, psychoanalytic approaches to the treatment of mental illness dominated U.S. psychiatry for several decades until 1980 with the publication of DSM-III. Although psychoanalytic enclaves have existed in most countries in developed nations, psychoanalysis has had little, if any, influence on the main thrust of psychiatric care and delivery of psychiatric services. For example, in Britain the tiny British Psychoanalytic Society with some four hundred members has had an enormous influence on American psychoanalytic thinking, although almost no influence on the delivery of medical services and psychiatric care in Britain. It is in itself an interesting issue as to why such a tiny group of individuals should have such an enormous impact on the American and world psychoanalytic scene, assuming that the British are not born with any better brains than Americans!

In the United States, as a result of combined chance, political, and perhaps personal charismatic elements, psychoanalytic thinking has until recently dominated treatment of mentally ill individuals, although it was often oversold, not only as a method of psychiatric treatment but as a solution for all the psychological woes of the world. Unfortunately, psychoanalytic approaches have failed dismally in this regard. Spearheaded by maverick psychoanalysts like Spitzer, psychiatry rejected the psychoanalytic approach to the etiology of mental illness and adopted instead a phenomenologically based, statistically derived syndrome approach to the classification of mental illness, resulting in the first edition of DSM-III in 1980.

Spitzer advocated what was later adopted by the American psychiatric scene as a return to "known for certain" fundamentals, which he hoped would allow the growth of a rational, evidence-based approach to the etiology of psychiatric illness. Subsequent additions beyond DSM-IV will likely revise and radically change the way psychiatric illness is classified, as new psychodynamic, neuroscience, and psychiatric genetic contributions become available, allowing multidimensional nonlinear etiological equations to the developed to include psychodynamic axes.

Psychoanalysts have reacted in an ambivalent and paradoxical way to this change in their political influence. Some have advocated a complete withdrawal from the third-party payment system and a return to the way in which analysts have usually functioned over the past hundred years, which is as the treaters of the tiny percent of individuals who can afford such intensive and extensive treatment. Some others of us have explored the possibility that psychoanalytic contributions might be of greater value in application to contemporary social issues rather than as a method of treatment per se (Twemlow and Ramzy, 1999). A third group is attempting to adapt psychoanalytic ideas to the DSM approach to psychiatric illness in order to provide a rapprochement with modern psychiatry. Today it is clear that psychoanalysis, whether it fails or succeeds as a treatment method, is seen by many powerful psychiatric leaders to be of little relevance to the general psychiatric scene in America at the turn of this century. Thus, analysts who suggest that we should withdraw from discussion with psychiatry if it does not accept our pronouncements, speak of denial of cosmic proportions!

It is my contention that many failures in psychoanalytic treatment in the United States result often from too narrow a paradigm of what is truly "a psychoanalytic process"[1] with a defensive overfocus on interpretation as a vehicle of cure and a relative neglect of contributions from the neurosciences and from the British, French, and Relational schools. Such rigidity often goes far beyond friendly professional discussion and argument.

A Comment on the Nature of "Failure" in Psychoanalysis

Prior to review of the clinical material, it will be most useful for us to take a look at the concept of failure itself. The *Oxford English Dictionary* (OED) defines failure as derived from the Latin "faillire"; that is, to disappoint expectations, to be wanting or defective. *Webster's Third International Dictionary* also defines failure in terms of not doing what one has promised. Such definitions imply a countertransference quality to clinical failure. In my experience, I have on occasion created trouble for myself in overpromising results to patients for whom analysis is economically and personally feasible, in a misplaced desire to maintain a psychoanalytic practice in a highly competitive environment.

From another perspective, failures in psychoanalysis can be classified into several types:

1. The failure is the patient's "fault"; severe ego defects not apparent during initial evaluation subvert the treatment process.
2. The failure is the analyst's "fault"; for example, an inflexible theoretical paradigm that precludes use of medications as part of the psychoanalytic process; countertransference scotomata.

---

[1]This term is often used to reject applications for certification in psychoanalysis by the American Psychoanalytic Association with such wording as—"there does not appear to have been a true psychoanalytic process in this case."

3. The failure is due to unavoidable reality factors; for example, changing financial circumstances, job transfer, or illness.

Philosophers, including Grünbaum (1984), have pointed out that none of these oft-cited causes of failure are seen by psychoanalysts as a failure of psychoanalytic theory as such. Although this is not the appropriate time to engage in a discussion of the scientific viability of psychoanalytic theory, I will mention my own experience over the past several years of teaching a course at the Topeka Psychoanalytic Institute, which has been reformulated and renamed several times, reflecting marked shifts in how psychoanalytic theory looks at technique factors important for a successful treatment outcome. Initially, it was taught in two separate courses: "Special Problems in Psychoanalytic Treatment" which considered the sorts of patients who didn't fit the classical model. It included reading assignments such as special problems of the supervised analysis; erotized versus erotic transference; silence and sleepiness in the analyst and patient; severe regressive phenomena in the transference, including psychotic and hating states; negative therapeutic reaction; and acting out. A parallel course taught at the same time was called "Parameters and Modifications," and dealt mainly with analysis of sicker patients, including classical studies by Zetzel, Kernberg, Klein, and Rosenfeld. This course naturally defined a parameter against an ideal analytic state as described in the landmark paper by Eissler (1953). The parameter was always the minimal necessary and would be "fully analyzed" before the analysis was considered complete. These two courses were collapsed into the one in the 1995 to 1996 curriculum, now called "Special Issues and Modifications," an unsatisfactory name that still implies some ideal of classical analysis. The topics covered in this course are not at all special, but quite mundane. Yet they are essential topics to deal with if the analysis is to be successful; and they are often not covered in other courses in the typical four-year curriculum.

A listing of topics reveals obvious factors with not so obvious complexity: extra-analytic contacts, the fee and missed sessions, and special challenges to the functioning of the analyst. These challenges include the sick mental health professional, the boundary violating therapist, physical illness and aging in the analyst, the pregnant analyst, the V.I.P., the dying patient, the impact of race, culture, and ethnicity on the psychoanalytic process, religion and spirituality, the influence of major life changes like divorce, childbirth, loss of a child, on the analyst, and the use of medications in psychoanalysis—not an exhaustive list. From this point of view then, failures of psychoanalysis may be due to factors that have no relationship to clinical or metapsychological theory per se, but instead have to do mainly with apparently peripheral topics that are part of the everyday reality of the clinical situation.

Now these courses have come full circle, as the proper role of clinical psychoanalysis is being redefined; the special has now become the ordinary and theory is less center stage. It is attention to these hidden yet obvious factors which often contributes to the success or failure of psychoanalytic treatment.

There is another set of more obscure factors inherent in the value structure of psychoanalytic treatment that can have a marked effect on outcome; and that involves how a "healthy outcome" is defined. Freudian concepts of health imply an undesirable isolationist philosophy where autonomy is seen as freedom from all needs, including the need for relationships. Beginning with Kohut, there has ensued a remarkably effective assault on that idea through the concept of self-object, which defines a "healthy" ongoing lifelong need for relationships. Many "subschools" have emerged that emphasize the curative value of therapeutic relationships above the rational use of insight. In spite of Freud's apparently relativistic emphasis on happiness in love and work as the main benchmarks of mental health, his theories had come to be seen by some to embody a cold, rigid isolationism. A strong emerging philosophical foundation for relational–intersubjective psychoanalysis is being developed by such writers as Hoffman (1998) and Strenger (1999). Hoffman, with his concept of dialectical constructivism, emphasizes how interpretation and interpersonal influences are inextricably, dialectically intermingled; one is not effective without the other. Strenger's concept of self-creation, a postmodern vision of man struggling to "author" him- or herself against strong social pressures, raises many thought-provoking questions about matters that psychoanalysts often take as givens. For example, Strenger explores in depth Phillips's (1996) observation that: "most psychoanalytic theory now is a contemporary version of the edict book; improving our internal manners, advising us on our best sexual behavior (usually called maturity, or mental health, or a decent self). It is, indeed, dismaying how quickly psychoanalysis has become the science of the sensible passions . . ." (1996, p. 87). Shockingly, Strenger makes a convincing argument for the healthiness of sadomasochistic sex in the case of one of his patients, seeing it not merely as an unsatisfactory defensive compromise. Only time (and well-designed outcome studies) will tell whether these paradigmatic shifts in psychoanalytic theory and practices will reduce failures and improve the patient's health and happiness. Perhaps then all psychoanalysis really does is convert neurotic misery into normal (acceptable) misery! But then again, perhaps that *is* success, and sufficient?

A Clinical Case: Negotiating the Nonnegotiable in the Psychoanalysis of a Narcissistic Woman

As I began to collect my thoughts about this case, I realized on a very personal level how difficult it is to admit to failure. Within the OED definition, failure has to do with expectations not being met. I find that I usually try to rationalize that some good has come out of an analytic process, even if it is interrupted, as in this case, perhaps because it is hard to admit that all the time, energy, and money spent has been for naught. I note that the use of the word *interruption* implies the possibility of continuing later. Although further psychoanalysis did not eventuate in this case, contact has been maintained on a once-a-year basis. The nonnegotiable in this patient, I believe, contributed to the premature termination of the formal analytic process. Stuart Pizer (1998) describes the nonnegotiable as follows: "Ultimately, the non-negotiable is a relational property, determined by the convergence of qualities and limitations in both members of the dyad (analysis and analyst)" (p. 108).

What is negotiated in the relational model of psychoanalysis is an interaction between the interpretive component that gives insight and understanding, especially of repetitions, and a relational component that is an interpersonal and real connection between the patient and the analyst in ways that promote nonverbal psychic healing; that is, by virtue of the existence of a variety of nonverbal nurturing and interpreting gestures derived from the analyst's mode of being, way of relating, tone of voice, as well as therapeutic self-revelations from the analyst. As Pizer says, if this does not happen, "The non-negotiable enters analytic space, like a deadness, or deadliness, eliminating space, time or process" (p. 108).

Pizer goes on to note that transference repetition is an enactment communicating nonverbally painful growth experiences or lack of necessary growth experiences. It is "as if trauma has corrupted the symbolic utility of words or disrupted the bridging process necessary between internal feeling states and that representational element garnered from the outside to describe experience in metaphoric terms" (p. 115).

According to Pizer, a nonnegotiable patient is one who functions in a concrete mode, continually reenacting and repeating who they are and what they feel, thus precluding the possibility of negotiation of meaning and relationship in verbal terms. Put in another way, words have ceased to be a very trustworthy way of representing what the patient feels. At this point, the patient becomes helpless, using only action defenses that obscure meaning and affect or dissociative defenses that disperse meaning and affect. Pizer lists a variety of nonnegotiable, psychiatric states, including compulsions, addictions, perversions, somatizations, and a variety of others. In fact, essentially what Pizer is saying is that certain types of conflicts, because they are not able to be expressed in words and thus have meaning assigned to them in a thinkable sense, remain as what Bion (1967) would call beta fragments or preconceptions, and are thus nonnegotiable because they are essentially nonrelational nor thinkable, and instead act to defend the patient against exposure to meaningful communication. In my experience, there is another more common and more important meaning for such defenses, and that is to prevent the catastrophic experience of endless and nameless dread; an isolating, meaningless, unthinkable state of cosmic terror that was first identified by Bion and later elaborated by Grotstein (1990).

Isabel was a mildly obese, Caucasian woman who first presented for analysis at the age of 40. She functioned in the superior range of intelligence and had nearly completed a graduate degree in geriatrics. She worked as an occupational therapist at a nearby for-profit hospital. She had thought of psychoanalysis for many years, since it intrigued her and she wanted to know more about herself. She was in no acute distress initially, although she had tried many ways of losing weight, including behavioral modification and hypnosis, and listed weight loss as one of her main problems. Symptom checklists, however, indicated a variety of other problems, including chronic headache, feeling of being burned out, job dissatisfaction, anhedonia, and difficulty in relating with others. She said of herself, "Initially, I feel like I'm standing on the edge of life, but somehow don't, won't get involved. I'm waiting for something to happen."

Psychological testing confirmed good verbal grasp, excellent ego strength, with an intellectualizing somewhat obsessive–compulsive cognitive style and some elements of narcissistic vulnerability. Painful affect seemed to threaten her, but there was no evidence of serious depression. She plainly described an aggravating personality style, her "smart mouth," with which she provoked people into angry responses, which gave her an excuse to avoid them. An early indication of complex transference and potentially countertransfernce models was given in her response to the TAT Card, 12 M: "This young man on a bed has decided to go to a faith healer because he has some incurable disease, or what he thinks is incurable. . . . The outcome is the guy never really had a bad disease in the first place; didn't understand what the doctor said. So, he didn't die, but he thinks the faith healer cures him of something he didn't have. So, he becomes a jerk to deal with because he can't convince him. And the faith healer becomes richer because he gets a lot of money to do this thing." The patient implies, clearly, the ease with which one can get into a power struggle with her, especially if trying to convince her of something. She also reveals the fear of being exploited, especially from those who need what she has, and she implies also a lack of feeling of inner strength to resist that exploitation.

The patient began a five-times-a-week psychoanalysis, completing about five hundred hours before premature termination. The first two years of the analysis revealed much about her family background: She had a brother, some six years younger, who had a long criminal record. Her mother was a woman raised to obey her husband, and she did so without question. Her father was often extremely bad tempered and had a severe alcohol problem. He was a career military officer and was frequently away on overseas assignments. He did not keep up communication with the children during these long assignments, some of which would be more than a year in duration. During one of those assignments, the mother became severely depressed and needed to be hospitalized for a three-month period. The children were cared for by an aunt, who continues a positive relationship with the patient. At the time of the mother's hospitalization, the patient was in the middle of the Oedipus complex with virtually no contact with stable male figures. She developed at that time several terrifying autistic defenses. She began bingeing and vomiting, she had violent dreams of being eviscerated and having her eyes cut out, and enacted repetitive head-banging to the point of bruising herself and needing emergency care. She became enuretic and encopretic and also indicated that her teeth rotted out at that time, later necessitating a complete set of dentures. Pathetically, she would get up early in the morning to wait outside for her father to return, although he never did establish a consistent pattern of contact with her or with his son. She was always looking for male figures, and on one occasion, when she was about 10, she was encouraged to pose for a picture taken by a military officer, a young man who then molested her sexually, though without violence. She did not describe this experience as negative at all; in fact, she viewed it as highly positive. She felt that after this experience, she began to feel more attractive to men and less critical of her body, which up to that time she had always thought was ugly and very overweight. Schoolwork was easy for her and she never had to work. In high school, she dated on very few occasions, and usually boys who would disappoint her by their macho brutality, deserting her, and leaving her not knowing what had happened.

During her college years and throughout her life, she had a number of relationships with men, all of which were "like a crush," as she described it, and very disappointing. These men failed to perceive her needs and usually eventually left her without warning. At the age of 38, she developed carcinoma in situ of the cervix and had a hysterectomy, with no recurrence of cancer. This premature termination of her childbearing potential seemed not to affect her much until the later phases of the analysis. She simply took it as something she would have to put up with. She felt that with her tomboy nature, she could tough it out. This way of numbing herself to disappointments was a long-standing and repeated enactment, especially with male figures. She reached the middle years of her life without completing her main degree, with no children, no husband, and few friends. She felt that she was grossly obese, although clinically she was only mildly obese. Although quite an attractive woman, she felt very unattractive and lived by herself in a tiny and rather ugly house in a poor part of town.

A typical session, highlighting the first two years of this process and illustrating the power struggle, the fear of being damaged by closeness, and a nonnegotiable lack of trust, is illustrated below. It occurred about six months before the interruption of her treatment, and after two years of analysis.

She was on time for this Monday session.

Patient: Thinking a lot about why I'm so antagonistic with you. I don't know what the core of it is. I'm being aggravated but don't know why. It has to do with what I expect. I have to change what I expect. I want answers. I'm wondering if one day, I'll figure it all out.

She remained silent for about three minutes and was lying in a typical rigid posture, in which it was hardly possible to see her breathing.

Patient:	I had the idea that there's something not right here. There's something wrong with you. I feel you're often in a good mood or a bad mood, that you're not feeling well, that you're distracted. Then I will change my mood depending on what you do. Then I get into trouble because I feel angry. I've been reading that dreams are important, they give the state of the ego and tell you about the relationship of the analyst. I'm very frightened of finding out anything about you outside of this room. I would feel the worst when there was that sort of crossover.
Analyst:	It seems like you feel like you have to accommodate to my moods and my problems, as if you've been subjected to it before.
Patient:	Yes, you're supposed to be an anchor.
Analyst:	Then you're disappointed.
Patient:	Didn't realize that until this morning. I didn't know I was going through all these things. So when you respond to me in this habitual pattern I realized I was not getting anywhere. Then I thought to myself, maybe I'm just getting whiny. It doesn't change anything and you're the person who knows me the best. (somewhat wistfully)
Analyst:	So, there were good and bad elements in relating to me?
Patient:	Some dreams came to mind. Only fragments, but they're hard to remember. In the first fragment, I am in a Chinese store in Chinatown. There are three little children, very tiny, like dwarfs, and I am trying to catch them. In a second fragment, I am in a familiar place, a restaurant, eating a special lunch that "I had never had before." And a third fragment: Some students were eating lunch after a session, I didn't know what the session was, but a friend says that the students would be accommodated eventually.
Analyst:	Where do you want to start with the dreams?
Patient:	When in Vietnam, I needed much more adventure in my life. I used to go to a town near a border. I

went with a girl friend of mine who had a boyfriend and we would hitchhike. We were spoiled rotten because we were the only women in the group. A colonel had lunch with us. Took us to a farmhouse and we had the best time, just partying.

Analyst: So you can have fun with a colonel and food sometimes does something for you other than make you fat and miserable. I wonder if what's going on is that at times you argue with me in a way that bores you and seems repetitious and that by now you've also seen how you're reenacting what went on, particularly with your father who was not there when you needed him and your mother who also, although physically there, was ill. You became extremely miserable and disorganized as a little girl when you realized how alone you were. And I notice that when you uncover those sorts of feelings, your voice gets very loud, as if you feel you have to shout at me in case I don't hear it, in case I'm too much like your dad and he can't hear you from a long way away in Korea. But I hear you.

Patient: I have to keep reminding myself that people are not my parents, that you are different, I hope; you say you are.

Although only a partial analysis of this complex session is possible here, the reenactment of the past struggle seems to be counterpointed by her feeling that I am also reenacting something with her by repeatedly behaving like a typical stereotyped analyst with my various reflective comments, rather than giving her the answers she feels that she needs, a guarantee of lifelong care and attention, I suspect. The session opened up enough material for me to be able to interpret on a deeper level my appreciation of the depth of her misery, her need for nurturance, and especially how miserable and alone she must have been as a child. She realized that minitransference psychoses occur intermittently and that she needs to be careful to remind herself that I am not her parent and that others aren't either. In addition, she wistfully and intelligently notes her lack of trust in me, in spite of my "performance."

At the next session she came in very disheveled and expressed a wish to leave analysis "right now." She also commented that there must be something wrong with her, that she doesn't pick things up very quickly (i.e., that I really might be untrustworthy), that as a child she was always considered the bright one and the good one and that her parents expected too much of her (that I do this to stress her out). She then set a termination date about a month ahead; however, as the time for termination came closer, she expressed a desire to see me once a week for a period of time. During the once-a-week sessions, she was a lot more comfortable, as the relationship pressure was much less.

During these less intense sessions, she reflected on how my stereotyped reflective analytic presence made her feel I was not real, and not trustworthy, since I may just be repeating meaningless phrases. The times when I reflected my personal responses to her, temporarily restored hope. In her view, I fluctuated between a human and nonhuman presence, which enraged and depressed her since it duplicated the childhood experience with her father. My own countertransference feelings reflected from the outset that I could not fulfill her needs, which at times seemed to require parental holding and nurturance. The premature interruption precipitated a guilty depression for which I received consultation-treatment. I have yet to experience in any other patient such an intense pressure to act in ways that I knew would be harmful to the patient. At times, my secretary commented that I seemed different after seeing this patient. At times I felt brain dead; for example, I "forgot" details of her life; projective identification, counterprojective identification, and extractive introjection processes set the daily tone of the analytic experience. I felt battered and bruised, the victim of the enraged acting in of her demands for answers (reparation) and revenge. I "became" the miserable encopretic 5-year-old with rotting teeth. What caused this analysis to be interrupted was mainly my failure to see that the intensity of the contact did not make the nonnegotiable lack of trust more negotiable; instead, once the patient had modulated the pace, the treatment became more successful.

She continued on for a three-month period without a definite termination date, but then was sent for overseas service by the military. In the final session before she went overseas, she made many statements that revealed an intense internal feeling of being disappointed and how "I'm afraid of certain people who love me and leave me," repeated in a variety of different ways. In one session, after a one-week absence on my part, she described feelings like "someone scraping my brains out of my skull, taking out my eyeballs and putting them in water," with a feeling of wanting to push her cheekbones real tight and push her eyes too hard, telling me, I believe, that there was something she could not see about herself, because if she did, it would result in severe psychic injury and destruction of her mind. During this time, she also became deeply depressed. She began taking Prozac, 40 mg a day, and achieved relief of depression. I reassured her that she could return anytime she liked after her military service and resume her analysis. That reassurance seemed to allay many fears that surfaced that she could not see me again because I would not like her since she'd not completed the analysis to my satisfaction.

She wrote me a quite fearful card just prior to leaving for military service, in which she reported that she had asked her mother to help her out for the first time in several decades. She felt good about that. She felt like this was a very important way to prove that she was a "real soldier" and was able to be open about her realistic fears of being killed, although she mentioned at that point missing her quiet and simple life. She said, "I am comfortable with who I am, although I still tend to be too independent."

This analysis terminated some ten years ago. I have seen the patient once each year for a renewal of her Prozac prescription, when she needs it over the wintertime. She has noticed definite seasonal affective disorder, and Prozac helps her maintain her moods during the bleak winter months. It also represents a way of keeping in touch with me. I noticed a significant shift from a cynical, fixed smile and physically rigid body, to a now much more settled individual who still has no close friends, but decides they aren't worth making herself miserable about. She seemed much less defensive and able to interact with her parents, by now very old. She asserted, interestingly enough, her right to be a hermit and controls very well her degree of closeness to her parents without guilt. She also says she's happy single without children and is much more comfortable making Topeka her home. The act of leaving the analysis, without my retaliation, and the experience of combat gave her a greater feeling of strength and a right to assert herself rather than be exploited. She is no longer paranoid, and lives in an attractive house in a nice part of town.

In retrospect, the TAT response suggested the existence of deeper level pathology, as did the history of what sounded like a psychotic regression at about the age of 5, with the mobilization of periodic states, reminiscent of sensory perceptual regression such as encompassed in Ogden's (1989) autistic–contiguous position. It seems that analysis conducted out of sight of the patient, with a focus on insight and with an anonymous analyst is peculiarly unsuited to the treatment of patients like this, as the British have recognized for many decades. First of all, the intensity of analysis is not necessarily suited even to those who appear to be well put together. The pace of analysis needs to be and perhaps should be set more by the patients themselves, as the best monitor of their own needs with, as Renik (1998) suggests, ongoing reassessment of the goals of the process with the patient. The analysis also taught me how important the relational aspect is, particularly in this instance with a nonexploitative male figure, who is willing to engage her in reflecting sincere therapeutic self-revelations, and not reject her in spite of the display of her worst and most horrible inner life. I also learned, as an interesting aside, that not all child sexual abuse is damaging but may instead be helpful. As McMillen, Zuravin, and Rideout (1995) indicated in a study of 154 women who were sexually abused, about half reported benefit, including knowledge to protect children from abuse, knowledge on how to protect oneself, and having a stronger personality with higher self-esteem. In this study, those who had perceived themselves as benefiting from the abuse were much better adjusted and got along better with others. For Isabel, the abuse was nonviolent and involved admiration of her body and appeared to be actually supportive of her self-esteem at that time, especially from a military male figure in the absence of her father, who was on duty. I also learned from this process that sometimes external analytic experiences are very important. For example, the experience of being in combat situations further reinforced her feeling of strength and capability to withstand physical assault on her body. And finally, and perhaps the most important of all the lessons I've learned from this analysis, concerns the danger of having rigid criteria about what a healthy analytic outcome is; such as realizing one's full potential, or being married with children, or achieving full genital heterosexuality; concepts derived from a particular theoretical approach to an ideal state that does not exist in reality. Adherence to rigid criteria could seriously damage the patient and prolong the analysis.

This patient did achieve her wish for a quiet and simple life, and finally, with the ongoing assistance of Prozac and without guilt, she had decided it is perfectly all right to live by herself without a husband or children and without very many friends. As Anthoy Storr (1988), in his work, *Solitude: A Return to Yourself*, says, "The happiest lives are probably those in which neither interpersonal relationships nor impersonal interests are idealized as the only way to salvation. The desire and pursuit of the whole must comprehend both aspects of human nature." He finishes, as Isabel might, with a quote from Wordsworth's poem, *The Prelude* (p. 202):

> When from our better selves we have too long
> Been parted by the hurrying world, and droop,
> Sick of its business, of its pleasures tired,
> How gracious, how benign is Solitude.

References

American Psychiatric Association (1980), *Diagnostic and Statistical Manual of Mental Disorders*, 3rd ed. (DSM-III). Washington, DC: American Psychiatric Press.

Bion, W. H. (1967), *Second Thoughts.* New York: Jason Aronson.

Eissler, K. (1953), The effect of the structure of the ego on psychoanalytic technique. *J. Amer. Psychoanal. Assn.,* 1:104–143.

Grotstein, J. (1990), The black hole as the basic psychotic experience: Some newer psychoanalytic and neuroscience perspectives on psychosis. *J. Amer. Acad. Psychoanal.,* 18:29–46.

Grünbaum, A. (1984), *The Foundations of Psychoanalysis: A Philosophical Critique.* Berkeley: University of California Press.

Hoffman, I. A. (1998), *Ritual and Spontaneity in the Psychoanalytic Process: A Dialectical Constructivist View.* Hillsdale, NJ: Analytic Press.

McMillen, C., Zuravin, S., & Rideout, G. (1995), Perceived benefit from child sexual abuse. *J. Consult. & Clin. Psychol.,* 63:1037–1063.

Nemiah, J. C. (1961), *Foundations of Psychopathology.* New York: Oxford University Press.

Ogden, T. H. (1989), *The Primitive Edge of Experience.* Northvale, NJ: Jason Aronson.

Oxford English Dictionary (1971), "Failure" c.v.

Phillips, A. (1996), *Terrors and Experts.* London: Faber & Faber.

Pizer, S. A. (1998), *Building Bridges: The Negotiation of Paradox in Psychoanalysis.* Hillsdale, NJ: Analytic Press.

Renik, O. (1998), Getting real in analysis. *Psychoanal. Quart.,* 67:566–593.

Storr, A. (1988), *Solitude: A Return to the Self.* New York: Ballantine Books.

Strenger, C. (1999), *Individuality, the Impossible Project: Psychoanalysis and Self-Creation.* Madison, CT: International Universities Press.

Twemlow, S. W., & Ramzy, N. (1999), Editorial. *J. Appl. Psychoanal. Studies,* 1:1–5.

Webster's Third International Dictionary (1971), "Failure" c.v.

5

From the Analysis of an Unsuccessful Painter

Cecilio Paniagua, M.D., Sc.D.

Eleven years ago, I was invited by a friend to the opening of a bookstore. On the wall hung two large abstract paintings created by the owner's husband. The paintings did not impress me favorably; I found them somewhat garish. I was introduced to the painter, and one year later I had him as a patient.

Mr. Ruiz (not his real name) decided to consult me about his general dissatisfaction with life, his obsessive worries concerning his family's safety, and his anxiety about losing his memory, which he feared was a harbinger of a general deterioration of his mental faculties.

At the beginning of treatment he was 44 years old, married for twenty-one years to a successful professional who was 42. They had two boys in their teens. Mr. Ruiz was an industrial engineer, and he worked part-time at the prosperous family business that his paternal grandfather had founded. His evenings were dedicated to painting. In the recent past he had also taught mathematics at a university, but he did not see himself as a mathematician, an engineer, or a businessman: he was a painter.

Born in postwar Spain, Mr. Ruiz was the middle child and only boy, with one sister eighteen months older, and the other, eighteen months younger. When he was $2^1/_2$ his 28-year-old mother was hospitalized for tuberculosis. She died six months later. Almost two years after her death the patient's still grieving father decided to live abroad in order to take care of family business overseas. He was out of the country for one and a half years, leaving the children behind with one of his sisters and a nanny. They lived at the grandfather's home, and upon his father's return, they continued living there with the same domestic arrangements, for his father led the life of a carefree single man, dating young women and often neglecting his parental duties. He had died of liver disease when my patient was 30.

At home, talk about the mother's illness and death was avoided, supposedly to protect his father's feelings. "I don't think my father saw us as his children, but as reminders of his widowhood." It was assumed that the children's interests were also served by that "conspiracy of silence." The children were also kept away from the "contagious" maternal side of the family, who lived in another city. While Mr. Ruiz had no specific memories of his mother, she was described as a beautiful blond, languid woman with an indolent personality. It was believed that this disposition had made her prone to morbid wasting. The family feared that the children might have inherited this characterological proclivity. Father had always wanted his son to become involved in sports, in order to counter what he perceived as passive tendencies in the child, but my patient as a boy did not particularly enjoy physical activity.

The aunt who took care of the children was a childless woman separated from a deranged husband. She was described as narcissistic, uninviting, reproachful, and obsessively worried about the children's health, height, and looks, which she saw as reflecting on her performance as surrogate mother. She seemed quite oblivious to the children's inner life. My patient remembered that once when he cried she just scolded him for ruining his neatly ironed shirt. The nanny was a rather cold and castrating spinster who would tell the boy things like, "Don't urinate a single drop outside the bowl for in the future you'll have to aim better." There was a second aunt living in the household who was fun but immature and perhaps mildly mentally retarded. There were also two live-in maids. His two sisters, like himself, were rather short in stature, and he felt embarrassed about this characteristic in them. He grew up surrounded by females, "a rooster-child in a henhouse," but he enjoyed looking at the naked bodies of these women through the keyhole of the bathroom door. Mr. Ruiz did manage somehow to garner sufficient masculine identification to develop his heterosexuality.

At the other end of the house lived his grandfather, a gruff old man; his grandmother, often experienced as warm by the boy; and his father, heir to the family business and traditions, and revered by his younger siblings. He was preoccupied with his outward appearance, and his son, as a boy, admired him from a distance. My patient was proud of being the only male child, and heir, of such an elegant and seemingly important man.

As a boy, Mr. Ruiz used to play with the seven children of a paternal uncle. They were his functional siblings. They frequently ganged up against him and his sisters, reminding them that their splendid home did not belong to them but to their maternal grandfather, an assertion that used to shake his precarious sense of security. His father never came to the rescue of his children's wounded pride.

Mr. Ruiz did well in school. He married at 23 before finishing studies at a Spanish university. Unlike his father, who did not finish his own studies in engineering. Mr. Ruiz eventually graduated. Mr. Ruiz and his wife moved abroad in order for him to get a Ph.D. in electronic engineering at a prestigious school. He obtained good grades, but one day decided that he was going to become a painter, abandoning his studies, despite his teachers' encouragement to complete the degree. This decision coincided with the announcement of his father's fatal illness.

I had three sessions of initial evaluation with this patient. He was highly intelligent and articulate, with a defensive tendency to use abstractions. He had an obvious psychoneurosis, both symptomatic and characterological, and he felt motivated for analysis. His stable marriage, his adequate social relationships, and his ability to persevere in his studies and job seemed good signs of analyzability. I feared, however, that his seriously deprived and traumatic childhood cast doubt on his suitability for such treatment. I decided to send him for psychological testing, trying to rule out a possible prepsychotic condition that perhaps I had been unable to detect, and also to ascertain that his dysamnesia was not a sign of presenility. The tests did not show any signs of organicity. His reality testing was more than adequate. He came across as a person with good internal resources who feared that something internal was getting out of control. I decided to start a four-sessions-a-week analysis with him.

I have selected material from this lengthy analysis related to the patient's identity as a painter and his professional failure as such. Before I met him, Mr. Ruiz had shown his paintings once in a public exhibit, selling only one of them to a friend. Later on, a couple of his paintings were shown at a joint exhibit, and at another time, in the aforementioned bookstore opening. During the ten years of his analysis he never exhibited the *oeuvre* that he cherished. Freud (1925) said of the artist that "His creations, works of art, were the imaginary satisfactions of unconscious wishes, just as dreams are. . . . But they differed from the asocial, narcissistic products of dreaming in that they were calculated to arouse sympathetic interest in other people" (pp. 64–65). The last part of this statement did not seem to apply to Mr. Ruiz.

The length of this analysis and the insightfulness of the analysand will throw further light on the multidetermined processes of plastic creativity and their sublimatory or maladaptive compromise formations.

The first painting Mr. Ruiz remembered having painted, at age 12, was of an oasis in the middle of a vast desert. This was painted at an age when he could not yet fathom the personal symbolism of this imagery. In late adolescence and early adulthood he was fond of painting uninhabited houses, expressing the absence but also curiosity about the stories of their past dwellers: "I wanted to reflect the solidity of the building without the fragility of life." He saw these houses as both beautiful and terrible. He became aware that they represented his mother. He wanted to paint them (her) as cold and desolate, but luminous (dead, but also alive).

Mr. Ruiz chose to study a technical career that his relatives considered useful for the family business. It soon became apparent, however, that his main interest was not directed toward industrial applications, but toward highly abstract mathematical theories. While living abroad he learned about his father's fatal illness, and it was then that he felt he had to become a painter. Obtaining a Ph.D. in engineering became for him an undesirable concession to conventionality. He clearly saw that his studies had been only a psychological maneuver to protect his fragility. Since he was going to be one of the heirs of a substantial fortune, he figured he needed neither the security of a doctorate nor a more advanced professional specialization. He also thought that, after all, he was approaching mathematics and engineering in an "artistic way," detached from practical concerns, and that his absentmindedness about concrete facts and numbers would disqualify him as a practitioner or teacher anyway.

Upon his return to Spain, to his family's dismay, he announced that painting was to become his central occupation. Ever since then, he has worked only a few hours a day at the family business despite many attempts by his relatives to have him dedicate more time to the firm's management. He was even promised the directorship of the company, but he never wavered in his decision. To the contrary, he often felt that he should be doing full-time painting. If he chose to spend some time working for the business, this was not out of fondness for his family, but because he sensed that it was an "anchorage to reality": an antidote against a fearsome regressive pull. He usually talked about his work at the family firm as "an evasive hobby," while he considered his artistic activity his "true job."

Mr. Ruiz saw his painting as "a cleft through which I can have access to a different plane of existence: a fissure to get out and see the light." He was unaware in the beginning of the obvious rebirth meaning of this statement. "I want to express my sequestered self," he would say. Since as a child he did not feel safe or supported, painting provided Mr. Ruiz with the opportunity to be playful, and childlike. "My painting is not pictorial, it's acultural; what interests me is that which is the most primitive and the least geometrical," he said; and he chose an abstract style for his painting "because I don't love objects."

Mr. Ruiz felt that what gave him the identity of a painter was not *how* he painted, but the fact that he *needed* to paint. Whenever he was traveling, he could not wait to return to the canvas. This did not necessarily mean that he enjoyed painting; as a matter of fact, he said, "It's much better not to have to create." Most of the time he suffered in this activity, feeling painfully insecure and frustrated. He was interested in an unseen netherworld, but expressed understandable doubts as to whether this world could be externalized through art. He felt that his responsibility as a painter was to put himself in a trance-like state in front of the canvas, letting his hand do the work. Sometimes he even felt an angelic presence behind him (the muse!) guiding his brush, almost hearing a voice telling him, "Now do this, now do that." He lamented, "If only I had finer ears to listen to that voice!" He wished he could emulate Picasso, who stated that his hand moved automatically, as though on rails.

Not only did Mr. Ruiz not plan any of his paintings, they were untitled. He would not do any preliminary drawings or sketches. "The painting itself is the sketch; the canvas is my palette," he would say. And, when facing it, ready to paint, he would not arrange the brushes, the paint tubes, or any other implements, in any orderly manner. He stated, "If someone asked me what do I paint, I would have to answer: 'I don't know. I paint the painting.' "

When immersed in painting, Mr. Ruiz wanted to feel that the outside world, where he "did not belong," disappeared. Blind self-confidence in his painting would spell a mental rest for him, and at times he managed to experience it momentarily. His painting, he insisted, had to portray feelings of porousness, evanescence, blurriness, and desolation, "as though on the brink of disappearance." The day Francis Bacon died in a Madrid hospital not far from my office, Mr. Ruiz compared the work of that famous British Expressionist to his own, stating, "My work is not ugly like his, and I try to make no impact; my paintings border on nothingness."

Mr. Ruiz was aware that he was trying to translate psychological states into esthetic forms. What he was really doing, of course, was transforming unconscious fantasy into art (Trosman, 1990). In the process, he experienced feelings of becoming estranged from external reality. He feared then that his art was nothing but a solipsistic accomplishment, and yet this was the only esthetic endeavor that interested him. He wondered what motivated him to paint when the gratifications were so scarce, and he would answer, "It's preferable to live in frustration than in meaninglessness." The tension of painting, although unpleasant, made him feel alive and fecund.

Through painting, Mr. Ruiz was searching for the revelation of something fundamental. He said he heard "like the Big Bang echo," feeling impelled to externalize in plastic fashion these powerful background sensations. Painting his "amorphous but authentic" inner feelings was painful; however, these were his "only reality." He feared though, that a purely contemplative stance would make him sink into a blissful but annihilating paralysis. At times he had the fantasy that he had not been born yet; his art would make his birth possible. He said, "I'm looking for vitality: for the kind of explosion that gives the baby his primordial sense of security." Understandably, his utopian ambitions did not meet with success.

In his painting, Mr. Ruiz wanted to portray "an unambiguous, crystalline and perfect world, an oriental nirvana" without feeling "too exposed." To render a "luminous presence" was a leit motiv in all his work. He wanted to condense through this impression his sense of feebleness with his wished-for solidity, yet, whenever he looked at his paintings he wondered "whether a house can be built with toothpicks." Mr. Ruiz figured that, due to its inherent subjectivity, his abstract style could not be the object of any questioning, therefore he could feel relatively safe with this form of expression. However, he feared that through inadvertent "crevices," his art could also reveal woeful feelings of inadequacy. He expressed hopes that the treatment could help him find solutions for his lacks, so that he would not need to hide or disguise them. He daydreamed of the eventual manifestation in his painting of a talent so great that it would erase all his deficits. Alas, this never happened.

Mr. Ruiz felt highly ambivalent toward the opinions of real or potential viewers of his art. A respected colleague once told him that one of his works showed plastic maturity and fullness; this description sounded to him like "heavenly music," and yet he also said, "If my art were highly esteemed, perhaps I could not bear it: the emotion would be as intense as learning that I was not an orphan." He would have liked to show more of his *oeuvre*, but he did not think it possessed sufficient quality or unity. His main exhibit, years ago, had a dissuasive effect on him because, despite the positive reception by the owner of the art gallery and favorable reviews in the newspaper, it did not fulfill his secret expectations to have "an anonymous public falling in love with my work." Anyway, he felt that favorable reviews could not be of great help, for he did not believe that his work was truly valuable.

Mr. Ruiz would ignore or deride other people's judgments about his art, as when a friend told him, "Please, paint something one can live with!" When asked what qualities a viewer would require to appreciate his art, he responded: "He would need to have the sensitivity of an insect's antennae; my paintings are purely sensorial." Simultaneously, he could not stand rejection of his paintings by significant others as evidenced by the way they glanced at them. Since childhood, Mr. Ruiz was extremely sensitive to any sort of disdain, real or imagined (as when he interpreted the analyst's smile as sneering). He dreaded that the grandiosity of his artistic ambitions would be the subject of mockery.

He felt that trying to make a professional career of painting would have defeated the genuine purpose of his artistic endeavor. Selling his work would have meant "behaving like anyone else." Entering any kind of competition would have been "vulgar." He had decided to become a painter precisely because he wanted to remove himself from the world of conventionality. The only prize he coveted was appreciation from others (without exhibits!).

Refinement and lack of spontaneity were, for Mr. Ruiz, a sign of distinction, but only in verbal exchanges, never in painting, where he could not even discern a relationship between his emotions and the brush strokes or the selection of colors. He once said, "I wouldn't want to eat or defecate like a monkey, but I wished I could paint like one." He considered any theorization on painting as futile and pretentious. He maintained that any true artistic expression was inherently ineffable, and the verbal language used to describe it was always suspicious. Indeed, despite the sophistication of his vocabulary, this man felt awkward when trying to talk about his work, for his words sounded insecure to him. He mused, "I draw in the same way I discourse, but my painting is completely different." For him, music had "no flesh," and literature was "postmaternal." He also dismissed sculpture because of its "coarse tridimensionality," whereas painting was "static and permanent, whatever angle you look at it from."

For Mr. Ruiz, painting was an activity that an artist ought to know without any formal training. He felt contempt for technical skills and dexterity. Among the many logical contradictions and seemingly impossible tasks this man wanted to accomplish through his art were the following: his personal intentions and will should not be at all visible in his paintings, although "there must be nothing between me and them"; nonretinal impressions ought to be reduced to colors; one should not be able to differentiate content from form; very concrete lines should convey very abstract notions materialized in images of "passionate coldness"; and his work devoid of construction should manifest the "robustness" of his insecurity. . . .

Mr. Ruiz's art represented, in his own words, "experiments in identification." He said, "I question my painting the way I question my very existence. When I look at it, I'm asking, 'Who am I?' and whenever I see nothing it's as if my reflection disappeared from the mirror." He expected the colors and forms to tell him something likable about himself, "but my fears are as intense as my hopes." He waited for intuitions to tell him to place a line here, a color there. Most of the time, Mr. Ruiz felt frustrated with the results but, occasionally, the work got imbued with "a miraculous sense of unity, and that's the joy of painting!"

For Mr. Ruiz, his painting possessed a life of its own. In the dialogue with his work he could not foresee what forces in it were going to pull him toward satisfaction or disappointment. He felt that he just planted some seeds that might or might not fructify; "something may emerge that gives shape to my emotions; that something may wield surprising meanings." Frequently, Mr. Ruiz would talk of his work as though it were independent of his intentionality; for instance: "unexpectedly, the painting started giving something back, and the colors came out fresh and shameless."

Mr. Ruiz was particularly interested in painting over some of his old paintings. He was fascinated by the transparencies and impressions that could be guessed under the new coats; he also liked the traces left on the canvas after erasing the paint, as well as any sort of accidental marks. He would thus discover unsuspected images, such as viscerae, secretions, excrements, or "organic forms like a repulsive, incomplete fetus." At other times he would distinguish ominous shapes such as strange birds or carnivorous flowers—never human faces. In many of his paintings, Mr. Ruiz detected three distinct elements that he associated to himself and his two sisters. Once, after painting a central column and two big shadows he was startled to discover in it a chest x-ray reminiscent, of course, of his mother's last illness. As the treatment progressed, the patient's own "Rorschachs" became less hideous and menacing. He began then creating and seeing more pleasant "inner spaces," usually with pieces of furniture; one of these was a headboard that made him exclaim, "I must have seen my mother sick in bed!"

Frequently, Mr. Ruiz reported dreams that he labeled *preverbal*. He would occasionally experience Isakower phenomena. He likened his painting to dreaming, as something more related to sensations than to ideas, although in painting he did not feel as passive as in dreaming. Indeed, painting was for him a revolt against sterility, an exercise in assertiveness.

Mr. Ruiz felt that painting placed him in another reality presided over by the absence–presence of his mother. He said, "When I paint I feel deep down that I'm glancing at my mother's eyes. I imagine that I saw myself in her. Her gaze must have penetrated my soul," demonstrating Winnicott's (1971) belief that the mother's face is the child's natural mirror. The patient realized that in his painting he always used gray and white—the colors of her eyes. In this homage he tried to reproduce her and her beauty. "I cannot talk about my mother, all I can do is paint what she represents," he said, adding, "the problem is that no one turns his head to say, 'Gosh, how incredibly pretty she is'!" His art tried to keep her alive, but in his creativeness he also identified with her: "To create is to be a mother." He equated the elaboration of a work of art to a pregnancy, but he wanted to be "maternal" in a special way: "I don't see my works as coming from my womb; I see them as coming through me; I wish to be only a medium, not an origin." He then voiced his sorrow for his "helpless children, the paintings," which would end up forsaken like himself. Additionally, he had the oedipal fantasy that his ghost-mother would have wanted him to become a painter against his father's wishes.

Mr. Ruiz imagined his mother with a halo, and he thought that perhaps he could remember her glowing face, her soft breasts. I was never able to detect phallic strivings in his evocation of these partial objects. Despite his enormous attraction for the maternal imago—or because of it—he said once in a while, "I wished my magnetic mother left me alone!" He thought that his preference for an abstract mode in his painting was related to his not having witnessed the reality of her final days, and also to the avoidant attitude of his family concerning the circumstances of her death. This could have made him develop a phobic distaste for realistic details. Also, he associated a figurative style to the odious tediousness of his childhood years. Owing to his family's atmosphere of concealment, as a child he felt that he could not ask or even consciously fantasize about his mother. If he inquired about her, he would find out that she was truly gone forever. Through painting he hoped to continue embracing his mother, extending his pregenital childhood indefinitely.

In his art, one of Mr. Ruiz's foremost goals was to attain a fusion, "a mystical reunion" with his mother. As in the early mother–child relationship, emotions would be transmitted in painting without any need for language. In front of the canvas he felt like a child waiting for his mother: "I'm still expecting her to return." Painting was seen at times as "surrendering to consumption," like his mother supposedly did. He felt that these potent though vague impressions glued him to his work. He experienced his paintings both as portraits and self-portraits, "since I am like a Siamese joined to my mother." When the painting seemed "agonizing" he had a chance to insulate life from it. In this way he hoped to save not only his mother, but himself. In his fantasy, he had died at 3; "I was me only until then and I'm still looking for paradise lost. I cling to my paintings like a puppy to its mother." While he liked evoking feelings of total protection and unconditional love, the idea of being unborn or fused to his mother generated anxiety. In analytic work we found that the dialogue he established between the mass of paint on the background and the arabesques he drew on it had as unconscious meaning the attempt to differentiate the child from his mother.

As in Plato's cave allegory, Mr. Ruiz held the belief that the beauty he found in feminine faces was but nostalgia for an ideal beauty. The latter could not be met in our earthly existence, "although I have this feeling of having experienced it," he said. One could attempt to reexperience it only through art: "Human beauty always ends in decay and death, whereas artistic beauty is generous and eternal: it's frozen time." It was Kris (1952) who remarked that "destruction of the real is fused with construction of its image" (p. 52). Mr. Ruiz needed to elaborate the unquestionable beauty he expected to regard with awe, but since he deemed his art insecure like himself, he feared that it would portray him as timorous and fragile. He wanted it to reflect not what he was, but what he wished to be. He stated, "I would like to be seen as a dazzling angel, to transmute the shit I am into gold, like an alchemist." He was fond of quoting the words of the painter Rothko: "One has to be capable of creating miracles whenever one needs them."

Mr. Ruiz said, "Perhaps what I want to achieve is painting the terror with nice colors, and the only way to come face to face with horror is metamorphosing it into Beauty" (a great definition of sublimination!). He wanted to become the secure boy he never was, and he figured that painting was the only way to exorcise the demons of his childhood. In counterphobic ways, he wanted to confront his fear of losing control of his reactions, freeing himself from the "psychological corset" that prevented him in childhood from asking "Where is my mother? Why did my father leave me?"

Painting was perceived by Mr. Ruiz as a tabula rasa that would permit him to relive his childhood; that is, a second version of it. He considered it a chance to shake the chronic feelings of numbness that had characterized his emotional life since age 3. Ever since his mother passed away, he had been "treading on quicksands." He wanted to recapture the sense of security that she provided for him, and be able to happily scribble with the irresponsibility of a small child, painting without self-consciousness. Recognition from others would be merely a secondary gain. Furthermore, he wanted to recapture the normal developmental path that leads from total lack of inhibition to adaptive restraint. Thus, he would try to impose some order and structure in the mass of paint he applied to the canvas, but, alas, only seldom did he manage to reproduce the effect of the healthy evolution that he sought.

As a child, Mr. Ruiz thought that his future had to be very promising. "It was the only thing that saved me from despair." His orphanhood had made him an "exception" (Freud, 1916). Something had to compensate him for his unfair destiny. The wondrous reparation he had expected would have to come from his art. "If they didn't love me for what I was, they'll have to love me for what I do," he thought. Simultaneously, he believed that his circumstances made him special in positive ways. He had an "ugly duckling" fantasy: through painting he was going to make his very valuable inner self evolve, and some day it was going to gleam, causing astonishment and envy in his relatives, especially those cousins whose circumstances and accomplishments he had so envied.

Among the partial instincts sublimated through his art, voyeurism was prominent. Indeed, painting reminded him of his childhood excitement when looking through the keyhole of the bathroom door. His associations led him to reflect on his wish to get to the naked essence of women who had hidden so much vital information from him in his childhood. Mr. Ruiz thought also of the solitary, onanistic quality of his painting, associating the opacity of its meanings to the need to hide his shame for masturbation, which he did occasionally around his paintings, equating the spurts of semen with streams of paint. When painting, he had the feeling that he needed to remove some obstruction to free internal fluids: "Something deep in me needs to flow; it's like when I vomit or when I blow my nose." Since he painted "with eyes turned inward, toward my entrails," he did not find it surprising that his style had "a jumbled, intestinal quality." He enjoyed dirtying himself with paint, which he clearly associated to feces, symbolically equating defecation with painting: "It's like the excrement that goes through you coming out transformed."

Early in the analysis, Mr. Ruiz felt that he was changing: his dysamnesia decreased significantly; he was less afraid of calamaties falling upon his family; he described more of a feeling of authenticity; he felt less envious and rivalrous; he became more generous and interested in other people; he felt less ambivalent toward his relatives; and he was better capable of realistic evaluations. In our sessions he talked with less defensive vagueness. Also, he reported that the problems in his business were interfering less with his painting and vice versa. He became definitely more adept in interpersonal relationships, and a better entrepreneur. What he did *not* become, reportedly, was a better painter. Indeed, his improvement seemed founded, in part, on the gradual concentration of intrapsychic conflict in his painting.

Throughout the analysis, Mr. Ruiz experienced ebbs and flows in his level of satisfaction with his painting. His moments of progress proved "a mirage," as his tormenting self-doubts made him think once and again that his work could not possibly have sufficient quality for exhibition. "My nuclei don't fertilize each other," he complained; that is, the splitting remained in place.

Mr. Ruiz resisted talking about many aspects of the process of painting, in part because this led to the frustrating acknowledgment of how little he had accomplished. He was disappointed that analysis did not make a successful artist out of him. He had expected the treatment to help him fulfill his dream of creating great art "with total spontaneity and zero perspiration." He would have wanted to find both in psychoanalysis and in painting, "germinal ideas" that strengthened his sense of self.

The similarity between the struggle for freedom in artistic expression and the resistance to free associations on the couch has long been recognized (Milner, 1957). This parallelism was very obvious in Mr. Ruiz's case. He very often paused at the beginning of the sessions, which reminded him of his usual initial hesitation to put his brush in contact with the canvas. Indeed, in both situations he experienced "the same fear of the plunge into no-differentiation and the disbelief in the spontaneous ordering forces," to use A. Freud's (1957) wording. He could not allow himself sufficient freedom of imagination in either activity. He commented in the beginning that the analytic setting felt as restrictive as a picture frame. In the sessions, as in his painting, he tried to push himself to start somewhere without reflection and let his associations wander. Owing to his basic mistrust, he was quite unsuccessful in both endeavors. He remarked, though, that with his painting he felt more courageous than with me.

He expected certain brush strokes to give him formidable revelations about himself, and he expected something analogous from my interventions. My silences felt to him similar to when the paintings gave back no satisfactory clues. When I did not utter a word—and I am not a particularly quiet analyst—his vitality decreased; he did not talk less, but his affect was toned down. Whenever he thought of giving up his artistic interests, he felt simultaneously tempted to terminate analysis. "I never know when a painting is finished, and I feel the same way about the treatment," he said. It was characteristic of him to think that the decision to terminate analysis was his alone.

He admitted that what he painted was influenced by what we talked about in the session, but he seemed unable to describe specifics. When asked to spell out details he tended to issue bewildering statements such as, "My painting is lyrical and ambiance-evoking, but also very hard, like German Expressionism." When the defensive aspect of pronouncements such as this was interpreted, he would acknowledge that he simply dreaded too much appearing childish to me. When I invited him to say more about concrete facts, once again Mr. Ruiz would increase his articulate intellectualizing.

He considered any psychoanalytic exploration of true art to be doomed—at least his. His painting was "ineffable and irreducible." Analytic interpretations were "mere descriptions" of deep, implicit sensorial memories. "Words don't cure!" he opined, because verbal language was inherently inauthentic; "words are the jail of true feelings," he said. Apparently, words in his case had not been sufficiently invested libidinally. Too much of his nondeclarative memory failed to progress toward "word representations" (Freud, 1915), and the result seemed an unbridgeable dichotomy.

My patient was seized by emotional conflicts and logical aporias that seemed impossible to resolve. "I paint right from the wound of my orphanhood," he said, "and I want to create out of nothingness. I want people to acknowledge my hollowness, the structure of absence, the life of the dead." He realized, though, that these goals were unreachable, and wondered how could he achieve invulnerability from a position of ontological insecurity. Even though he felt that the artistic transmutation of maternal love was an absurdity, Mr. Ruiz could not give up painting for one vital reason: he could not renounce the enclave where he had placed what little was left of his beloved infancy. He said, "I disappeared with my mother, and painting gives life to the part of me that died." He could not forgo that "most genuine" part of him, the source of "those few ephemeral moments right out of paradise." Although Mr. Ruiz often considered his art "a false solution," for him it represented "the meal I need for my survival." He lived most of his youth repressing such need. Once it became sublimated instead of simply repressed, he felt he had to hold onto it; without it he feared he would drift into "malignant indolence" (i.e., a maladaptive form of identification with his mother).

He did not like dwelling only in sensorial nostalgia. He wanted for his painting to be also "an arrow aimed at the future: the hope that perhaps I can love again." Most of the time this hope did not materialize. He fantasized that after a lifelong fruitless wait for "something to happen," he would burn all his paintings and himself in a pyre, leaving nothing for posterity, thus actively exterminating himself and his mother instead of perishing passively. He said, "perhaps the only security would be self-destruction."

He often considered that his lack of success in painting was proof of his failure in life: "In the beginning of the analysis I had hopes that my painting could take me somwhere. Ten years later I reproduce the same basic split that makes me feel unwhole and sterile."

Why did Mr. Ruiz continue in treatment? First of all, my attention had an important trophic function for him. He also had not given up hope for a satisfactory consolidation of his personality through painting. Interrupting analysis would have meant conceding defeat.

And, what of my reasons for prolonging a seemingly interminable treatment? First, I shared his hopes of finding better solutions for his splitting fixation. Second, I thought he was psychologically more fragile than he saw himself. I knew that any empathic failure on my part could precipitate an abrupt termination, which was something I considered dangerous. I thought of the case of the Armenian-American painter Arshile Gorky who killed himself. He also was an orphan, his father had abandoned him, and his painting served similar transitional functions (Gediman and Lieberman, 1996).

I wondered whether painting was functioning as a form of nonverbal acting out, since intrapsychically it was so similar to psychoanalysis for Mr. Ruiz. I was aware from the beginning of the limitations imposed on the treatment by the early events in his life. Indeed, I had serious doubts that exploration at the level of the preoedipal basic fault could bring forth appropriate material for mutative analytic work (A. Freud, 1969), but this notwithstanding, I thought that psychoanalytic work could help this troubled man reach more adaptive compromise formation in life.

There was an unusual biographical coincidence that made me feel specially alert to probable countertransferential interferences: he and I shared birth dates. Mr. Ruiz was born a few hours before me. This stimulated all sorts of fantasies in me, rescue ones among them. I realized as well that, although our lives had been very different, we had shared many *zeitgeist* assumptions. These points of identification at times rendered quite difficult my analytic attempts at objectivity. For instance, narcissistically identified with him—and remembering my negative impression of his paintings before he became my patient—I found myself wishing that he became successful in his painting, as though this was a legitimate goal of the analysis, disregarding Ticho's (1972) dictum that treatment goals need not coincide with life goals!

I did not know, nor was it my function to find out, how much artistic potential Mr. Ruiz had, but I could not help wondering whether a basic lack of talent was partially responsible for his failure as a painter. I remembered with special poignancy Freud's (1927) lament, "Before the problem of the creative artist analysis must, alas, lay down its arms" (p. 177). Was Mr. Ruiz perhaps not creative enough? Was his failure not intrinsic but conflict related? Or both? Certainly, his precarious self-confidence had to do with his failure. His inability or refusal to transcend in his art preverbal–preconceptual experiences, channeling them through secondary process, may have made his painting difficult to "digest" for the ego. Gombrich (1954) wrote: "It is our ego which, in resonance, receives from these . . . multiform crystals of miraculous complexity we call works of art . . . the certainty that the resolution of conflict, the achievement of freedom without threat to our inner security, is not wholly beyond the grasp of the aspiring human mind" (p. 411). How could Mr. Ruiz possibly transmit for resonance any of this? But, on the other hand, how did other, no less disturbed artists manage to do it?

In the plastic arts, recognition seems contingent on the capacity to create images especially apt and syntonic as projective screens (Grinberg and Paniagua, 1991). Mr. Ruiz rejected the idea of an adaptation of his painting to any artistic trend. He would exclaim, "no concessions to any conventional harmony!" (or size, I thought, since his canvases were an unusual and unwieldy 2 × 2 meters). He said, "I'm not about to abandon myself to the wish to be praised." Naturally, this contradicted his intense narcissistic needs; greater than these needs, however, was his fear of losing his hard-won individuation through isolation.

Most artists have to struggle early in their careers to obtain recognition. Mr. Ruiz recoiled at the slightest sign of dislike or indifference by the few viewers of his paintings. Of course, his narcissistic vulnerability was the main cause of his inhibitions concerning the exhibition of his *oeuvre*. He wished he could really accept Oscar Wilde's pronouncement that "A true artist takes no notice whatever of the public," but, at least in Mr. Ruiz's case, this statement was totally a reaction formation. He did not even consider the idea of using his extensive social contact to make his paintings known. "My painting is no merchandise," he would say proudly. Is it at all surprising that Mr. Ruiz was a manifest failure as a painter? And yet, his decision to dedicate so much time and effort to his peculiar form of art making served many functions, and seemed to constitute the best possible compromise formation in his circumstances. His artistic failure was at the same time a psychodynamic success.

References

Freud, A. (1957), Foreword. In: Marion Milner's *On Not Being Able to Paint.* In: *The Writings of Anna Freud,* Vol. 5. New York: International Universities Press, pp. 488–492.
——— (1969), Difficulties in the path of psychoanalysis. In: *The Writings of Anna Freud,* Vol. 7. New York: International Universities Press, pp. 124–156.
Freud, S. (1915), The unconscious. *Standard Edition,* 14:159–204. London: Hogarth Press, 1957.

———— (1916), Some character-types met with in psycho-analytic work. *Standard Edition,* 14:303–333. London: Hogarth Press, 1957.

———— (1925), An Autobiographical Study. *Standard Edition,* 20:1–74. London: Hogarth Press, 1959.

———— (1927), The Future of an Illusion. *Standard Edition,* 21:1–56. London: Hogarth Press, 1961.

Gediman, H. K., & Lieberman, J. S. (1996), *The Many Faces of Deceit.* Northvale, NJ: Jason Aronson.

Gombrich, E. H. (1954), Psychoanalysis and the history of art. *Internat. J. Psycho-Anal.,* 35:401–411.

Grinberg, L., & Paniagua, C. (1991), The attraction of Leonardo Da Vinci. *Internat. Rev. Psycho-Anal.,* 18:1–10.

Kris, E. (1952), *Psychoanalytic Explorations in Art.* New York: International Universities Press.

Milner, M. (1957), *On Not Being Able to Paint.* London: Heinemann.

Ticho, E. (1972), Termination of psychoanalysis: Treatment goals, life goals. *Psychoanal. Quart.,* 41:315–333.

Trosman, H. (1990), Transformations of unconscious fantasy in art. *J. Amer. Psychoanal. Assn.,* 38:47–59.

Winnicott, D. W. (1971), Mirror-role of mother and family in child development. In: *Playing and Reality.* London: Tavistock, pp. 111–118.

6

A Sense of Failure in Analysis and the Phenomenon of Serial Analyses

Johanna Krout Tabin, Ph.D.

Introduction

It is a common experience for psychoanalysts to see patients who return for further work after a previous period of analysis. The implications of second or third analyses nonetheless do not appear to have been explored in the literature. It is particularly strange that no one has explored the effect on the analysis of those patients returning for further work (with the same or another analyst) where the patients count the first analysis as a failure. There is a twofold purpose in focusing on this issue: first, in terms of considering psychoanalysis as an extension of the developmental process all personalities are engaged in throughout life; second, in terms of encouraging the utilization of material from previous analyses as part of a present effort—rather than, as seems to happen more usually, to discount what can be learned from the series.

The name *serial analyses* applies in general to the occurrence of episodes of analysis (even prolonged ones) that follow upon each other with notable lapses of time in between. Most often, one thinks of these as returns to analysis at a later time because of the benefits achieved from an initial analysis. Freud's case of the Wolf Man famously illustrates serial analysis. A special case of it is the familiar set of serial analyses we analysts often undergo ourselves. As frequently noted, first analyses that are associated with meeting training requirements at an institute may seem to be useful enough, but, after a while, the results do not seem comparable with the experience of patients who come into analysis for deeper reasons. A second analysis may thus be motivated by a desire for one that is more completely satisfying, based upon confidence in the method. The particular examples to be considered in this chapter are of another type. In these, the patient feels that an original analysis (or prior analyses) was a failure, yet returns to pursue the work again—sometimes with the same analyst and sometimes choosing a new one.

For anyone to undertake another analysis after a failed analysis suggests that the sense of failure is not absolute. This raises the question of definition of success or failure. For purposes of this chapter, the patient's assessment is the criterion of success. It is possible, of course, for a patient to feel an analysis was successful in dealing with what the patient came to deal with, and yet for the analyst to feel uncomfortable about what was not dealt with. The fact still is that the patient's satisfaction with the analysis reflects an ongoing increased satisfaction in life. When a patient declares that an analysis was a failure, however, the analyst must be careful to avoid defensiveness in trying to understand why the patient retreated from further analysis, unsatisfied. The patient's assessment in this case inevitably requires significant introspection about the countertransference. Nonetheless, the transferences that influenced the course of a prior analysis further affect the patient's assessment of the analysis.

We psychoanalysts, not our patients, usually provide the literature through which we may hope to learn from each other. Information from patients is difficult to procure. Follow-up inquiries are problematic about analyses that are evaluated as successful by both patient and analyst because it seems quite properly for the former patient, to regulate the ensuing psychological space between that patient and the analyst (Nathan, 1999). Still less accessible is information from patients who may feel that an analysis was a failure. The closest one can come to this kind of information is from analysts of patients in their second analyses. The trouble is, a previous analysis is seldom given importance in accounts of subsequent work.

Review of Relevant Literature

The literature on failed analyses, in any case, is sparse; on serial analyses, it is nonexistent. Occasionally, the fact of several prior disrupted analyses will be mentioned before discussion of a particular case (e.g., Silverman, 1996), but the significance of this as a pattern is not addressed. Some insight can be gleaned from what has already been written, however.

In "Analysis, Terminable and Interminable," Freud (1937) expressed doubt that any analysis can be complete. Nonetheless, Glover (1955) cited a termination phase as an essential part of the analytic experience; Novick (1990) echoes subsequent theorists who agree that this is true. In all of the cases reported in this chapter, the patients, in addition to complaining about the inadequacy of previous analytic work, experienced abrupt disruption of their first analyses. The possibility of a termination phase, this essential part of the work, was precluded.

Frank (1999) examined the critical nature of a termination phase. He points out that more is involved than reprocessing the earlier work of the analysis—to enable still tighter integration of the ego, and to deal especially with the issue of separation and loss. There is the specific loss not only of the analyst, but also (either in replay or anticipation) the permanent loss of the parental figures whom the analyst represents. This opportunity for ultimate freedom from the parental introjects is perhaps unique to the termination phase. In the forepart of serial analyses, this profound work has not taken place. There can be an approximation of it in the serial patient's taking abrupt departures and learning in the interim that it is indeed possible to exist without the parental figure—returning to the analyst to find out that the "parent" has not been destroyed by the patient's having an independent life; or proving that there is always "another streetcar" by finding a different and even more adequate (seeming) analyst-parent another time around.

Milner (1949) had an opportunity to write about a case that both she and the analysand felt terminated most unsatisfactorily. When they chanced to compare notes long afterward, they could agree nonetheless that much had happened in terms of the analysis that was of value to the patient.

Glover (1949) suggests that there is the factor of spontaneous recovery to help us to maintain proper professional modesty: "Sometimes it is impossible to prevent patients from curing themselves." Another way to say this is that psychoanalysis is a hothouse for psychological development and sometimes growth spurts by our patients are beyond our expectations and can take place during the postanalytic period.

This observation directs attention to psychoanalysis as a developmental process. There are ways in which universal and continuous issues are dealt with by the ego (Tabin, 1985, 1996). Psychoanalysis can be thought of as a method by which someone can accelerate progress toward dealing with these issues and their formidable, formative interrelationships (such as attachment-separation, autonomy-dependency, sexuality-pleasure/safety, goodness-badness). These are not abstractions. They are integral with what it means to be oneself in regard to other people and the personal bodily and affective experiences that make up a person's life. Dealing with one's human complexities engenders symbolic means of coping, the origins of which slip beneath consciousness. Psychoanalysis offers a chance to translate symbolic constructions into language that is consciously recognized and to trace their interpersonal effects as these become conscious in the transference manifestations. Countertransference behavior, when so used, can help the patient appreciate the cyclical effects old patterns create interpersonally. With sufficient awareness of all that is involved, a person may develop an adult life that is relatively harmonious inwardly, yet well enough adapted for achieving goals in the outer world that are ego syntonic and in keeping with a self-concept as a good person. This goal can be very elusive if the criterion used for evaluating an analysis is either a mythically complete success or a complete failure (Nathan, 1999).

One way to evaluate the possible benefits of analysis is to anticipate changes in character that would mean a patient's being able to handle the universal issues of humankind on a higher level. McWilliams (1994) and Kumin (1996) underscore the relationship between character and behavior during an analysis. McWilliams believes that individual character does not change during analysis, but within the dictates of a set personality organization, one can through psychoanalysis utilize one's psychic abilities for relating in more satisfying ways. Kumin sees the possibility of changes that affect character, as the relationship between deep issues and current circumstances become clear and can be dealt with—notably by means of the transference.

Patients must be active in the analytic process in order to make fundamental changes in ways of relating, even if their styles of relating remain (as McWilliams portrays the role of character). In relation to serial analyses, it is possible to discern an active role on the part of the patient in setting the analytic course.

Understanding the roles of patient and analysts in evaluating success and failure includes questions of diagnosis. In Wallerstein's (1986) collection of forty-two Menninger clinic patients, who were treated either psychoanalytically or by means of psychodynamic psychotherapy, he rated 25 percent as failures. (There were a number of examples of serial analyses, but he did not pursue this issue and the published data are not informative.) He considered diagnosis as a key to failure. Severe difficulties with attachment and separation were apparent in the failure group, suggesting borderline organization.

The reader will quickly note that all three of the cases described in this chapter fit the characteristics of a borderline personality. These examples are all of people who are talented and successful in the work sphere, but like many others with borderline organization, maintain grave difficulties in regard to separation and attachment. Thus, the acute but unstable tansferences they demonstrate fit their using serial analyses in a pattern of successive, seemingly severe failures.

Borderline patients take much analytic work in the process of their maturing into a more contented adulthood. Serial analyses, which mean taking attachment and separation squarely into their own hands, can be a surprising tool in this process.

Introduction to Case Material

It may be useful to think of psychoanalysis as an important phase in a lifelong process of personality development. Just as in the childhood phase, personality development during an analysis is an amalgam of interpersonal and intrapersonal experience, with mixed results in terms of adaptiveness for happy living. An analysis performed by two imperfect human beings is likely to obtain mixed results. Thus, Balint (1950) states that his ideal of an analysis—resulting in firmly established genital primacy, accompanying a capacity for tenderness and identification with a love choice by a strengthened ego, able to cope well with tensions—occurred in only 20 percent of his cases that continued past an exploratory period. We do expect, however, that the total sum of the analytic effort will result in the patient being better able to capitalize on an inner potential for improvement.

Thus, when a patient calls an analysis a failure, but is willing to try it again, this may provide an opportunity for increased general understanding of the analytic process. One plausible lesson from the following clinical material may well be to emphasize a developmental approach to psychoanalysis as process.

A Case of Serial Analyses with
Different Analysts

I was the third person to see Agnes in analysis and her fifth psychodynamic therapist. The first therapist saw her when she was a college student. Mixing psychotherapy with general medicine, he persuaded her to let him give her a total physical examination, which required her to take off her clothes. She reports nothing else unethical from that experience, which she felt was helpful to her in dealing superficially with her anxieties at the time.

After graduation, Agnes was employed in a city two hours away from a large center for psychoanalysis. She had earned an MBA and felt well placed in her first job, but she did not want anyone to know that she required psychoanalysis. She arranged for analysis through the Center. She felt that her personal life was so limited, it did not matter that four times a week, she would drive to her appointments, and back, after work. At this time, her concerns centered upon her drinking and drifting off with strange men whom she met in bars. The analytic relationship sufficed to relieve her of the need to continue these compulsions, except when the analyst was away on vacation. She wrote him letters that she never gave him in which she expressed how important he was to her. The letters did not include overtly erotic content.

After two years of the analysis, Agnes found employment in the same city as the analyst's office, which was in his home. Among her achievements during this period (which predated the recent surge of interest in childhood sexual abuse), was the recovered memory of an episode when she was 9 years old and a gardener seduced her in the potting shed. This memory was dynamically useful in her dealing with the pattern of allowing strange men to pick her up.

Gradually, over the seven years that the analysis continued, Agnes became aware of arguments between the analyst and his wife. He began to tell her details of his annoyances with his wife. One day, she vented anger toward him by flinging the pillow from the couch back at him. She recounts that he then stood up, told her that her acting out was unacceptable, and immediately terminated the analysis.

After some months, Agnes sought short-term help from a woman. This person was old enough to be Agnes's mother and Agnes quickly developed a strong positive maternal transference to her. She assumed when bills were not forthcoming that the therapist felt so strongly for her in her plight that she was not going to charge for the time-limited work. This permitted a flight into health. Agnes felt capable of taking trips, permitting herself to make friends at work, and generally to feel comfortable. She was aware of encouraging words from this therapist that occupied her mind instead of the inhibiting messages from her mother which usually resided there.

Then a bill arrived. Agnes felt betrayed. She paid the bill without voicing her disappointment. The old messages from her mother again filled her thoughts.

Agnes recognized that she needed further analysis. She again sought help from a woman. For two years, she believed that the analysis was going well. In the third year, the analyst let her know that the analyst's mother was in the process of dying and it would be difficult for her to maintain the analytic schedule. Agnes was distraught. She insisted that she would be flexible, if only they could continue. The next crisis occurred when the analyst, whose mother by then had died, was due to leave for a month away. Agnes was in a panic. The analyst instructed Agnes to see a psychiatrist who would prescribe medication for her. Agnes followed through even though this meant driving on the highway, which she feared to do.

The psychiatrist prescribed an antianxiety medication. Agnes returned, as suggested, in two weeks. At this time, the psychiatrist's evaluation led him to change the medication to an antidepressant. When the pharmacist informed Agnes that the medication was one that was used also as an antipsychotic, she was furious. Resuming her analysis upon the analyst's return, Agnes felt that their former rapport was ruptured and that the analyst did not wish to continue with her.

Agnes received my name from a friend who was in treatment with me. She telephoned me, saying that she believed her present analyst did not want to continue with her and furthermore spoke at length in language Agnes could not understand. I responded that it sounded like a "glitch" that could become useful when understood by both parties, since there had been such a productive alliance in the past. We had three conversations along this line before, some weeks later, I agreed to see her.

Agnes produced six audiotapes from her handbag. She had recorded sessions without her analyst's knowledge, to prove to me that she was accurate in describing how the analyst was treating her. The countertransference was apparent as I listened, lending credibility to Agnes's account of her experiences.

At this point, I agreed to begin analysis with Agnes. Some months later, I learned how wary Agnes was with me, as she felt (wrongly) convinced that I must be recording our sessions. This concern reflected her typically borderline confusion as to self-identity and identity of another. She maintained a borderline organization for many more years of work, gradually expanding her range of ego control and capacity for fusion of aggression and libido.

Agnes is a good case for the present purpose because she had two failed analyses. In neither case was there a proper termination. Even though the second one involved a decision on her part to stop, there was no processing of its meaning to her with the analyst at that time; let alone another integrative course on her deep issues; nor the relationship between giving up the analyst completely and the permanent loss of a parent (Frank, 1999).

Yet, the positive aspects of each relationship were adequate for Agnes to continue to seek further analysis. In both failed analyses, symptomatic behavior was improved on the basis of strong positive transferences. More important, however, in each analysis there were some advances in developing greater structural balance. In the first analysis, the recovery of memory of childhood sexual involvement with the gardener enabled her to reduce the importance of the fantasy that sexual expression required her to be victimized. The erotic transference to her analyst, although eventually the stumbling block to further progress, enabled her to refrain from alcoholic consumption she guiltily associated with closeness to her father.

In the second analysis, a strong positive maternal transference freed Agnes to make friendships with her coworkers on a more ongoing basis than in the interlude while she was seeing the psychotherapist. It was possible for her to manage the rupture between the second analyst and herself without losing sight of the useful first years of their work. Integration of aggressive and libidinal impulses was only begun, but the degree of fusion she achieved in that relationship brought her beyond the total dismissal she experienced in regard to her evaluation of the first analyst.

The third analysis was also lengthy, giving an opportunity to understand how painfully slow Agnes's reconstructing of her relationship to her past has been, as a theme in all of the stages of her serial analysis. She often did not recall what she herself had said only a spoken paragraph before. Still, it continued to be true that whenever she recovered feelings encased in previously repressed memories, the effect was to free energy for the present. Gradually, she began to hold connections between her thoughts. An early achievement was managing a continuity of impressions in the present with connections to life in her family. Arranging order in her stockpile of photographs seemed to make possible her reporting for the first time vivid sensory impressions; for example, how blue the sky, how green the grass. Fusion of aggressive and libidinal impulses increased at first to the point of seeing a resemblance between the evildoer in a horror movie and the facial appearance of the third analyst, without needing to stop looking at the film, overcome with horror. Tolerating, even enjoying, romantic films was a later accomplishment. Hard work on her alcoholism finally yielded stability, maintained with membership in Alcoholics Anonymous. Whereas formerly the slightest official review of her financial accounts created a crisis in her anticipation of severe legal difficulties, she came to a matter-of-fact attitude. She could bring her concerns to colleagues, whose reassurance she could accept.

The work of the third analysis clearly flows from what preceded it in the previous analyses. The pattern of forcing a disruption of the analysis was repeated many times. By the third analysis, however, forewarned by Agnes's account of the previous disruptions, the analyst was not susceptible to taking on the role of dismissing her. Agnes gradually recognized that the analyst expected her to continue with the work and that it was she who was trying to leave because of her disappointment in the analyst. With this base, it was possible to approach the meaning to her of someone (the analyst, well-defined in the transference) repeating an inability to listen to her and an unwillingness to talk to her that she identified with her mother.

Case of Serial Analyses in the Face of Repeated Failure with the Same Analyst

Maura came into analysis after a consultation about her troubled son. Her two older children, both girls, were, relatively, going about their lives in a constructive way. The boy, aged 11 at the time, had worried her with his acting-out behavior from the time he was a preschooler. Although he had been evaluated several times by various professionals, he was in treatment for the first time. Maura followed the recommendation of the boy's therapist in coming to see me.

There were two immediate significant transferential communications. First, Maura brought me a small but lovely ceramic flower arrangement because she wanted "something pretty to look at." Second, she gave me a copy of *The Giving Tree,* the story of giving unconditionally and uncomplainingly to a small boy who takes from the tree in different ways as he grows up. Finally as an old man, he sits on the stump that is all that is left of the tree.

Maura related the value of the book to her concerns about being diagnosed as schizophrenic, with bizarre thoughts. The flower arrangement led to emphasis upon finding the good Maura while she felt overwhelmed by bad feelings. She developed a strong positive maternal transference, concentrating her negative feelings on her mother. For several months, she broke with her mother entirely. She reported making friend easily, but giving up totally on people who disappointed her and cutting them off. Interestingly, she also showed greater loyalty in her actual commitment to her husband (although highly critical of him and while fantasizing steadily about a boyfriend from her adolescence). Her need for control in relationships was at odds with her genuine wish for her son to gain autonomy, making her behavior with him erratic. As he matured physically, his libidinal demands echoed prior demands upon her in growing up with an older brother, further complicating her relationship with him.

Maura broke off treatment with me eight times. In between, several of the times, she sought help from other mental health specialists—analysts, psychiatrists, and social workers. She never felt understood by any of them, eventually returning to me with a dismissive account of the shortcomings of the others she had consulted. I believe that my deep confidence in her as a person was the source of her bond to me.

Unfortunately, my countertransference interfered in two ways: I repeatedly responded inwardly to the fact each time that Maura returned to treatment with me, that she came in despair, explicitly demanding immediate relief. I felt the pull strongly, fostering my feelings of inadequacy. In addition, the pattern of Maura's abrupt departures added a sense of urgency to offer something profoundly meaningful before the opportunity disappeared. This was in contrast with my usual comfort with the expectable pace of analytic work. My enmeshment took me very long to sort out in terms of all that was operating within me.

The good thing about this sarabande was that each time Maura satisfied herself that I was not good for much, after all, she proceeded constructively with her life. I would learn during the periods of contact that she had completed a graduate degree or fulfilled on a high level the challenges of a new job, or expanded her social circle.

The ruptures consistently occurred on the basis of her feeling highly critical of me, but finding it unacceptable to admit the reasons to me. Thus, it was always on the basis of my not having enough to offer her. The subtext was her feeling both competitive with me and superior to me. Her fear of destroying me through her success was what I understood. Whenever she approached such a crisis, she left me.

The last time I saw her could hardly be called analysis. It consisted of a single session. It was apparent to me that although Maura reported feeling almost immobilized by depression in a litany of causes for despair, including what now was clearly a pattern of self-attack that included agony over the state of her hair and her belief that she must fire a maid (a consistent euphemism for myself over the years), the key thing was her having engineered the buying of and erecting a town house upon a magnificent property. Maura was angry with what she experienced as my unsympathetic attitude toward her pain and ignored my underscoring of her conflict over whether to allow herself enjoyment with her latest success (far beyond what her parents ever managed for themselves). By chance, I have since learned that Maura has subsequently entered another period of productive contentment.

Case of Serial Analyses with Two Analysts

Spike, a man of 48, has been in analysis with his present analyst for five years (Berenbaum, 1999). Before that, he had two rounds of analysis with another analyst, the first time for four years, afterwards for eight months.

This patient also revealed borderline organization. By his report, throughout both stages of his first analysis and for a long time in his second, he opened each session with a disclaimer that there was any point to the work, or that it had been of any use to him at all. One obvious gain that he made by nearly the close of the first segment of the first analysis was to make a major change in his professional situation, the ostensible reason for his entering into treatment.

In addition, Spike had managed as an achievement to enter into a rewarding financial arrangement that he kept secret from his wife. This secrecy was plausibly an important part of his management of his need to establish autonomy. Unfortunately for the shape of the analysis, his wife learned about it. She insisted that she join in one of the patient's hours, to confront the analyst. The analyst took a nonjudgmental stance, which pleased neither the wife nor his patient (who hoped for backing). Shortly thereafter, the patient left the analysis. He returned for an eight-month stint when he observed that the change in professional circumstances did not provide happiness. When this patient sought further analysis with a new analyst, he said that the only good that came out of the first one was permission from that analyst to be able to make a change in his career. He then proceeded to denigrate the value of the second analysis. Nonetheless, he persisted in it.

At the five-year point in the second analysis, no structural change seems to have solidified in relation to primary figures. The general level of character expression (McWilliams, 1994), however, no longer requires a disclaimer of the analyst's value before the session can proceed. Spike was able to note spontaneously a contrast between his calm reaction to an unexpected interruption during an hour, compared with the almost violent rage he felt under such circumstances previously. His giving voice to his amazement with himself was probably as significant as his perception of his gain. Spike is now able to connect with memories of earlier states when he was easily disrupted, and revel in his own improvement.

Discussion

What is noteworthy in all three cases is the length of time it takes for further ego integration to take place once a superstructure exists that holds personality fragments apart. None of these patients had developed rigid isolation of such fragments to the degree occurring in true multiple personalities. Like those extreme cases, however, the conscious egos of the people described in this paper had limited access to connections between feelings, thoughts, and memories. In details of the clinical material that are beyond the limits of this chapter, they each revealed a basic borderline organization by the intensity yet shallowness of their attachments; difficulty with time that operated against a sense of change (the only moment in the present one and it will remain the same forever); concern about fundamental dichotomies like good/bad, omnipresence/total disappearance, autonomy/dependency; ambivalence that appeared unconnectedly, through closely stated contrasting statements, each of which held complete sway while being uttered; concentration upon appearance rather than roles (a quality not obvious in the third case); domination of oral and anal concerns, with sexuality enveloped in confusions relating to personal identity.

These patients sought out help. They could thus fixate on the possibilities of psychoanalysis. Yet, their unsettled, highly ambivalent attitudes made for treacherous difficulties in the process. Woloshin (February 18, 1999, personal communication) tells of a case reported to her of a depressed patient whose therapist felt there was a remarkable breakthrough in the closeness of their collaboration. Subsequently, he learned that the patient had committed suicide the night before the next appointment with him. Fortunately, in the cases in this paper, the patients disrupted analyses rather than asserting autonomy so drastically.

If one views these cases developmentally, it is possible to appreciate the progress each made in each segment of analytic work. One can, of course, take a lofty view of evident countertransference complications. Nonetheless, from the standpoint of a patient's development, these cases illustrate an overall constructive thrust in what takes place. Although Agnes could see only the failure in her first analysis, while she could maintain a more balanced view of the second (though eventually failed), it becomes clear that her ability to integrate her gains increased during every therapeutic episode. The coconstructivist aspect of her interchanges can be traced. The first analyst allowed the reality of his marital problems to enter the analysis (whether they were characteristic or not of his marriage in general), perhaps affecting his ability to keep an analytic stance with Agnes's reactions. Yet, before the disruption, she felt safe enough with him to gain access to important sexual material that once had been repressed at some psychic cost; and was able to acknowledge anger toward him enough to provoke him—instead of repressing and denying it.

In the second analysis, the analyst had to deal with Agnes's intensified dependency while dealing in her personal life with the imminent and then actual loss of her mother. By this point, however, Agnes had attained enough ego integration that she could maintain a sense both of her gains with the second analysis and her disappointment at the end. Although Agnes coconstructively provoked an end to the second analysis, as well as the first—in the work of her third analysis, she was able to return from her bursts of dismissal to continue the work.

Maura encountered the countertransference limitations of her analyst repeatedly in the analyst's difficulty to deal with her pain and need to emphasize positives for Maura. Nonetheless, Maura was able to use the insight she generated during each course of analysis, returning when she felt the need (much like the person in *The Giving Tree* who could keep coming back to the tree for further help that was appropriate for the tree to give in the successive times). The fear that she, like the person in the story, would use up her "tree," making it feel dangerous for her to continue when she became critical of the analyst (or needed to wrest her autonomy back from her felt-dependency)—meant that she had to disrupt the analysis. The hard work during the analytic periods enabled her to put her isolated memories into relationship, to maintain themes in her associations, and to be increasingly productive in her daily life, with a much improved relationship with her husband.

Spike, who switched analysts, encountered his first analyst's ambivalence when the analyst permitted the man's wife to enter into the situation, and furthermore promoted his own appearance of objectivity rather than using the interview exploratively. Nonetheless, the patient's insistent declaration that all that analysis was good for was his achieving a change in his professional status ignores the growth that permitted this achievement. His managing a stab at autonomy from his wife by holding a major secret from her suggests that he moved significantly toward becoming his own person. With the second analyst, continuing the process for another five years, Spike has come to the point of ego-integration where he can recognize and even enjoy his sense of stability in the face of frustration.

Serial analyses are to be understood as linear because they are stages in a single person's development. Senses of failure and disruption in analyses are significant in the same way as their predecessors in the person's history. They are an important part of the story, but by no means describe the entire situation. No child nor analysand survives if there is only failure and lack of connection. Given survival, the child who struggles on and the patient who persists in serial analyses utilize the margin of good that we analysts are charged to find and hope we can enhance.

These cases do not show that failed analyses do not exist, although a completely failed analysis is perhaps debatable. Serial analyses generally demonstrate that whatever went wrong in various efforts, enough ego strengthening was accomplished (or remained) to enable the person to continue the process. The fact that the person has not given up on the analytic process may be a sign that significant growth did take place in preceding attempts. Not only may the patterns of disruption prove meaningful, but the growth that did take place may noticeably facilitate the ongoing work in subsequent analyses.

Ego integration with a patient in analysis is in parallel with physical healing when tissues exist in a disrupted state. The initial stages of producing a healthy form are detectable only microscopically; then one can observe changes that are apparent, but still tenuous; and finally firmly knit tissue is in evidence. The analogy to physical healing is perhaps not far-fetched. In both kinds of progress, one can assume an underlying impetus toward such development, emanating from the forces that promote maturation from the beginning of life.

Final Note

We assume that in the ordinary course of events, the analytic process continues for a long time after termination. If we interpret our work as facilitative for further psychological development, then it is tempting to assume that further growth is at least partially a consequences of what was achieved during the analysis. Failures of empathy and other sources of failures as are contributed by an analyst remain subjects for the analyst to regard soberly. The inevitable fact of some degree of participation in the failure of an analysis is a starting point for the analyst's own greater self-understanding.

At the same time, the failure of the analysis from the standpoint of the patient's contribution is best contemplated in the context of the patient's developmental tasks. Serial analyses give us a window on what happens in the aftermaths of formal analytic periods. It would be an excellent subject for in-depth study: What does the patient report about why a previous analysis was terminated—especially if it was on the basis of a judged failure? What has the patient experienced in the interim period? What brought the patient back into analysis? Why the choice of either the same or a different analyst—and in what way, if different? Can one discern in what ways the ego states in the prior analyses differ from the ego states of the patient in the present analysis? Are there demonstrable ways in which the patient begins subsequent analyses with greater strengths, traceable to the preceding analyses? Such a project would enrich our understanding of our work in general. This chapter is offered as a beginning.

There is a saying that one never steps into the same river twice. Each analysis in a series proves to be a unique experience, but one that proves the dynamic quality of all human experience. The patient is not the same as before any analysis took place. Previous analyses are helpful sources of information as the patient continues toward becoming the person the patient wants to be.

References

Balint, M. (1950), On the termination of analysis. *Internat. J. Psycho-Anal.*, 31:196–199.

Berenbaum, H. (1999), The case of Spike. *Audiotape Library*. Chicago: Chicago Center for Psychoanalysis.

Frank, G. F. (1999), Termination revisited. *Psychoanal. Psychol.*, 16(1): 119–129.

Freud, S. (1937), Analysis terminable and interminable. *Standard Edition*, 23:209–253. London: Hogarth Press, 1964.

Glover, E. (1949), *Psycho-Analysis*. London: Staples Press.

———— (1955), *The Technique of Psycho-Analysis*. New York: International Universities Press.

Kumin, I. (1996), *Pre-Object Relatedness: Early Attachment and the Psychoanalytic Situation*. New York: Guilford Press.

McWilliams, N. (1994), *Psychoanalytic Diagnosis: Understanding Personality Structure in the Clinical Process*. New York; Guilford Press.

Milner, M. (1949), A note on the ending of an analysis. *Internat. J. Psycho-Anal.*, 30:191–193.

Nathan, M. (1999), *Structural Change in a Case That "Failed."* Unpublished dissertation. Chicago: Chicago Center for Psychoanalysis.

Novick, J. (1990), Comments on termination in child, adolescent, and adult analysis. *The Psychoanalytic Study of the Child,* 45:419–496. New Haven, CT: Yale University Press.

Silverman, D. K. (1996), Polarities and amalgams: Analytic dyads and the individuals within them. *Psychoanal. Rev.,* 83(2): 247–271.

Tabin, J. K. (1985), *On the Way to Self: Ego and Early Oedipal Development.* New York: Columbia University Press.

———— (1996), Transferences and the gender of the analyst. Invited paper for Psychologists Interested in the Study of Psychoanalysis, Toronto, August 11.

Wallerstein, R. S. (1986), *Forty-Two Lives in Treatment: A Study of Psychoanalysis and Psychotherapy,* New York: Guilford Press, pp. 561–573.

7

Reconsidering an Analytic Outcome: Success or Failure?

ROBERT S. WALLERSTEIN, M.D.

In 1967, I published a paper on the concept of the "transference psychosis" built around a report of two cases. This was at a time when the development and then the resolution of the so-called regressive transference neurosis was viewed as *the* central technical and conceptual vehicle of psychoanalysis as a therapy. It was the heyday of the hegemony within (American) psychoanalysis of the ego psychology metapsychological paradigm, and Merton Gill's statement of the nature of psychoanalysis as a therapy was widely accepted as the most succinct and definitive expression of that conviction within the ego psychological framework: "Psychoanalysis is that technique which, employed by a neutral analyst, results in the development of a regressive transference neurosis and the ultimate resolution of this neurosis by techniques of interpretation alone" (1954, p. 775).

Acknowledgment. I thank Joseph Reppen for his highlighting—in an exchange of letters—the range of perspectives on my 1967 paper on the transference psychosis that lend themselves to reconsideration from the standpoint of psychoanalytic success or failure, as seen within the framework of psychoanalysis today.

By contrast, but within that same ego psychological framework, my paper dealt with two patients in whom the analytic
transference lost its as-if quality and became (temporarily at
least) delusional. In these cases, the patient's observing
ego—from the ego split into an observing (introspective) ego
alongside the experiencing ego, as posited by Sterba
(1934)—failed, during the course of the analysis, in its guardian function of maintaining distance from, and exerting reality
mastery over, the transference illusion, with a severe disorganizing and dereistic episode then ensuing. The following citation from my 1967 article illustrates what I meant:

> A highly emotional woman with a hysterical character structure[1]
> had been adjudged suitable for psychoanalysis,[2] despite her po-
> tential for being swept away by surges of affect, because of the
> penetrating realism with which she could subsequently see her-
> self and her reactions after the storm had passed. One evening
> toward the end of the second year of her analysis she tele-
> phoned me in an anguished and guilty rage to inform me that
> her aggressions had overwhelmed her, that she had choked her
> tom cat to death, and that she "knew" as she did it that it had
> my face. Also, her father's first name had been Tom. For several
> months during this period of her analysis this patient lived
> through such fusion experiences and, under their sway, at times
> exhibited just such bizarre and violent behavior. Some six to
> nine months thereafter, when she had reconstituted, she re-
> ferred to these ideas and actions from this period as having
> been "deluded" [1967, pp. 551–552].

In that 1967 article I differentiated this "transference psychosis" from the psychotic transference ideation and behaviors
of borderline or psychotic patients taken into analysis, particularly by British analysts (see, for example from that period, H.
Rosenfeld [1954]; Little [1958, 1960]), and I reviewed the then
sparse literature on the psychoanalytic treatments of putatively
neurotic patients who, like my two, developed transitory psychotic reactions within the transference unfolding, though

---

[1]See Wallerstein (1980–1981) for my specific conceptualization of the hysterical
character structure.
[2]This judgment had been made on the basis of the two-week-long diagnostic evaluation of prospective patients, the modus operandi at that time of The Menninger Clinic,
an evaluation process that included the Rapaport-devised psychological projective
test battery.

none of those reported by others, to that point, spilled over into the patient's ongoing life situations as extensively, or for as long a duration, as did mine. Actually, I found a total of six well-enough described comparable cases, starting with an initial description of this phenomenon on a very transitory basis and totally encapsulated within the analytic hour (under the name of "passagère symptoms"), in two early papers by Ferenczi (1912, 1919), and going up through a 1961 paper by Hammett on the "delusional transference," in which the author raised the question as to whether a *forme fruste* of such a development, a periodic intensely, almost delusionally, held system of beliefs within the transference, does not occur in almost every analytic case.

What I did not state in my 1967 paper was that both the patients I described were psychoanalytic control cases from my candidacy days, and that the first of the two, from whose case description I have just quoted, was my very first supervised case, and had been offered to me as an ideal psychoanalytic first control case. It was on this basis of experiencing two such instances during my candidacy that I undertook to support Hammett's proposition as follows:

> Hammett raised the question that perhaps every analysis pursuing its "usual" course contains a *forme fruste* of this phenomenon here seen [in my two case instances] in exaggerated and therefore highlighted form: a tendency at the height of every transference involvement to blur the saving "as if" transference awareness. Two such quite extreme derivations from the more usual transference course in a still small analytic experience lend some support to this suggestion. A continuum of degrees of loss of reality mastery over the transference illusion undoubtedly exists in "usual" analytic practice [1967, p. 578].

When I published my 1967 paper, my intention was to describe these two very extreme instances of this transference psychosis phenomenon, which were of an intensity, scope, and duration that was beyond any that I could uncover in my literature search at the time. I wished to describe the (quite similar) circumstances under which the regressive and disorganizing psychotic transference process erupted in the two cases, as well as the circumstances of the gradual reconstitution in both instances within a quite comparable process of reconstruction and mastery (hence the article's title). It should be noted that the two patients presented with quite different character organizations, the one, already cited, who was flamboyantly hysterical, and the other, very obsessional. Implicit within that account was the conviction that therefore such patients could be treated "classically" psychoanalytically—albeit requiring, for periods of disorganized and delusional functioning, the resources of a psychoanalytic sanatorium where temporary hospitalization could be combined with the full maintenance of the ongoing psychoanalytic treatment. It was expected that reasonably successful outcomes would result. The focus was on what *could* be accomplished psychoanalytically, even under such difficult circumstances.

In this present article, geared to the consideration of psychoanalytic treatment failures, I am endeavoring to reconsider the whole treatment process of individuals who develop such a psychotic reaction within the transference (within the parameters I have set forth). I will look at this from the standpoint of the limitations of the treatment process and the outcome achieved, to what extent it could have been more effective (or not), and to what extent then the course and outcome described could be marked as a relative failure rather than a relative success. I do this, of course, within the framework of the technical and theoretical advances that have characterized our psychoanalytic world over the four decades since these treatments were carried out. I am quoting in full the case description of the first of the two cases I presented in my 1967 article, the flamboyantly hysterical patient from whose case I have offered the illustrative vignette. I do this for two reasons: (1) the transference psychotic episode in this case was the more extreme, the longer lasting, and the more dramatic, and therefore, more transparent, and (2) it is the only one of the two on which I have some follow-up data, albeit slight, that can be of some aid in fashioning a judgment of the effectiveness of the treatment outcome. The original case description was, verbatim, as follows:

The patient was a 32-year-old housewife and mother of three children who came to analysis because of recurrent acute depressions ostensibly linked to her second husband's periodic overseas assignments as an air force officer. Actually she suffered from an intense chronic unhappiness and lifelong severely disturbed and highly turbulent interpersonal relationships. At 19 she made an extremely serious suicide attempt. She had first married at 16 with the conscious intent of escaping the unhappy, strife-ridden atmosphere at home. It was a loveless wartime marriage to an air force man whose passivity and inability to meet her need for love she deeply resented. At a time of separation from this first husband, and after being told by his mother that they would be better divorced, she had gone to her husband's room, taken his shot gun, and in front of her mother-in-law fired at her heart, succeeding in blowing a hole in her chest from which she recovered only after a prolonged and critical illness.

From the first, the patient dwelt on her hateful dependent relationship to her mother and her guilty feelings over the two hospitalizations for psychotic episodes of her two-year-older sister, the only sibling. The picture of her father emerged more slowly and somewhat later, and was initially much overidealized. He had died by suicide when the patient was only 4. She remembered that she was hurried off with no explanation other than that her father had gone away to the country. She was not allowed to participate in the funeral. Although she occasionally referred to him as the father who had hurt her by leaving her and deserting her, more often he was the good father who had been driven away by the wicked mother.

In relation to this idealized image of the father, there had been a succession of good fathers in her life—a Jewish businessman friend of the father who after the father's suicide had offered to adopt the patient; the mother's second husband, the patient's stepfather, a kindly though ineffectual man dominated by the mother; and a courtly colonel, twenty years her senior, who carried on an intensely gratifying wartime romance with the patient. It was actually the frustration over the dissolution of this relationship (under the shadow of the colonel's reconciliation with his wife) that precipitated the patient's suicide attempt when she shot and nearly killed herself when she was 19.

Neither of the patient's two husbands was anywhere in this line of "good fathers." The first marriage rushed into at 16 was unhappy from the start. The second husband, also a flier, was a childhood friend. He too had been shot down, had been a prisoner of war in Germany, and courted and married the patient upon his return after the war. It was the paradoxical depressive episodes in this marriage that followed her husband's returns from overseas assignments that had precipitated her coming for treatment.

What emerged in the treatment was her feeling that she had never really loved this husband either, that she saw him as a "fussy old woman" and a "nagging mother" just like her own mother. Neither husband nor mother, in her eyes, had ever wanted her or chosen her. The patient bitterly remembered her mother's frequent, angry statement that she was "nothing but a slip," and hence, never wanted. The counterpart with the husband was that the patient had married him through a ruse. Sensing his indecisiveness about the courtship she had pretended to be pregnant and was thus guilty of tricking him into the marriage. When she confessed the ruse years later, he said that he had known it all along, but this did not dispel her feelings that he also had neither wanted her nor chosen her.

Through the analysis the patient's relationship with her husband pursued an ambivalent zigzag course. Violent quarrels, dramatic acting out, and periods of estrangement alternated with tearful reconciliations. Divorce was talked of often, culminating in periodic separations. The patient would always demur at actual divorce, however; she would become guilty and depressed and be driven to seek reconciliation. Divorce would repeat too closely the childhood loss, the man driven away, the family members deprived of father and husband. When they reconciled it was with restitutive fantasies of bringing back the man who was gone, restoring the man to the woman.

The transference development was marked by the same intensity and volatility. It was alternately a deeply erotized transference to the father or a hateful transference to the nagging, domineering mother. During the "positive" phases there were undisguised fantasies and wishes for direct love making with outright refusals to work analytically with this material and even threats to quit the analysis if she were made to do so. Once she wore her overcoat in the analytic hour because she had forgotten to put a skirt on before she left the house, and then expressed extreme guilt since simultaneously there was an absence from her life of any sexual feelings toward her husband. Concomitantly death wishes were constantly voiced against my wife. Periods of "confession" of erotic feelings were followed by expressions of active dislike and spiteful efforts to disrupt the treatment. Once when the patient thus angrily stayed away, she regaled a friend with recitals of her sexual fantasies about me.

It was in the second year of the analysis that the material began to revolve more closely around the father's death and that simultaneously the harbingers of reality-deviant behavior began. The patient reconstructed that her father had rejected her and had indeed preferred her elder sister just as mother had always openly rejected her with her lifelong preference for a boy. In the patient's guilt-laden fantasy she had revengefully brought about her father's death and had simultaneously revenged herself on mother and sister by depriving them of husband and father. Parallel to the theme of hostility and guilt toward the father, and preoccupation with his desertion and rejection, there were dreams of reuniting with the long dead father only to have it turn into a frustrating, unrewarding experience. In the most vivid such dream the father was seated in a chair, somehow newly returned to life, but making no overture to her and she felt unable to make contact with him. This led to a feeling that the analysis would never give her what she wanted and a deepening hatred in, what became, more clearly at this point, a predominantly mother transference. The patient said, "I came to analysis looking for a loving father, and what do I run into but a denying mother." It was at this time that the first grossly bizarre and violent behavior occurred, the choking to death of the tom cat that had my face, and her father's name. In killing the cat-analyst she was thus not only destroying the hated mother, but repeating the earlier crime against the father. This turned out not to be the first such episode. Years before she had been so enraged by the family cat that she had gotten the family shotgun and blasted and killed the cat. She had then gotten into her car, driven along an abandoned roadside, and guiltily thrown the body out into a culvert. Some other car was passing at the time and she wondered whether she had been seen and whether the police would come to arrest her as a murderess.

The decompensating trend was shortly reinforced by a number of life events. The patient's kindly stepfather died of a heart ailment. His memory was much idealized. Simultaneously there were increasing clashes with the husband, who was seen as linked ever more strongly to mother. The patient asserted that a sign of her "improvement" in the analysis was the lessening of the sense of guilty obligation which had always tied her to this husband. At the same time she was intensely intolerant of my forthcoming three-week summer vacation and stormily proclaimed that she would be taking an additional three weeks off before that vacation with the announced intention of terminating completely.

She was back at the end of the six weeks. Her initial depressive, guilt-ridden state had returned and she begged to be taken back into treatment. I had the patient sit up during these first hours when we discussed the conditions of her return to treatment. On occasion she seemed dazed and to drift in and out of contact with her surroundings. She was cautiously taken back to treatment.

In the first period after her return the patient was preoccupied with the "homosexual" nature of her tie to some of her close women friends, who were also patients in analysis. She saw in the tensions of these relationships the recapitulation of aspects of her lifelong difficult relationship with the two-year-older sister. Memories of childhood sexual play with the sister emerged as well as an increasing awareness of the extreme ramifications of the guilt she had always felt in relation to the sister's two psychotic episodes. Out of the patient's "badness" in her sexual play with her sister, the sister subsequently became crazy, daddy had been driven to kill himself, but the patient had escaped scot-free.

This same period of return to treatment was marked by an infantile dependence within the transference in which the patient established a childishly trusting relationship to the image of a (for the first time) nurturing, good mother. As a mark of her trust at this time she gave up the "secret" that she had maintained throughout more than two years of analysis. She divulged the name of the Colonel who had been her lover during the war. She told her husband that she was convinced that her analysis had reached a turning point and that from here on she would go on to get well. She used this so provocatively with him that he felt driven to state defensively that as far as he was concerned things were no better between them but actually worse and he might as well get a divorce. Once offered, the patient eagerly seized this gambit and within a few days engaged a lawyer and filed suit. To her this divorce was a realistic and logical outcome of the analytic work that had been accomplished thus far. It would be, to her, a betrayal of all she had learned about herself to go on in what she felt was an untenable marriage, bound by ties of guilt to a nagging hostile "mother." She rationalized in fact that getting the divorce was essential to the continuation of her treatment. At the same time she vehemently denied all transference meanings in it, especially that it represented a giving up of all other objects in her life and throwing herself completely and dependently onto the nurturing analyst. This made her bitterly angry, and each time that she was strongly advised to defer the divorce and maintain a separation, if need be, until she had more thoroughly worked out the attached problems, she would berate me severely for my lack of understanding and faith.

During this period of awaiting the divorce hearing and holding to her fixed positions in the therapy, the patient became clinically more openly and acutely disturbed. She began to have "fugue states" in which she transiently lost reality contact, these occurring both in her life outside and in connection with coming to her treatment hours. She was now sitting up in treatment, and when especially agitated, was given extra hours. She was concomitantly seeing an internist who had her on substantial doses of a nonbarbiturate sedative[3]—which helped intermittently. Her care of her children suffered markedly and they were often thrown upon her friends to care for when she proved totally incapable. On one occasion she left them with a friend and disappeared with an expression of intense urgency that something had to be done, lest she kill herself. I, as well as the husband (who was at the time separated from her pending the divorce), a number of her friends, and the police were all activated in searching for her. She showed up matter-of-factly the next day, having spent the night in a local hotel. She stoutly denied that any of these upsets were consequent to the divorce action; they were to her additional proofs that she had to get the divorce proceedings over with quickly in order to be able to "settle down."

When the divorce came, its impact was minimized and narrowed down only to the guilt she acknowledged in relation to the youngest child, the 4-year-old daughter, who was being deprived of her father at the same age that the patient herself had lost her father by suicide. The murder of the father and the deprivation of the family were enacted in double measure, since the patient's daughter and my daughter had the same name—a fact which had infuriated her ever since she had chanced to find it out. The upsets pyramided after the divorce was final and resurgent suicidal impulses led (despite the patient's total lack of available money) to a long overdue month-long emergency hospitalization in the maximum care section of our hospital.

During this period of hospitalization the patient reconstructed—out of dream fragments, fantasies past and present, and bits of circumstantial evidence that seemed to "fit"—in great anguish, and with tireless and horrifying detail, her vision of her father's death by suicide. In her reconstruction fantasy

---

[3] This was in the 1950s, prior to the era of modern psychopharmacology and the widespread availability of psychoactive medications.

the father died by jumping out of a second- or third-story window, crashing through the glass, landing on the pavement in the middle of the street below and being immediately cut into pieces by a streetcar running over his body, the patient all the time having been a petrified onlooker. There was an urgent pressure to vividly recreate each detail in sequence and to reexperience the intensity of feeling that would have been appropriate at every moment of this presumed episode. The meaning of an episode shortly before the hospitalization, during the period of increasingly disturbed and uncontrollable behavior, was now much clearer. The patient had brought a heavy hammer to her hour with the double fantasy of smashing my head in, or, alternatively, of smashing the window and making me jump out—to recapitulate the father's death jump. (Incidentally, she left the hammer with me at the end of the hour and never tried to reclaim it.) She now associated the recent panicky episodes which had occurred when she felt trapped in glass-enclosed public telephone booths. The first "fugue state" in which she had momentarily lost all reality awareness had occurred in a phone booth in a department store downtown. When she passed the home of a psychiatrist colleague who lived near her, she had a number of times—well over a year before—been startled by the fantasy of "the penis at the window." In this image she thought she saw the colleague, or just his penis, at the window (a third-story window) and that something was coming out the window, or perhaps that he was urinating out the window. In connection with this she recalled her childhood fantasy that rain represented God urinating upon the world from out his window.

Accompanying these "reconstructions" in the analytic hours the patient inaugurated a steady pressure through letters to her mother, to her sister, and to her lawyer to find out the "truth" about her father's death. She felt that her mother had always evaded and outright lied to her. Now she wanted the unvarnished truth. She instructed her lawyer to look into the newspaper and legal records of the time but she never did secure outside verification of the facts. There had always been a vague memory or a fantasy—she was not sure which—of a policeman coming up the stairs, to notify the family that the father was dead, was no longer going to be coming home. Many times during her married life the patient was frightened when it was only her husband coming up the stairs to bed; on many another occasion she awakened in the middle of the night with the almost hallucinatory impression of somebody coming up the stairs, pounding heavily, coming up to convey bad news or to "get her." Perhaps her father had died by committing suicide in the park and been found dead on a park bench. Once she was driven into a very agitated state by seeing a mannikin lying on a park bench as a window display in a business building downtown.

The precise description of the reconstitutive course from this point on would seem anticlimactic when compared with the drama—and the violence—of the treatment adventure to this point. With the repetitive reworking of these many interlocking fragments of dream and fantasy and childhood memory in endless variation and in full detail, the accompanying affective charges gradually diminished. After a month the patient was allowed home from the hospital to reassemble her children who in the meantime had been separately boarded out with various friends in town. This was a period of intense dependency and demandingness within the analysis. The patient brought repeated emergencies and demands for immediate actions to stave off disaster; on one occasion this involved getting nursing help into the home within an hour; on another occasion getting the local social welfare agency involved to help provide housekeeping service on a sustained basis. Throughout it all, the patient kept repeating that her treatment was "all shot," that everything the analyst did was wrong, that she no longer could trust him—the stupid, mistrusted, and hateful mother; but on the other hand interpersed this with pleas not to give up on her no matter what she said or did. She went into the summer vacation period after three years and over six hundred hours of analysis with alternate expressions of intense desire to go on in treatment versus accusations of indifference and malevolence on my part. The extremes of anger would be followed by contrite statements that she could not remain angry and fixing more firmly the return date after the vacation.

There was one further month of formal treatment in the fall. In the interim she had reintegrated to the extent that she was again living an organized life, able adequately to take care of herself and the children. Her disturbing symptoms, the depressive sweeps, the severe guilt, the troubling nightmares were now gone; she was no longer on medication of any kind. She thought she wanted to go on in treatment in order to work out more fully the core of still unresolved problems, centering around the hostile relationship to the mother. She consciously tried to discount the possibility that further analytic work might open the gateway to another regressive sweep of total dependency and the fierce reactive hostility generated with it. Yet she seemed at least preconsciously aware of this potential expressed in her "disappointment" that somehow this renewed period of treatment was not what she had anticipated it would be. Thus she indirectly voiced her wish for the return to the infantile dependence that had characterized her psychotic phase now several months behind her, a wish which consciously must be perceived as a danger to be feared and warded off. She now began to express that she was satisfied with her life; her overall adjustment she declared better than any she had heretofore known. She said that although she had gotten much sicker at the height of her illness than many other people in analysis, she felt she had reconstituted to a much better state. Admittedly her current life had limitations, especially as a divorced woman with three children, and with a severely restricted social life. This was a lack which she might be fortunate enough to remedy, but in any case she declared it much preferable to the guilt-laden marriage in which she had been caught when she came into treatment. She felt the analysis had accomplished for her all that it "reasonably could." In the relationship with the mother (and the sister), the intensity of the hate was gone, being replaced by a relative estrangement and mutual forbearance.

Thus she officially terminated her analysis. Continued therapeutic contact occurred over the next six months, however—in the form of about ten once weekly sessions. They provide an epilogue. These further contacts were initiated by the patient about two months after stopping her treatment. She was in an automobile accident and was surprised when she realized that it was her ex-husband she wanted most to see. This apparently stimulated a serious rethinking of her situation. What she conveyed when she was seen by me could be condensed as follows: that her ex-husband was no longer mother, he was just himself; that I was neither mother nor father, just myself; that she had been driven by her need to perceive her husband the way she did, to do this cruel thing to him, to divorce him; but how now she was aware how much she wished she had let me talk her out of it. The divorce was an expression of the illness, to which she had been compulsively driven. Now she wanted a chance to make up and to love him. She wanted to stop hating. She had been hating long enough in her life.

Concomitantly these same sentiments were being expressed to the ex-husband. He was bewildered but pleased. He began to court her again attentively and cheerfully but not without some wariness. He had reasons not to rush tempestuously back into a remarriage.

It was during this period of his making up his mind, of the cautious courtship on both sides, that I saw the patient on a weekly basis. Despite her eagerness for the remarriage she was not without doubts and fears. During this period—toward its end—there was a recurrence of an amnesic episode lasting an hour or two, during which the patient wandered around downtown, oblivious to her surroundings. She said she had suddenly "flipped" again. It happened the day after a man committed suicide by jumping off a high building downtown. The newspaper account remarked about a woman who had seen him on the ledge before he jumped and had gone to call the police. The patient insisted that this was no way to deter a man from suicide; she should have gone and told him she loved him (a perfect stranger to her). Thus the patient stated how she should have been able to save her father. Her complaint about all this in her next session with me was that she had all this insight but was still not secure in her ability to keep past and present firmly differentiated, at least not in the moment in which it was occurring.

The last note. Some six months after the end of her analysis, the patient and her ex-husband quietly remarried. He was shortly transferred to another city. They were not unhappy to leave Topeka and to start again in a new milieu. (I have just a little follow-up information. The patient is living tolerably with her husband and is free of her major neurotic symptoms—the depressions and the panic states. A major gain she feels from the treatment is a restored capacity to enjoy her relationship with her young daughter.)

This dramatic psychotic episode in this flamboyantly hysterical patient occurred over a time span of many months—in the midst of a psychoanalytic treatment—with a considerable prodromal period marked by episodic fugue states and grossly reality-deviant behavior outbursts and with a similar prolonged restitutive phase marked by persistent efforts, not just to seal over, but to reverse and undo the damages inflicted in the compulsive reenactments of earlier traumatic situations within the psychosis. The driving fantasy of the psychosis centered around the father's death by suicide when the patient was 4; the good father driven away by the cruel and hateful mother, or alternatively, the victim of the patient's "badness." Subsequent figures in the patient's life stood either in the line of good fathers, mostly distant, unobtainable—or ineffectual—or of bad mothers, vindictive and nagging. The husbands, both of them, were "fussy old women," "nagging mothers." The yearning within the transference was for the kindly father; the major perception within the transference was of the hateful, denying mother.

The patient's major, and so close to being devastatingly successful, suicide attempt came ostensibly over the tension in the first marriage to the petulant, small boy first husband, a demanding and controlling mother figure in her life, but actually as well over the loss of the 20-year-older good father figure, the romantic lover. The depressive swings that brought the patient to psychoanalysis focused around the overseas tours and enforced absences from the second husband, most particularly when the reunions with him never made her as happy as they were supposed to—as the fantasied restitutions that they should have been.

When the analysis too basically "disappointed" her, when it did not lead to the loving dependent reunion with the good father, now restored to life, both the patient's frustration and guilt mounted to an unbearable degree. When the death of the kindly stepfather and the pending summer vacation from the analysis were additionally imposed, the patient's integrative resources stretched past their breaking point. The impulse push occurred in two divergent directions. The first was the reenactment of the father murder by the divorce of the husband. In identification with her daughter, she was again the 4-year-old, losing her father. Through the linkage of names between her daughter and mine, I was being destroyed as well. Simultaneously the divorce also represented the driving off of the husband as the bad mother so that she could throw herself unreservedly into the incestuous relationship with me as the father.

At the same time that the patient was seeking the divorce, with all its overdetermined meanings, the pressure within the treatment was toward reconstruction of the fantasies of father's suicide and reexperiencing in their horror the accompanying affects that seemed then to have been suppressed. The reconstruction fantasy was gradually transmuted from the more bizarre (the horribly detailed scene of the body crashing through

the window onto the streetcar tracks below) to the more plausible (being found dead by the policeman on the park bench).
Accompanying fantasies and behaviors—the appearance in my
office with the hammer in order to make me reenact the father's
death; the panicky episodes in the glass-enclosed phone
booths—were each reworkings, at first on an increasing scale,
afterwards on a diminishing scale, of the same trauma. In the
earlier choking of the cat as the combined representation of
analyst and father, the patient had taken the lethal action most
directly into her own hands, and felt, properly, most directly
guilty.

How much of this fantasy reconstruction—of the man going
out the window and chopped to bits by the streetcar below—was
a reconstruction of fantasies with which the patient had consciously reacted to her father's death when she was 4, fantasies
and ensuing behaviors which might then have been of sufficient
intensity to have warranted designation as an infantile psychotic
reaction, is from the point of view of retrospective reconstruction, probably unknowable. Certainly in all the intervening
years, even before the regressive pressures of analysis, there was
fateful evidence of potentials for ego rupture, the self-murder
when she shot and almost killed herself, the animal murder
when she shot and killed the family cat (and feared arrest as
a murderess).

Reider [1957] has stated, as already pointed out [in my detailed literature review on this subject in 1967 which has not
been quoted in this article], that such psychotic reactions within
the transference occur either as reenactments of childhood psychoses or as an identification with a psychotic early attachment.
This patient qualifies on the second count as well. Her only
sibling, the two-year-older sister, had twice been hospitalized for
psychotic episodes over which the patient had always been both
embarrassed and guilty. As children they had committed a mutual "sex crime"—mutual masturbation—out of which they had
driven their father to his death. The sister was punished by her
mental breakdown. Mother was punished through losing her
husband. Father was punished through his death. Only the patient had gotten off scot-free until, overburdened by the intense
guilt, she had now been driven crazy like her sister.

Yet with all this, despite even being choked in effigy, I neither
died nor abandoned her and thus did not do to her what her
father had done—and thus gradual restitution was likewise possible within the transference. For a time even, I was not only

the loving father, but the patient could—briefly—transcend the mutually hating interaction with the mother to reach behind to a trusting infantile dependence on a protective and nurturant good mother figure.

To give closure to the restitutive efforts, mastery had to be successfully carried through in behavior as well—through the remarriage. The divorce had most directly repeated the infantile crime. In addition, since the patient had initially tricked her husband into the marriage, and since she could never dispel the idea that he had married her reluctantly and only out of a sense of obligation, she bore a feeling of guilt that could be undone only by releasing her husband to his original freedom of choice. In the remarriage both these needs could be met. In the most appropriate way for the pursuit of her life in reality, the original crime against the father could at last be undone and finally put to rest; and this could be on the basis of a second chance, and a freer choice for each [1967, pp. 556–569].

Discussion

In the discussion section of my 1967 paper, after presenting the clinical account of my two cases, I began with the statement that I had tried to trace the transference unfolding, and the circumstances under which the ego splitting that normally acts to maintain reality mastery over the transference illusions, failed in this guardian function, with the consequent psychotic regression within the transference, in which the mature ego was overwhelmed by the intensity of the liberated affects. But beyond the main thread of that presentation, the delineation of the reconstructive function served in that psychotic transference regression, I stated that the clinical material lent itself to further discussion from a variety of additional standpoints—"diagnostic, therapeutic, and conceptual issues of significant current concern" (p. 577). These issues are still of "significant current concern" several decades later, and it is these issues that I want to rediscuss in terms of current-day psychoanalytic understandings, as set, for purposes of this volume, into the framework of considerations of therapeutic success and failure, or stated differently, treatment reach and limitation.

Diagnostically, I stated the problem (in 1967) as that of the nature, extent, and incidence of such severe regressive phenomena within the transference development. I opted for the rubric "hysterical psychosis" to emphasize two related considerations: (1) the lack of evidence within the psychotically regressive analytic material of a concomitant emergent thought disorder that would denote a schizophrenic process; like the transferences with psychotic or near-psychotic patients (cf. H. Rosenfeld, 1954, 1965; Little, 1958, 1960; D. Rosenfeld, 1992), and (2) the implications for the readier reversibility of the psychotic episode under proper psychotherapeutic management, which links of course to the major question—to which I will turn further on—of what is the best kind of psychoanalytically guided treatment in such situations, or put differently, how close, or not, is that "best kind" of treatment to the effort I maintained in the original therapy at a full, or proper, psychoanalysis (as conceptualized at that time).

Such a nosological distinction that I advanced in 1967, of a "hysterical psychosis," while familiar enough (albeit not often used) to the psychoanalytically informed audience of that time, has of course now all but disappeared, as even the psychoanalytic world has been swept up into the DSM-III and now DSM-IV nomenclature system with its avowedly atheoretical bias, grounded essentially in symptomatic and behavioral clusters, rather than in psychodynamic motivationally based formulations that are geared as much as possible to etiologic understanding and explanation. In this current world of Axis I and Axis II disorders, which even psychoanalysts must use, at least in connection with third-party reimbursement claims or research proposal applications, there is no room any longer for such an anachronistic (and seemingly archaic) diagnostic formulation as "hysterical psychosis," though I would submit that conceptually this rubric still fits best for the case just presented (and also for the other, not reproduced in this article) in terms of illuminating the nature and basis of the phenomena under study and in offering the best guidelines to their therapeutic management.

Concerning the prevalence of this phenomenon, I was prepared, on the basis of having two such patients within my very first handful of psychoanalytic cases, to believe that such instances were far more common than the sparse array of clinical reports to that time would lead one to expect, and to accept Hammett's suggestion that some *forme fruste* of this phenomenon existed in very many (if not almost all) psychoanalytic experiences, if only we could be properly alert to them. On the basis of my four decades of analytic work since those treatments took place, in which I have never again encountered such a disorganizing process within a proper analysis of a neurotic patient, I feel forced to reconsider these discrepant findings and to revert to the more traditional viewing of them as an extreme, rather than a commonplace, phenomenon.

This revised perspective can be accounted for in a number of ways. Traditionally, many patients have come or been sent to The Menninger Clinic because outpatient treatment efforts in their home communities had not succeeded, but with the feeling nonetheless that an intensive analytic treatment effort was still warranted, and could have a better chance of success if carried out within the frame of a sanatorium setting with hospitalization or lesser degrees of life management (day hospital, therapeutic community, etc.) readily available if needed, either temporarily, or for more extended periods. These are the kind of patients that Glover (1954) clearly had in mind when he separated the indications for psychoanalysis into three groupings, ranging from those whom he felt to be the most amenable, the so-called ideal analytic prospects, together with a statement of which diagnostic entities fell into that category, down to the third, those for whom the prospects with psychoanalysis were problematic, even dubious, but with the feeling that no other treatment could offer even as much hope for effective change, those with so-called "heroic indications" for psychoanalytic treatment. However, only one of my two cases (the one whose case history I have not recounted in this article), a chronically alcoholic woman with an obdurate obsessional character formation, who was brought to The Menninger Clinic for prolonged hospitalization concomitant with the ("heroic") effort at psychoanalytic treatment, could be clearly placed in Glover's third category. The other, the flamboyantly hysterical woman, whose case history I have presented here, was living in Topeka, came as a "usual" kind of outpatient, with depressive and anxiety symptoms, and was adjudged initially as an appropriate first psychoanalytic control case for a neophyte analytic candidate. And today, of course, almost a half-century after Glover's statement, we would hardly think in terms of a group of patients, with dubious indications for psychoanalysis, but who should nonetheless be offered a trial with that treatment modality on the basis that no other therapeutic strategy could offer even that modest hope; we would think today rather in terms of the range of psychoanalytically based supportive–expressive therapeutic approaches for such more disturbed patients.

From another viewpoint perhaps, our seeing less of such disorganizing and dereistic transference eruptions in neurotic patients now, than when I treated these two individuals (in the 1950s), could reflect greater attention during the initial evaluation process nowadays to some potentially ominous indicators in the patient whose case I have presented. There was, for example, the intensity of her affect surges, the disturbing vividness and wildness of her fantasizing, and her overgenerous tolerance for derivatives from the unconscious, which were all duly noted, albeit measured alongside her capacity for quick restitution and for penetratingly realistic self-scrutiny (which latter capacities were clearly, in retrospect, unduly weighted). Perhaps with such indicators, and in connection with such historical material as the guilty involvement and identification with the psychotic sibling, and the degree of ego rupture represented by the kind of suicide attempt that the patient had once made, the ominous signals might nowadays bulk sufficiently large as to temper the push to a full psychoanalytic effort, in favor again of a more supportive–expressive approach, and again, of course, psychoanalytically based. Given this greater cautiousness of approach, we could again wonder whether the florid transference psychotic reaction that threatened might have been much diminished in intensity, and even perhaps completely forestalled.

This brings me to the important *technical therapeutic* considerations, also still of "significant current concern," and the whole set of issues of relative therapeutic success and failure. Since my publication of 1967 we have entered with a vengeance into the era of the "widened scope" of psychoanalytic therapeutics heralded by Leo Stone, actually as far back as 1954. In America, we have had the elaboration and flowering of Heinz Kohut's self psychology (1971, 1977, 1984), built upon his efforts to bring the theretofore excluded narcissistic personality disorders within the realm of amenability to full psychoanalytic treatment. This was to be achieved through an analytic focus on what Kohut came to call selfobject transferences (as distinct from the traditional well-recognized object-directed transferences) and the selfobject countertransferences that they characteristically evoke. These are an array of distinguishable transference (and countertransference) dispositions that had to that point not been clearly delineated or significantly attended to, other than by considerations of tact and intuitive engagement. At the same time, and side by side with Kohut, Otto Kernberg (1975, 1976, 1980) articulated a "modified psychoanalysis"—declared to be psychoanalytic in contrast to just psychotherapeutic—designed to also bring the borderline personality organizations, at least those whom Kernberg called the "higher-level" borderline personality organizations, within the orbit of psychoanalysis, rather than being consigned to psychoanalytic psychotherapy.

Along with these invasions by Kohut and Kernberg and their adherents to extract the cohorts of narcissistic disorders and the "higher-level" borderline personalities from the domains of psychoanalytic psychotherapy (varingly expressive and supportive) where they had previously rested, and to bring them squarely within the scope of proper psychoanalysis itself (albeit "modified" to some extent, in some instances, by Kernberg), there has been a concomitant major infusion into the American psychoanalytic scene of the theoretical and clinical precepts of the British object-relational perspectives (from the British Independent Group), with its specific focus on the psychoanalytic management of regressive transference phenomena (deemed at times even to be necessary preludes to progressive reintegrations, akin perhaps to my own patient presented here), as well as of British Kleinians with their established willingness to treat psychoanalytically the whole

spectrum of sicker, and even "over the border" psychotic patients (as witness again, H. Rosenfeld [1965], and his Latin
American follower, D. Rosenfeld [1992]). All of this has made
for a progressive blurring of what were once—in an era of
what I have called "converging consensus" (Wallerstein, 1995,
chapter 5)—clear-cut crystallizations and distinctions between
the realms of proper psychoanalysis and the range of expressive
and supportive psychoanalytic psychotherapies. Each of these
modalities at that time had a well-defined ensemble of techniques, each indicated for a specifically different portion of
the psychopathological spectrum, and each avowedly geared
to differing goals and with differing expectable (and expected) outcomes.

The foregoing paragraphs may of course be seen as stating
opposed and contradictory trends. Would my patient have
been better off, have done better, with less life disruption, and
with a firmer, more durable treatment result, with a less rigor-
ous psychoanalytic approach, one tempered by a greater cau-
tion, and the readier deployment of more supportive, ego-
stabilizing interventions undertaken in the light of what I have
noted were then insufficiently attended to, ominous indicators?
Of course I did come to these interventions in full measure, but
only when faced with the actuality of the unfolding psychotic
reaction. But how does this square with the *enlargements* of the
domain of full psychoanalytic effort through the extraction
from the sphere of the less intensive and more supportive psychotherapies of whole categories of patients, not traditionally
deemed amenable to proper psychoanalysis, as pioneered in
the United States in the work of Kohut and Kernberg and their
many adherents, and in the United Kingdom by both the Independent Group and the Kleinians? This apparent paradox can
perhaps be in part resolved in terms of the conceptual and
technical advances of the past several decades, with the greater
understanding in today's praxis of the sophisticated deployment of psychoanalytically conceived interventions in response
to the changing specific clinical exigencies of each individual
patient, wherever placed on the psychopathological spectrum.

But in greater part I feel that this apparent paradox is to be
comprehended in terms of our greater understanding today

of the inextricable imbrication of psychoanalysis and psychoanalytically based psychotherapy than existed in the 1950s,
when psychoanalysis and psychoanalytic psychotherapy seemed
so distinctly demarcated from each other in terms of different
indications, of different appropriate techniques, and of differing achievable goals (Wallerstein, 1995, chapter 5).

This was certainly one of the major findings of the Psychotherapy Research Project (PRP) of The Menninger Foundation
(Wallerstein, 1986, 1988a). In summarizing the therapeutic
processes and outcomes of the forty-two patients studied in
that thirty-year-long research program (from the early 1950s
to the early 1980s), I stated, "A first major finding was that
psychoanalysis was not actually carried out in fully 'classical'
form with a single one of the 22 of our PRP patients recommended for and ostensibly started in analysis, if by 'classical'
form we mean that the therapeutic activity within the treatment hours was steadfastly and constantly focused upon the
interpretive uncovering of intrapsychic meanings, a constant
internally directed scrutiny of the manifest therapeutic content" (1988a, p. 133). After detailing some of the kinds of
departures from this austere model that occurred to some extent in every case, I went on to state:

> In all, we ended by (somewhat arbitrarily) declaring 10 of our
> 22 patients designated for psychoanalysis as having had treat-
> ments that adhered "well enough" to the model of classical
> analysis, albeit with some clear departures in every instance,
> which were however "minimal" within the context of that
> group of quite sick individuals treated within the traditions and
> expectations of that setting. . . .
>   With another six of these psychoanalytic patients, the analyses
> were *more* significantly "modified" along a variety of parame-
> ters, mostly differing from those felt to be more fully proper
> psychoanalysis along *quantitative* dimensions of alteration, of
> how often, how intensely, etc., but still adjudged overall to be
> essentially psychoanalyses, albeit with modifications. And with
> the other six of this overall twenty-two, there was either a modi-
> fication of analytic procedures substantial enough to be ad-
> judged—by independent research judges—a "conversion" to
> psychotherapy, or an explicit conversion to psychotherapy,
> clearly presented and acknowledged within the treatment.
> Clearly, in the experience with these twenty-two patients taken

into psychoanalysis, there occurred a marked blurring of the supposedly clear conceptual interface between (proper) psychoanalysis and intensive psychoanalytic psychotherapy [1988a, pp. 133–134].[4]

In that 1988 paper, in addition to outlining the then accepted mechanisms of the expressive–analytic approaches, of interpretation, of insight, of working through, or uncovering (analyzing) intrapsychic conflict, I also spelled out the dozen different operating mechanisms that we discerned in our research population that we felt were differentially characteristic of psychoanalytically derived supportive psychotherapeutic approaches. This was a more comprehensive listing than any we had encountered in the psychoanalytic psychotherapy literature to that point. These were each illustrated in my 1986 book by the clinical accounts of those of our research patients for whom we felt that they were especially salient. Our overall assessment of the integral place of these so-called supportive techniques in even the most expressive–interpretive of putative "classically" conducted psychoanalyses can be captured in one of the summary paragraphs of my 1988 overview paper on the findings and conclusions of PRP:

The predictions made for prospective therapeutic courses and outcomes tended to be for more substantial change and for more permanent change (i.e., more "structural change") where the treatment plan and implementation were to be more expressive-analytic, and where these changes were expected to be more based on thoroughgoing intrapsychic conflict resolution through processes of interpretation, insight, and working through. And pari passu, and again in terms of the conventional psychodynamic wisdom, the more supportive the treatment was intended to be (had to be), the more limited and inherently

---

[4]The text went on at this point to discuss the comparable situation that existed among the twenty patients in the project recommended for psychoanalytic psychotherapy along the expressive–supportive dimension. In the great majority of those twenty, plus in the six converted from psychoanalysis to psychotherapy, the issue over the whole therapy was constantly one of the varying admixture of supportive and of expressive–interpretive techniques that would properly fit the particular clinical needs of the specific patient at each moment during the therapeutic course. That is, here too there was a blurring of boundaries between the expressive and the supportive approaches, despite their being supposedly geared in opposed directions, to uncover and express inner conflict versus supporting an ego struggling to contain conflict.

unstable the anticipated changes were predicted to be. What our research study has revealed in great detail is that all of this was (again, overall) consistently tempered and altered in the actual implementation in the treatment courses. The psychoanalyses, as a whole, as well as the expressive therapies as a whole, were systematically modified in the direction of introducing more supportive components in widely varying ways, and by and large accomplished more limited outcomes than promised (hoped), and, as indicated, with a varying but often substantial amount of that accomplished by noninterpretive, i.e., supportive, means. The psychotherapies, on the other hand, often accomplished a fair amount more, and in several of the spectacular cases a great deal more, than initially expected and promised, and again, however the admixture of intervention techniques was originally projected, with much of the change on the basis of more supportive modes than originally specified [Wallerstein, 1988a, pp. 148–149].

Quite aside from my statement here on the related, but separate, issue of the reach of psychoanalysis vis-à-vis the psychoanalytic psychotherapies in relation to idealized and/or achieved goals, that was one of the central issues to which PRP was directed across its thirty-year time-span, the aspect of the above citation most relevant to my present context is the statement of the constant and inextricable intermingling of expressive–interpretive and supportive ego maintaining techniques across the entire spectrum from the most classically psychoanalytic cases through to the most singlemindedly supportive psychotherapeutic cases, albeit in different proportions of course, across that spectrum of intervention techniques. That is, we have come in today's world into an era of blurring what were once felt, in the 1950s and 1960s, to be very clear-cut distinctions between the nature, the indications, the technical implementations, and the goals of the psychoanalyses and the psychoanalytic psychotherapies. This makes much more problematic today than when PRP was conceived and when my two cases of "transference psychosis" were in treatment how we prescribe and characterize psychoanalysis vis-à-vis psychoanalytic psychotherapy.

This language of expressive and of supportive techniques is of course the idiom that was common parlance when PRP was constructed in the heyday of ego psychology dominance in American psychoanalysis in the early 1950s, and for purposes of consistency of communication was the language maintained when I was writing my overall final clinical accounting of PRP in the mid-1980s (Wallerstein, 1986), and though it has found continued useful clinical application over the years since—see, for example, the psychoanalytic books devoted specifically to "supportive psychotherapy" by Werman (1984) and Rockland (1989)—our language of therapeutic (mutative) processes has gradually shifted to the juxtaposition currently within each treatment of interpretive-insight aiming factors vis-à-vis relationship factors (less now a language of supportive intervention techniques). And with the real paradigm shift that has been occurring in America over the past two decades to the growing prominence now of the object-relational, interpersonal, constructivist, and intersubjective perspectives, all embedded in the tenets of what is called a "two-person psychology"—as opposed to the intrapsychically focused "one-person psychology" of the ego psychological, drive/structural era—a shift that I have dubbed elsewhere "The New American Psychoanalysis" (Wallerstein, 1998), the supplanting of the language of expressive and supportive by the language of interpretive-insight aiming and object-relational has become quite complete. But the phenomena being described and accounted for remain the same, the complete imbrication of insight and relationship, even of insight via the relationship, in all psychoanalytic therapies, psychoanalysis and (psychoanalytically conceived) psychotherapy both.

Again, all this makes more difficult (and less important?) today the teasing out and designation of the most properly calibrated technical approaches to the patient with the "transference psychosis" presented in this article (and the other patient described in my 1967 account as well). How much should it be a reasonably clear psychoanalysis (in today's terms) and how much a deliberately focused more clearly psychotherapeutic approach, more supportive, or, put differently, with heightened focus on its supporting relational elements? What does seem clear is that my effort in the 1950s to maintain a typically

classical psychoanalysis, with all its austere and even rigid aspects, abetted of course by my need as a neophyte psychoanalytic candidate for my work to pass muster within the
proscriptions of Eissler's (1953) severe model of proper psychoanalysis, which was the accepted benchmark of the time,
would be today much more automatically, or deliberately, soft-
ened. Indeed it was drastically altered into a clearly supportive
therapeutic direction when the emerging psychotic transference eruption drove me to it. Whether such explicit modification and lessened austerity might have served to mitigate and
even to forestall the psychotic transference development for
my two patients, is unknowable today. If so, the treatment
course would have been less anguished for the patient presented here, and clearly less disruptive of her life and the life
of her family. Clearly in that case it might even have been
possible that the enacted divorce and the subsequent remarriage would not have had to take place, again, with far less
suffering by all the concerned family members.

But, even if all that were so, would the end result, in terms
of restored life functioning at the termination point—and with
some confirming follow-up data—have been more complete
and with greater certitude for its enduring character? That is
a somewhat different question and here another set of considerations, also based on the findings of PRP, enter the picture.
Among the forty-two patients in the research sample, there
was a cluster of six, all women, of basically hysterical character
structure, with varying combinations of anxiety, depressive,
and phobic symptoms that brought them to treatment. All were
felt to be excellent candidates for psychoanalysis (and none
developed the severe psychotic transference unfolding that
marked my patient, who was not in the PRP research sample),
but to our surprise, as a group, these patients achieved psychoanalytic treatment outcomes that fell short of the ambitions/
goals originally posited for them. Characteristically, they mostly
reached very (or at least reasonably) satisfactory *psychotherapeutic* goals in terms of symptom amelioration and favorable
change in life functioning, and they expressed that satisfaction
at the treatment termination and follow-up (though mixed
with some disappointment and some awareness of limitation).

At the same time, they fell short of psychoanalytic goals in terms of resolution of intrapsychic conflict, and became clear that they did so in very similar ways.

The patient that we considered paradigmatic for this group (the Adoptive Mother) has been described in detail in *Forty-Two Lives in Treatment* (Wallerstein, 1986, pp. 295–302) and in condensed form in several different contexts (Wallerstein, 1988b, 1992a, 1992b). I won't here recount any of the treatment course and outcome except what is specifically relevant to my theme here of (expectable?) treatment limitation. It had initially been predicted that this patient, who had come to analysis in an acute anxiety state consequent to a failed effort at adoption, which had eventuated in a return of the adopted baby to the social agency, that her chronic panicky "fear of losing control" could lead her, at a point of achievement of good enough symptom relief, and of substantial if not complete gains toward more adaptive reaction patterns, to prefer to consolidate and "quit while she was ahead" rather than to face the dangers of continued analytic work with its regressive threats. She could always do this by invoking reality pressures and supports from without, and by remobilizing her potential for counterphobic mastery from within.

Further it was also predicted that with such an outcome, the area of incomplete work would be in relation to the negative mother transference and the patient's hostile identification with the malevolent, feared, and hateful preoedipal mother imago. Actually all this is exactly what seemed to have happened. In fact, the very life solution that she came to at the end of the analysis, to have a grateful feeling to mother figures, to maintain her marriage with its problems glossed over, and to try again to adopt children even at the price of considerable inner turmoil, was itself an expression of the unresolved identification with mother—she chose to be a martyr, like mother, burdened with children, and with an unsatisfactory husband.

A corollary prediction, which was based on the expectation that the analytic result would be incomplete and that the patient would be left liable to recurrent anxiety and perhaps even transitory symptom formation in the face of continued environmental triggering of her core conflicts, had to do with the form of future treatment. It was stipulated that this should not then be an effort to analyze further what had remained unanalyzed from the first treatment (for the same reasons), but that this should rather be a supportive–expressive psychotherapy aimed at helping her utilize the previous analytic accomplishments to stabilize herself in the face of new stresses.

In effect, this is also what happened. The patient did not seek further psychotherapy in an explicit way. She rationalized this on the basis of the higher treatment fees in her new community, which she declared she could not afford. What she did instead was to call on a variety of helping hands—none explicitly for psychotherapy. There was the priest who admonished her regarding her duties to her husband and to their future life together—including the child he encouraged her to adopt. There was the family physician who prescribed medications to help her cope with the tensions and anxieties any such moves would generate. There was the understanding adoption agency social worker, sympathetic to her plight, to whom she could pour out her burden of grief, of worry, of discouragement. The patient thus combined the ingredients of her supportive–expressive psychotherapy, and ensured that any more ambitious psychotherapeutic effort was precluded.

On this basis the patient was able to go ahead and adopt two children, albeit with considerable psychological strain. With the consolidation of the success of the first adoption, a girl, there was enough accrual of circular gratifications and enough increment to her self-esteem and her self-confidence, to enabler her, three years later, to adopt a boy. Thus, with an analysis that was adjudged incomplete and with important transference components unanalyzed, the patient could nonetheless achieve her original treatment goal—to be able to be a proper wife and mother. Indicative of the nature of the incompletely analyzed transference fantasies which underpinned these significant treatment changes, was the patient's voiced desire, on the occasion of her research follow-up visit, to see her ex-analyst and to show him her adopted daughter, the successful "fruit of his labors."

Although, obviously, the life histories, treatment courses, and circumstances at termination, varied individually in this

cluster of "good" analytic cases, the six women, with comparable hysterical character structures, and with similar presenting
symptom pictures, all shared the same limitation in their psychoanalytic outcomes, terminating their treatments while they
were ahead, but with significant unanalyzed conflicts, in *each*
instance some variation of a hostile identification with a preoedipal mother imago. And this we can say was true as well of my
patient with the hysterical psychosis presented in this article. I
refer here to a central driving fantasy of the patient's psychotic
period, the good father driven to his death by the cruel and
hateful mother, and all the subsequent figures in the patient's
lifetime, good fathers, but ineffectual, unreachable, and bad
mothers, vindictive and nagging. The husbands, both of them,
were experienced as "fussy old women," "nagging mothers."
And in the divorce enactment the patient recapitulated the
father murder by divorcing the husband, identifying with her
own hated mother in destroying the man, simultaneously identifying with her own daughter, becoming again the little 4-year-
old girl, losing her good father. To what extent the remarriage
brought enduring closure to these tormenting conflicts we can
only speculate; certainly they were not psychoanalytically resolved.

Which brings me to the question, the last in this article: Are
these less than full psychoanalytic outcomes of all the patients
presented here, albeit with good or good-enough therapeutic
outcomes; what is to be expected with such patients with hysterical character formations because of the patients' inherent lim-
iting characteristics (despite the conventional wisdom that they
are among those most ideally amenable to full psychoanalytic
treatment)? Or are we dealing rather with our own collective
personal and technical limitations that allow us to carry these
treatments only to a point of limited psychoanalytic results (a
relative treatment failure?), again despite the patient's achieving both substantial symptom amelioration and also her therapeutic life goals—therefore a treatment success? Or, put
differently, could the psychoanalytic work be so carried on with
the full awareness of the conditions of the complex failures
of full analytic resolution in the cases here cited, that these
difficulties could be overcome psychoanalytically, with a more

successful psychoanalytic outcome? Or must we, in the present
state of our capacities, settle for the more limited treatment
achievements of the Adoptive Mother, which to her were indeed "good enough"? Where indeed does all this leave us on
the axis, success-failure?

References

Eissler, K. R. (1953), The effect of the structure of the ego on psychoanalytic technique. *J. Amer. Psychoanal. Assn.*, 1:104–143.
Ferenczi, S. (1912), Transitory symptom constructions during the
analysis (Transitory conversion, substitution, illusion, hallucination, "Character regression," and "Expression-displacement").
In: *Sex in Psychoanalysis.* New York: Basic Books, 1950, pp.
193–212.
——— (1919), On the technique of psycho-analysis. In: *Further Contributions to the Theory and Technique of Psycho-Analysis.* London:
Hogarth Press, 1950, pp. 177–189.
Gill, M. M. (1954), Psychoanalysis and exploratory psychotherapy. *J.
Amer. Psychoanal. Assn.*, 2:771–797.
Glover, E. (1954), The indications for psycho-analysis. *J. Ment. Sci.*,
100:393–401.
Hammett, Van B. O. (1961), Delusional transference. *Amer. J. Psy-
chother.*, 15:574–581.
Kernberg, O. (1975), *Borderline Conditions and Pathological Narcis-
sism.* New York: Jason Aronson.
——— (1976), *Object Relations Theory and Clinical Psychoanalysis.*
New York: Jason Aronson.
——— (1980), *Internal World and External Reality: Object Relations
Theory Applied.* New York: Jason Aronson.
Kohut, H. (1971), *The Analysis of the Self: A Systematic Approach to the
Psychoanalytic Treatment of Narcissistic Personality Disorders.* New
York: International Universities Press.
——— (1977), *The Restoration of the Self.* New York: International
Universities Press.
——— (1984), *How Does Analysis Cure?* ed A. Goldberg with P. E.
Stepansky. Chicago: University of Chicago Press.
Little, M. (1958), On delusional transference (transference psycho-
sis). *Internat. J. Psycho-Anal.*, 39:134–138.
——— (1960), On basic unity. *Internat. J. Psycho-Anal.*, 41:377–384.

Reider, N. (1957), Transference psychosis. *J. Hillside Hosp.*, 6:131–149.

Rockland, L. H. (1989), *Supportive Therapy: A Psychodynamic Approach.* New York: Basic Books.

Rosenfeld, D. (1992), *The Psychotic: Aspects of the Personality.* London: Karnac Books.

Rosenfeld, H. (1954), Considerations regarding the psycho-analytic approach to acute and chronic schizophrenia. *Internat. J. Psycho-Anal.*, 35:135–140.

———— (1965), *Psychotic States: A Psychoanalytical Approach.* New York: International Universities Press.

Sterba, R. F. (1934), The fate of the ego in analytic therapy. *Internat. J. Psycho-Anal.*, 15:117–126.

Stone, L. (1954), The widening scope of indications for psychoanalysis. *J. Amer. Psychoanal. Assn.*, 2:567–594.

Wallerstein, R. S. (1967), Reconstruction and mastery in the transference psychosis. *J. Amer. Psychoanal. Assn.*, 15:551–583.

———— (1980–1981), Diagnosis revisited (and revisited): The case of hysteria and the hysterical personality. *Internat. J. Psychoanal. Psychother.*, 8:533–547.

———— (1986), *Forty-Two Lives in Treatment: A Study of Psychoanalysis and Psychotherapy.* New York: Guilford Press.

———— (1988a), Psychoanalysis and psychotherapy: Relative roles reconsidered. *Ann. Psychoanal.*, 16:129–151.

———— (1988b), Assessment of structural change in psychoanalytic therapy and research. In: *The Concept of Structure in Psychoanalysis,* ed. T. Shapiro. Madison, CT: International Universities Press, 1991, pp. 241–261.

———— (1992a), The goals of psychotherapy reconsidered. In: *The Technique and Practice of Psychoanalysis,* Vol. 2, ed. A. Sugarman, R. A. Nemiroff, & D. P. Greenson. Madison, CT: International Universities Press, pp. 63–90.

———— (1992b), Follow-up in psychoanalysis: What happens to treatment gains? *J. Amer. Psychoanal. Assn.*, 40:665–690.

———— (1995), *The Talking Cures: The Psychoanalyses and the Psychotherapies.* New Haven, CT: Yale University Press.

———— (1998), The new American psychoanalysis: A commentary. *J. Amer. Psychoanal. Assn.*, 46:1021–1043.

Werman, D. S. (1984), *The Practice of Supportive Psychotherapy.* New York: Brunner/Mazel.

8

The Troubled Seminarian

W. W. Meissner, S.J., M.D.

Introduction

The reasons why analyses fail or end prematurely are legion—like the devils of scripture. Of all the possible things that can go wrong, it may only take one factor or a minimal number to put the process offtrack and lead to a disappointing outcome.[1] There are cases that seem to go well only to come to grief in the throes of a mishandled or otherwise unfortunate termination; there are cases that run afoul of the disruptive and distortive power of transference and falter in the face of an irresolvable impassee or transference–countertransference gridlock. Then again, there are cases that never really get off the ground, cases that may sputter in uncertainty and trepidation so that the patient never really makes a commitment to the analysis and a meaningful alliance is never achieved. The case I wish to discuss is of this latter variety.

---

[1] I am reminded of an old scholastic maxim—*Bonum ex integra causa, malum ex quocumque defectu*—which I translate loosely as "the effect is good when all the causes are working right, but it only takes one thing going wrong to spoil it." Analysts can readily

153

Cases that never get going may run afoul of precipitant transference reactions preventing the patient's engagement and commitment. But often the precipitating factors involve more than transference and bring into play a variety of extraneous factors that are introduced from beyond the analytic frame from the real circumstances of the patient's life. One way of conceptualizing such situations is by a threefold understanding of the analytic relation as compounded of transference (along with related countertransference), the real relation, and the therapeutic alliance (Meissner, 1996). In these cases, the combination of transference distortion and reality conspires to undermine or inhibit formation of an alliance, so that the analytic process is more or less thwarted from the start.

Circumstances

The case I am discussing also presents a number of subsidiary issues reflecting the complexity of circumstances that serve to undermine analysis. The patient in question was a young man in his midtwenties who was a seminarian preparing for ordination as a diocesan priest. Alan came from a devout Catholic family in which he was the second son, having an older brother and a younger brother and two sisters. As the story unfolds, the interweaving of transference elements and aspects of the background reality will become clear. The reality issues had to do first with his situation as a seminarian and his relations with his superiors, and second with the fact of my own religious profession and the way it fed into his fantasies. The combination of these factors and the fears related to them contributed to the failure of this analysis to get very far at all—from beginning to end it lasted only twenty-three sessions.

Other factors contributed to the circumstances surrounding the analysis. The patient came to see me at the behest of the rector of the seminary where he was studying. I had only recently opened my office and had let it be known that I was interested in seeing any religious persons at reduced rates.

---

resonate with this sentiment. As the case material will attest, there was more than one thing that went wrong in this case.

Alan, who was well regarded in the seminary and was an excellent student, had been bothered by a series of depressive anxieties and problems in self-esteem that had begun to affect his studies and left him with a considerable degree of doubt about his vocation and his worthiness to proceed to ordination. His decision to seek help and to contact me, therefore, was motivated only partially by his own desire for deeper self-knowledge and relief from his difficulties, but also by what he felt was pressure from the superior—an aspect that left him feeling that his position at the seminary was in jeopardy and that he would certainly be thrown out and rejected as a candidate for priestly orders.

The Analysis

The initial contact was made by the patient's rector to inquire whether I was available, whether I was interested in seeing the patient, and establishing my fee arrangements. I indicated my availability and my willingness to accept a reduced fee commensurate with his ability to pay, but insisted that the patient had to negotiate the fee himself and arrange other details of the treatment. Alan himself then called to make an appointment.

The initial interviews were innocent enough. Alan described some of his anxieties and difficulties sufficiently enough to persuade me that he needed therapy and that the treatment of choice would be analysis. We discussed the pros and cons of analysis in a second hour, in which we explored superficially some of his doubts and ambivalence about undertaking analysis rather than psychotherapy, particularly his feeling that analysis—at four or five times a week—must mean that he was very sick and that doing the analysis would mean that he would not be able to go on to ordination. He had previously had a year of psychotherapy that did him little good and made him feel that his problems were more serious than he had thought. He seemed to accept my view that doing analysis and resolving some of his difficulties would make him a better priest, and he agreed to begin the analysis in the following week.

We discussed and agreed on a schedule, the fee and arrangements for payment of the fee, and other questions regarding vacations, confidentiality, and so on. Regarding payment of the fee, we agreed that I would give him a monthly bill and that he would make whatever arrangements were necessary for payment. That usually meant that the treasurer of the seminary would issue him a check that he then gave me. Confidentiality was a matter of deep concern for him, especially regarding what would be communicated to his superior of what went on in the analysis. This concern was to resurface repeatedly in the analysis. I emphasized that nothing of what he told me and what we talked about would go beyond my office walls—a stance that seemed to reassure him and diminish some of his anxiety, but, as I found out, did not lay the issue to rest. He could not get beyond a basic distrust and suspicion that his secrets would come back to haunt him and that when his superiors found out what was going on in his mind they would cast him into outer darkness and deny him ordination.

The first hour started surprisingly with a dream—"There was a child in a room with me, a man came in and told the child to come with him or else their relationship would be broken off, I told child he could stay with me." The associations led directly to the troubled relations in his family. The child was a part of himself that was threatened by having to face the world and by intimate personal relationships, and wanted only to retreat from any confrontations or involvements. He hoped that conflicts and friction would just go away or somehow be smoothed over. The difficulties with his mother came quickly into focus. His older brother had married a girl of whom his mother did not approve—the result was that she cut him off totally: "Mother cut him off because she feels he rejected her. She's so insecure. There's still a wall between her and my brother; she doesn't want his name even mentioned. Even my father is afraid to talk to her about it; she goes into a tirade then shuts him out with a wall of silence. It makes me sad; they haven't talked for over a year."

He went on to describe some of his difficulties with his mother and the difficulties other members of the family had with her.[2]

---

[1] In these verbatim accounts, my interventions are placed in brackets [ ].

My sister tried to help mother in the kitchen. She feels obligated to help, but mother has to have things just right. She started frosting a cake, but didn't do it right so mother blew up. I tried to show her she was wrong in not wanting help, but I couldn't get anywhere. [What were your feelings?] I felt she was irrational, unhealthy. I wish she'd get help. I felt sick inside but tried to act as if nothing had happened. Just like my father, I walk on eggshells with mother. I'm afraid she'd be angry, reject me. I stuck close to home; my brother wasn't afraid to leave. I only left when I went to seminary.

One result was that he found it difficult to visit home. His vacations were spent at home out of a feeling of obligation and fear of what would happen if he didn't, while his friends were traveling or enjoying themselves. He went on to discuss his feelings of inadequacy and inferiority:

This colors my relationships with women: I'm afraid to make demands that I couldn't meet sexually or emotionally. In high school I picked innocuous girls to date; Susan was like my sister, safe. There were other girls I wanted to take out but I was afraid. They probably had stronger and more manly boyfriends. If I took them out they'd find out I wasn't much of a man. I shied away from sports, because I was afraid I would look stupid or clumsy. I played football until high school since I was the biggest kid on the block, but the kids in high school were bigger. I retreated from challenges, and settled for second best. When I was teaching I had to keep control in class; I was afraid to experiment or give more freedom. I got frantic and tried other teachers' methods, but they never worked because they weren't my own. I feel different now, but I'm still ashamed that I did such a bad job. I used oppressive tactics to keep control. . . . I had a dream last night; I was in bed and a friend approached me. I pulled up the covers and said No. I was afraid of a homosexual advance. I'm still afraid of homosexuality. I was on a trip with Ellen and her cousins in Maine; we stayed at her house and she gave me a backrub. I felt uncomfortable. I didn't know if it was right because of my vows. I didn't feel frightened; she liked and accepted me. We kissed goodbye, it was beautiful. I'm not afraid to kiss on the lips. If I ever married it would be to a girl like her. She's not like mother, she's happy and outgoing, not a sulker. My relationships to women have changed but they're still ambiguous. I can joke with the girl in the library, but my relations with girls are only a joke, they can't be anything more. I was more with Ellen. Superficial relations are protective;

I'm afraid to lose out but I lose out anyway when they're superficial. Celibacy is ambiguous for me. I feel immature sexually;
I'd rather fantasize than risk a relationship. I fantasy that I'm a
more masculine person having intercourse. I thought I could
be more confident now, but I was ashamed of my body in high
school. I wasn't good looking or strong; skinnier guys were taking out good-looking girls. I was self-conscious about my light
beard; I joke about it but it still bothers me. I noticed pubic
hair at 12 or 13; I didn't want to grow up and be like that. It
meant leaving security. I was a thumbsucker for a long time. I
was afraid of growing up, leaving home. When I went to the
seminary, I went from one womb to another; it was structured
and met all my expectations. I knew where I stood, and wasn't
in danger of rejection.

This much of the analytic dialogue makes it clear that Alan's
relationships with his parents on both sides were troubled and
provided the basis for powerful transference paradigms that
contributed significantly to his difficulties. The picture he
painted of his mother was of a hypersensitive, vindictive, controlling, and punitive woman whose narcissism demanded that
she had things on her terms and that the people around her
should pay her court and cater to her every whim and wish. If
there were any conflict or deviation from her wishes, her response was to treat the offender with rejection, cold indifference, often not speaking for extended periods. Often she
would not speak to Alan's father for weeks at a time, and when
his brother married against her wishes, she ostracized him and
refused to speak to him for over a year, complaining that he
had betrayed her, leaving home and forgetting her in favor of
a girl. She got her way by working on others' guilt, sulking
when offended, and demanding apologies and compensation
in the form of accepting her demands. She was expert in playing the martyr role, manipulating others and getting them to
do what she wanted by playing on their guilt. Giving her presents was always a problem, regardless of the occasion—the gifts
were never right and she never seemed pleased. Christmas, on
this account, was a miserable time.

It was always an effort to talk with her, and he had to be
careful not to turn her off or offend her. It infuriated him that
she would not kiss his brother or say goodbye. As he put it:

She wouldn't accept his apology unless he crawled on his knees. It made me furious. She gets pleasure out of sulking, getting others to pity her; that's her self-pity—she let's herself be controlled by it. I have to worry that if I visit friends will she feel deserted? I can't sit home all the time and hold her hand, but I'm afraid she'll say I spend more time with my friends than with her. I wonder if I really love her; I feel controlled, and have to fight against a small-minded and jealous woman; but I still miss her.

Alan described the relation between his parents as devoid of any real affection, even though they had been married for over thirty years. They lived as two separate individuals without any expression of physical love. She sometimes let his father kiss her but she never embraced him. When Alan found out how babies were made, by the man putting his penis in the woman's vagina, he couldn't believe it because he could not imagine his parents getting that close. He definitely saw his mother as the more powerful figure. She wore the pants in the family and controlled his father, who could not afford to stand up to her.

Alan operated in dread fear of rejection from his mother and loss of her love and affection, such as it was. He reported dreams in which mother was doing something apparently self-sacrificing—cooking or washing dishes—while he was torn between feeling that he should help her and wanting to do something on his own. If he offered help, mother would say she didn't need any help from him and went on doing the dishes, then crying in a fit of self-pity and resentment. He would try to comfort her and reassure her of his love, but feeling resentful and helpless in that he could do nothing to help or change her attitude. She made him feel obligated to work around the house, showing her that he cared and would thus stay in her favor. His fear was that she would cut him off—he recalled that when he was about 7 or 8, she locked him out of the kitchen, because she was mad about something—underlining his fear that if she were mad at him he would be locked out of her love. His further reflections were that his mother was really sick and needed help. He felt indebted and burdened by all her hard work and sacrifices for him, and felt he owed it to her to make it up to her in some fashion. Striking out on his own became a rebellion against and rejection of her, and he felt torn between needing to lead his own life and feeling tied to her by his guilt and obligation and fear of rejection of him, like she had rejected his brother. At times he tried to express his anger at her, but to no avail—she would only feel hurt, cry, and make him feel worse than ever. Such attempts only made matters worse. And she held onto grudges for years—she would remind his father of things he had done wrong twenty-five years before, and then sulk over such old "garbage."

In one dream, he was in his bedroom at home, and his little sister had found his journal. He accused her of reading it, but she denied it. But he noticed that the paperclip marking the page had been removed and he slapped her, accusing her of violating his privacy. He then felt guilty, feeling that he had done wrong and hadn't controlled himself. He then commented, "I keep a diary and mark the pages with a clip and a note asking anyone not to violate my privacy. There are childish and emotional parts, that deal with feelings about mother. I was scared that Suzy might blurt something out, and mother might break off our relationship. I was afraid she would see my thoughts about how sick she is, and would be hurt. I'm the only one she talks to, not to my father." And later:

> I have to keep a balance of payments in relation to mother, I had to do things to keep in favor so she couldn't say I hadn't done anything for her. I was always appeasing her; I couldn't do enough to stay in her good graces. [You felt that you were never good enough?] I feel that about anything I create, never satisfied, always trying to please. That relates to my concern about satisfying women, having to be able to pay them back for everything. That's not the view of love I preach. Mother was constantly saying I didn't appreciate what she gave me.

One of his escapes from this pressure took the form of visiting a woman he called "Aunt Ann" who was an old friend of mother. He looked for any excuse to visit her, because he found her so easy to talk to. He enjoyed her company more than being with his mother, and would spent a lot of time there, even staying for lunch or dinner. But he dreaded his mother's reaction and her getting the idea that he preferred

Aunt Ann to her. When he talked to her about his visits to Aunt Ann, he would make up excuses to minimize her fears. If she ever found out what he talked to Aunt Ann about, she would disown him and never speak to him again.

Despite his ambivalence and resentment toward his mother, there were also glimmers of the ways in which he identified with her. If friends or fellow seminarians offended him, he would give them the cold shoulder and the silent treatment for long periods, showing them that he didn't need them and could be very self-sufficient without them. On one occasion, he recalled, "I had prepared a special dressing, but this guy threw it out. Damn nincompoop! I just sulked—I had put time in on it and he just threw it out, stupid. I felt slighted and wanted to retaliate. I wouldn't eat any food he prepared. I just sulked and hid, the way mother behaves when she's slighted."

So far as I could tell, Alan's father seemed to provide the primary object for internalization, especially as subordinate to his mother. He saw himself and his father as emotionally and temperamentally alike. Like his father, he was proud of his knowledge and found it hard to admit that he had been wrong about anything. When he and his father argued and Alan was right, father would only admit he was wrong reluctantly and would complain that Alan made him look stupid. Alan recognized that he had similar feelings, getting defensive when his knowledge was questioned and feeling insecure when he was challenged. And like his father he did not feel manly or assertive, qualities he disliked in his father and in himself—neither of them could come right out and ask for what they wanted or say what they thought, but had to hedge so their requests wouldn't sound too strong out of fear that they wouldn't be accepted.

He saw his father as weak and as incapable of dealing with his mother. Both he and his father had to walk on eggs, fearing his mother's anger and rejection. He thought his father was unable to make decisions on his own, that he was not manly or assertive—a quality that he disliked in his father and in himself. His father had been a vice president in a large corporation, but was fired when the business changed hands. After that he was completely at a loss, and hasn't been the same since. He was without a job for two years. Alan could not help but wonder why he had been fired if he was such a good employee. He was an unhappy and frustrated man who got no support from his wife. He was so afraid to offend, walking on eggshells with mother. He had a good business head and dealt in stocks, but was cautious and indecisive.

Emotionally, Alan's relationship with him was uncertain and ambivalent. Father had been a math major, and if Alan asked him for help with math problems and didn't see the solution right away, father would be impatient and irritated. Although Alan felt he was proud of some of Alan's work, for example his drawing, Alan felt it was not masculine work, and that his father paid more attention to his older brother, who was the apple of father's eye—they built and flew model planes together. Alan felt he could not criticize or confront his mother because she would just take it out on his father. Father just hung his head and moped—why didn't he stand up to her? He just couldn't afford to. Why was he such a weakling? He was so insecure after he lost his job, whereas before he had been so strong and confident.

Gaining father's approval was also a problem. In a dream, Alan was left alone in a restaurant with his brother's two children, one a year-old baby. The baby climbed out of the highchair and fell, crying. He tried to pick the child up, when suddenly his father returned. He was anxious about picking up the child, and worried whether his father would approve or blame him for the accident. While it seemed impossible to please or gain much approval from his mother, gaining approval from father became all the more important. In high school he worked hard to perform well and please the important people, living up to their expectations, and making his father proud of him. He found it difficult to accept that someone else might do better and constantly felt that he had to prove himself.

Even in the brief compass of this analysis, Alan made it clear that his difficulties in the area of sex, especially his concerns over his own sexual identity, were paramount. He had difficulty relating to girls, fearing that he would be seen to be inadequate as a male and that he would be overwhelmed by the girl. He was afraid that the woman would make demands, sexually or emotionally, that he would not be able to meet. In high school he tried to pick innocuous girls, whom he thought safe, that is, not sexual. If he was attracted to more sexual girls, he was afraid to ask them out, imagining that they had boyfriends who were stronger and more manly than he, and that if he took them out they would find out he wasn't much of a man. With more sexually available girls he was afraid of closeness, afraid of not having anything to say, of being superficial and having no substance. He recalled bringing a girl home from the senior prom at 3:00 A.M. He was afraid to stop the car and pet, felt confused about what the girl wanted, how far should he go, would she think him dirty? At the same time, he was afraid she'd say Yes. He was concerned with his image, and unwilling to take a risk. His anxiety was increased by the fact that he knew his parents would be up waiting for him. What would mother say?

He felt himself to be immature sexually, preferring to fantasize about sex rather than risk a real relationship: his fantasies were often about a more masculine person then himself having intercourse with the girl. He did not feel good looking or strong, but felt ashamed of and self-conscious of his physique. He did not want to grow up and become a mature man because it meant leaving behind the security of home and mother and having to face the uncertainties of relating to women on his own and standing on his own feet. He had resolved the conflict by turning to the seminary, which he saw as a safe heaven from these anxieties and self-doubts—as he put it, he moved from one womb to another. If he could only get hold of himself and grow up, everything would be fine and he wouldn't need analysis.

Related to these anxieties were his doubts about his own sexual orientation and fears that he was homosexual. He had several dreams involving homosexual activity and had engaged in some homosexual activity with another seminary student. He felt comforted by the closeness and affection, something he had never had from his parents and felt he could never get from a woman, but felt ashamed of these feelings and was terrified of the stigma and the implicit threat of getting thrown out of the seminary. He had homosexual fantasies, usually casting himself in the passive role and imagining the other male as a giant with a huge penis. If his lover did not treat him as he expected, he would get furious and sulk, much like his mother. His fantasies were bisexual—including images of a strong man having intercourse with a woman: the woman has no face; she is unimportant, but the man is brutal, takes the woman by force, like the rape scene in *Young Lions*. He felt attracted more to the man, but didn't think of himself as masculine. With women, he got flustered; a real man would be more aggressive. He felt his homosexual fear and feelings were sick, constantly comparing himself with other men. In puberty his fantasies were largely homosexual and sadistic—men being castrated and cannibalized were erotically stimulating. He often used the images of strong guys being castrated to masturbate. He described once confessing masturbation, fearing that he would die in mortal sin; the priest, so he reported, threatened him with castration and he left the confessional terrified that the priest would somehow expose him. When I commented that his fantasies seemed more aggressive than erotic, he replied that he thought he was making up for what he didn't have—he was skinny, afraid of sports, awkward, and shy. The fantasy of a powerful male giant holding and protecting him was very comforting. He still used such fantasies, both heterosexual and homosexual, to relieve tension.

He was preoccupied with and ashamed of the appearance of his body, feeling that he did not look manly and that physically he looked like a homosexual. He recalled pictures taken on a camping trip—he was not happy with how he looked: he didn't feel that he looked manly, he wasn't standing right; he was afraid of looking effeminate, worried that he looked like a girl, soft and limp and round, sitting with his knees together and blushing like a girl. He tried to improve his appearance by exercise, but it didn't help much. He directed the choir in the parish and the old ladies would congratulate him, but he was afraid to talk to men, because he wouldn't appear manly—he was afraid of the male prejudice that leading singing was effeminate, protesting that men were carpenters or played football. I inquired whose prejudice he had in mind; he acknowledged that it might be his and that he had a prejudice against effeminate men. I also challenged his stereotype, observing that the Boston Symphony was predominantly male, and he distinguished between professionals and amateurs: professional men could have such interests, but not amateurs. When I commented that his answer suggested some confusion, he replied, "I know they are stereotypes intellectually, but I make them work in my case; I refuse to believe that I'm like other men, I'm sick. I hang on to that way of looking at myself, even though I'm not happy with it." He tried to enlist me to support this persuasion—"Am I getting anywhere? I still have the same urges to fantasize and masturbate. Can I ever shake them off? It's a constant struggle; I have to stop using my body for my own pleasure. I want you to tell me if I'm homosexual, am I making it worse by my fantasies? I can believe someone else, but I either wouldn't believe you or I'd make it a self-fulfilling prophecy. You shouldn't tell me no matter how much I want it. I look for ideal men rather than women, someone strong, appealing to women, and confident, not like me."

These difficulties were compounded by the basically narcissistic organization of his character. Although he was at the top of his class in high school, he felt guilty and tried not to appear too good, fearing jealousy and ostracism. In his current work he felt that he was actually smarter than some of his professors. But in writing papers, he tended to rely on authorities, feeling that his own opinions were inadequate—preferring what he thought would please the professor rather than what he thought himself. He couldn't relax because others might get ahead of him—he had to be first: he recalled how competitive he had been with his older brother who was first in his class. Alan complained with some bitterness, "I ended up third and it made me sick. I never did anything just because I liked it."

Slipping below the level of his expectations created anxiety—a B− in an exam when he expected an A was upsetting because he was not living up to his ideal. The courses were more difficult than he had expected. He had failed to live up to the standard set by his brother; he was always a couple of points behind him, and was constantly comparing himself with his brother. He tried to make himself an ideal religious, but that was unrealistic and upsetting when the theology didn't come easily. He had always been able to accomplish by pushing himself. Parents and teachers all told him he should be doing better. He was concerned with impressing them rather than understanding the material. Performing and pleasing the important people worked in high school; he could live up to what others expected and protect himself from attack, but he could never accept that someone else might do better.

Despite his wishes to succeed and be better than anyone around, he was often self-critical, putting himself down and questioning his motives and sincerity. He felt he had to be careful of becoming proud—if he thought he was really good, then the ax would fall. The solution was not to do too well or not try to outdo others, so that if you fail you won't look so bad. But he tried consciously not to appear intellectually conceited, fearing criticism and retaliation. But alongside these feelings, he was constantly seeking perfection in his work, looking endlessly for the approval that always seemed to elude him. If he were to buy anything, say a coat, he would become preoccupied with whether he could have gotten something better at a cheaper price, being unhappy if someone else had a better coat, but then worrying whether the coat he bought would look too expensive for a seminarian and he would be criticized for buying it. He was severely critical of any of his colleagues were they not to adhere strictly to religious observances, but envious of their flexibility and freedom, torn by his need to live up to the religious ideal yet resenting the restraints and limitations it imposed on him, fearing that he was missing out and that others were gaining ground while he was falling behind.

It would not be hard to guess from this material that Alan suffered from authoritarian conflicts and had highly ambivalent and conflicted relations with authority figures—both within and outside of the analysis. These conditions emerged around his relationships with his superiors. He distrusted all superiors and his attitude toward them was overshadowed by his fears that his homosexuality would be discovered and he would forthwith be thrown out of the seminary. One of his

friends had been thrown out—Alan felt unjustly. He complained bitterly about the immaturity and lack of judgment he
saw in his superiors, and about his fears of being misunderstood or misjudged by them. He saw his rector, his immediate
superior, as immature and manipulative, trying to get people
to feel sorry for him and threatening to resign if things didn't
go right. The analogy to his mother came readily to mind,
along with the wish that someone else were rector, just like he
had wished that someone else—say Aunt Ann—were his
mother. He also saw the rector as like his father, weak and
unable to make decisions on his own, not manly or assertive—qualities that he had disliked so much in his father.

While he despised the rector for "walking on eggshells," he
felt intimidated and afraid in his presence: "He has knowledge
about me, and I have to do what he expects. I break out in a
cold sweat, like a little kid, I have to please him so he can't
hurt me. I'm in a delicate position, my future in his hands,
he's a threat to my future so I try to impress him." It was much
the same, perhaps worse, with the bishop—worse because the
bishop had more power and was therefore more of a threat.
The pressure to please him was even greater, along with the
feeling of indebtedness because the bishop was footing the bill
for the analysis. The image of mother again loomed large insofar as she had made him feel burdened and obligated as well.
Alan felt conflicted about the analysis and guilty for imposing
such a burden on the bishop, yet at the same time resentful of
the obligation and indebtedness he felt imposed on him. He
commented, "If I could repay my mother and the bishop, they
would continue to look at me with favor; the bishop is doing
me a big favor." I observed that he had a right and a need for
help, but making it into a favor made him feel indebted, and
further that the indebted feeling was his alone, not anyone
else's. He replied, "But I'm afraid they'll try to get rid of me;
I have to pay my debts to make sure they don't." The bishop
might use the fact of his being in analysis against him in some
way, the way his mother had used things against him and held
things against his father for years. Alan felt his position to be
highly precarious such that he had to assure himself that he

was in the bishop's good graces and that anything that might threaten that confidence was avoided.

Transference

These problems were not slow to surface in the analysis in Alan's relating to me as an authority figure. In his previous psychotherapy, the same issues had arisen in the form of Alan's fear of the therapist and his efforts not to offend him. He could recognize the projective aspect of this attitude, but nonetheless he saw both the therapist and me as strict and stern judges around whom he had to watch his step—walk on eggshells, as it were. He felt threatened and anxious about my judging him with disgust as depraved and perverted for his sexual wishes, especially for his homosexual inclinations. He was constantly preoccupied with what others thought of him, and that concern was intensified in the analysis. Whatever they thought, he was convinced that it couldn't be anything good. With me he tried to be lucid and logical and careful about what he said or by being vague and ambiguous in order to protect himself and not offend me. He was afraid of being misunderstood, and afraid that I would not think well of him, judge him as harshly as he judged himself. Part of him wanted me to be stern and judgmental, but he was threatened by what those judgments might be, just as he was terrified of judgments from any of his superiors or teachers. If any of them, even his professors, got to know him they would see through his facade and see his weaknesses and judge him less of a man.

None of this, of course, prevented him from turning his critical guns on me, as he did with any and all who had any authority over him in his eyes. He compared me to his previous therapist, generally negatively—I said things that were obvious and unnecessary suggesting that I didn't really understand him. He expected something better, something new and different that would bring quick and easy results. Even if he felt more relaxed with me, he thought I was too friendly and smiled too much. More to the point, he wondered whether I was as good a therapist as his previous therapist, especially since I charged so much less. He felt the reduced fee was also a favor that made him feel indebted, as he had so often felt indebted to his mother, and that made it so much more difficult to feel or express any anger or resentment toward me.

He repeatedly expressed doubts about the analysis. He felt unconfortable and anxious, wanting to hide his thoughts and feelings. He worried whether he was worth the expense of the analysis—after all other people, like his mother, were worse off, and he felt guilty about spending the bishop's money. Was he deserving? Why should he get help while others didn't? Did he build up a need for help in his mind? What would it be like if he weren't in analysis? He reported an early dream in which I was a background figure and which had to do with his anxiety about getting to an appointment on time while keeping the analysis a secret, especially from his mother. There was a sched-uling conflict between a piano lesson and analysis; he thought he was late and was afraid that I would be displeased, thinking that he was irresponsible and not worth the effort.

Termination

These concerns suddenly came together in a rush to terminate. He desperately needed to please the bishop, feeling that he had become a burden on him, especially financially, and that this put him in the position of feeling burdened and indebted. What he really needed was to control himself and grow up. The feeling with the bishop was the same as the feeling he had toward his mother when she made him feel so indebted and that he had to prove himself and work to avoid any disfavor. He announced suddenly one day that he had gone to see the bishop and had decided to stop the analysis.

> I went to see the bishop about analysis. I asked if the diocese could afford it. He said I should be able to do without it, so I decided to terminate this analysis. It's a luxury that we can't afford. I'd like to terminate Wednesday, and I'd like to know where I am. [What feelings?] I wonder about this decision; it was precipitated by the bishop asking about Blue Cross/Blue Shield. It's a question of finances. But I'm afraid of the bishop

and what he can do to me. I had to talk with him to see how
he felt. I asked if he could afford this analysis, but he left it to
me to decide. [What did you think of that?] In the past I made
decisions on the basis of what other people thought, but I'm
curious what will happen without it. He asked if I could do
without it. I still have questions about my sexuality and self-
condemnation, but they're not causing any anxiety now. Besides, organizing liturgy in the parish can be therapeutic. I feel
now that I can do without it; the sex question doesn't bother
me so much. [I wonder if we shouldn't be cautious about the
suspicious aspects of your decision.] I felt pressured: I knew I
should talk it over, and I don't know why I didn't wait. I was
really telling him that I wasn't sick, I was really a good candidate
for the priesthood.

In the following hour he continued:

I was thinking about my decision—it was precipitant, but I
needed to tell the bishop that I didn't need analysis. As soon
as I said it, I felt a sense of relief. I felt guilty for going to
analysis; if people knew they wouldn't think so well of me. It
was an admission of weakness. And I wanted to be free of the
feeling of indebtedness, using analysis as a crutch, an excuse
for not improving. I decided it was better to face things without
analysis. [You saw it as an admission of weakness?] I wouldn't
have undertaken it if I felt strong. . . . I felt analysis was jeopard-
izing my career. The bishop seems to understand about analysis,
but I don't trust him. That's my way of looking at anyone in
authority—if he knew about me he would do me in, force me
out of the seminary. And I'd feel obligated to him; he'd have
control over me, like mother made me feel so obligated to work
around the house. [It seems that you act out the same thing
with the bishop as with your mother; it's not much different
than the situation with your mother and Aunt Ann, is it?] If my
mother knew what I talked to Aunt Ann about she'd disown
me; if the bishop knew what I talked about here he wouldn't
understand. He might start asking questions and threaten me.
I had to minimize his fears like I had to minimize mother's
fears. There's no buffer between me and him. [I guess you felt
that at home too?] My father couldn't afford to stand up to her.
[And you feel the same?] Definitely my feeling, I was afraid; he
threw out my closest friend. [Just like your mother threw your
brother out?] I don't know why I should be afraid of mother
now, I'm leading my own life. [It doesn't really sound like it; it
seems more that you substitute the bishop for your mother.] It

bothers me that I can't take the risk—that's one reason why I don't feel manly. I did risk something to undertake analysis, but now my fears have gotten the better of me. The choice is to change through psychoanalysis or religion; religion is safer, analysis is more threatening to my vocation. [The bishop seems to be understanding and quite cooperative?] But I don't trust him. He manipulates people and I've seen it happen to better men than me.

The next hour was the last. There was a note of regret and a sense of his overwhelming need to capitulate in the face of his anxieties and doubts. He thought we were beginning to develop some rapport, but he was the one to "drop a brick into the pie." He was afraid of making me angry for destroying the analysis. It was, he said, a breech of contract, against the rules of the game, but he felt he had to stand by his decision:

> I thought the bishop was worried about finances, and that he thought of me as a poor risk for orders. [You seem to see analysis as an obstacle to your vocation rather than as a path to it?] I guess the obstacle is in me. The bishop represents a threat. My position is precarious; I always felt any love or favor was precarious, I guess that's because of my experience with my mother. . . . I just wanted to put the decision in his hands—I often put people in a position of making decisions for me.

Discussion

The salient points that seem related to this abortive outcome are Alan's basic insecurity, his conflicts over dependence and independence, his ambivalence and conflicts with authority figures, and the intense transference overlay that colored all these dimensions of his life experience. These would merit discussion in their own right, but I feel that the material more or less speaks for itself and any other analytic reader would draw conclusions similar to my own. I would rather focus the discussion on the aspects of the analytic relation and examine the extent to which certain critical failures in that regard were determinative of the failure of this analytic process. The aspects I will discuss are the transference, the real relation, and the alliance—the components of the analytic relation I have described in detail elsewhere (Meissner, 1996).

The transference elements took the form of his seeing me as both the critical, harshly judging, and condemning figure on the one hand, and the self-sacrificing favor giver who would put him in a position of dependence and indebtedness. The derivation from his parents, especially his mother, was impressive and powerful. The judgmental side was partly from his father, and the fears of hurting me by any critical or aggressive attacks of his own had to do with his mother. But if his father was critical and judgmental, he was also weak and inadequate—unable to handle or stand up to Alan's mother. And if his mother were the masochistic martyr-figure, she was also the powerful wielder of love, acceptance, and approval, and could cut him off and cast him out at her whim. These transferential derivatives came into play not only in the analysis in relation to me as a transference object, but in his relationships and dealings with his religious superiors as well.

The reality components played a decisive role in setting the frame within which the analysis proceeded. The fact that the analysis was conducted with the approval and financial support of Alan's superiors cast a dark shadow over the whole proceedings. All of his anxieties related to his transference determinants and the resulting conflicts of authority, his basic distrust of his superiors, and the fear that in the course of the analysis he would be exposed, condemned, cast out of the seminary, and thus denied ordination to the priesthood, were provided ample scope for playing themselves out. This despite the fact that Alan's superiors were quite supportive, involved themselves minimally and constructively in making the necessary arrangements, and were in no sense discouraging or interfering. The fact of my own religious affiliation and identity may also have played into this aspect of the problem. Despite the fact that I had no connection or communication with his superiors (other than the one initial contact before the analysis started), Alan could not develop enough trust in the privacy and confidentiality of our work together to feel secure and accept that his superiors would know only what he chose to tell them about his analysis. Regardless of my reassurances, he lumped me in the same category as his superiors, and could not dispel the idea that we would somehow be in collusion that would result in his downfall. His fear of falling into disfavor seemed to settle on the money issue—whatever the diocese spent on his analysis would be too much and would put him in the vulnerable position of feeling indebted and obligated and to stir his fears of disapproval, of becoming a burden on the bishop and the diocese, and of being judged unworthy of ordination. This conviction was again maintained in the face of the fact that the fee was significantly reduced and that the diocese had generous insurance arrangements for precisely such purposes.

One of the unstated premises that Alan retained and that did not come to the fore, until the very end when termination had been decided on, was that his turning to psychoanalysis for help was in some sense a mark of his religious failure, of his inability to find peace of soul and a more positive and constructive outlook on the difficulties in his life through prayer and religious devotion. This set up in his mind an opposition between psychoanalysis and his religious commitments, which led him to assume that to the degree that he engaged in and committed himself to the analysis, he was turning his back on and betraying his religious commitment and his reliance on God alone to solve his problems. His was a basic conviction that I have found to be pervasive in many religious persons, high and low. Exploring underlying unconscious motivations is threatening for all analytic patients, but in the case of religious the threat is often felt to be directed not only at their sense of themselves but at the roots of their religious convictions and faith. This sheds some light on why Alan repeatedly protested that his vocation was endangered.

The dichotomy and opposition is spurious, of course. Freud himself, in his correspondence with the Lutheran pastor, Oskar Pfister, acknowledged that psychoanalysis could very well be used by religious persons for religious purposes, even though that was not his cup of tea (Meissner, 1984). I am also reminded of the paradoxical maxim of St. Ignatius of Loyola—"Pray as though everything depended on God, but act as though everything depended on you" (Meissner, 1999). For the religious who is dedicated to seeking to fulfill God's will, psychoanalysis may be a vital, and even in some cases necessary, means to that end. In retrospect, it seems very clearly that Alan's appeal to religious observance and practice as his preferred channel for resolving his difficulties was no more than a rationalization of his precipitant and misguided decision.

While these factors were sources of difficulty and fed into each other in potent and destructive ways, they would not in my view have been sufficient to derail the analysis had there been available a meaningful and solid alliance. The alliance in this case—to be generous and put the best face on it—was fragile, tenuous, troubled from the start, and riddled with problematic misalliances. The misalliances that I could identify were rooted in both transference and reality; that is, any meaningful alliance between Alan and myself was undermined and constantly threatened by discolorations deriving from transference elements, as discussed above, deriving from both parents on one side, and by the actuality of his position as a seminarian and his relations with his superiors on the other. His engagement in the analysis was hesitant, fearful, lacking in trust, and cloaked in fears of judgment and retaliation, almost to the point of a paranoid misjudgment. Any idea that we were involved in a process of mutual exploration and inquiry, that we were collaborators in a process in which neither one of us held an advantage over the other, or that the imbalance of power and vulnerability that he perceived was a figment of his imagination, found little or no place or acceptance in his mind.

The effect was not complete rebellion and resistance on his part, since if he was terrified of the threatening consequences of his pursuing the analysis, he was also compelled by his desires to please and to be accommodating to what he also understood to be his superiors' wishes and mine for him to do the analysis and resolve his difficulties. But this motivation to make the analysis work and help himself, which would have served the alliance purposes well, was quickly and decisively overwhelmed and silenced by his countervailing anxieties and fears. In consequence, his participation, while it lasted, was half-hearted, although at times he seemed to get into it and the material flowed easily, suggesting that if the negative factors had been sufficiently resolved, he would have made a good analytic patient and probably would have benefited greatly from the process.

However, I can only say that with some regret. Looking back over this case, I have asked myself what I might have done that would have gotten Alan over the considerable hump or humps that thwarted his analytic effort. But my own inexperience and analytic naiveté as a recent graduate carried their burden of limitations. Were I working with Alan today, my approach might differ—but how? I have thought that better interpretation of the transference components might have helped. These were touched on at several points, enough for Alan to have some initial awareness of their effects, but far from enough to enable him to shake loose from them in any effective way. These were obviously major contributing factors to the undermining of the alliance. But on the other hand, had we been able to effect a sufficiently effective alliance, these transference derivatives might not have weighed so heavily, or we would have had better opportunity to explore and interpret them.

Sitting in my Monday morning quarterback's chair, I also thought that one aspect that was missing and might have served the analysis better, was a more direct approach to the alliance itself. By this I would mean a more direct focus on the difficulties he was experiencing in engaging in the analysis and the potential threats and impediments he imagined in that connection. While such an approach might have clarified some issues and resolved some of his anxieties, it would also have played into his view of me as a powerful and judging figure of whom he would have to be suspicious and with whom he would have to be cautious. This, however, is an exercise of reading my current understanding of the alliance and its role in analysis back into the material of this case. When the case was happening, I did not appreciate those aspects of the alliance as deeply and tended—to my regret and Alan's misfortune—to more-or-less take them for granted. Whether the outcome would have been any different I find it hard to say.

Alan's case also raises some interesting questions specifically about the analysis of religious personnel—patients who are by profession religiously committed and oriented. The issues in this truncated analysis never got around to specifically religious issues, although based on my experience I would hazard a guess that Alan's deeply rooted transferential concerns would have played a role in his religious thinking—his God would have been cast in much the same character as his superiors and myself. More to the fore were the conditions of his engagement and participation in the analysis—specifically the meaning of the analysis vis-à-vis his relations with his religious superiors. In my experience, religious superiors tend to take a fatherly concern in the welfare of their subjects; I have never run into a religious superior, in a secular or religious order, who was not entirely supportive of analysis for one of their subjects. They are usually intelligent men and women who understand and accept the advice of medical or psychiatric–psychological professionals regarding the physical or mental well-being of their subjects. They have never intruded on or interfered with analysis in my experience.

But that does not mean they could not. Especially in virtue of vows of obedience, superiors have the right and obligation to both know their subjects thoroughly and decide in their best interest. There have been cases in which superiors have made inquiries, wanting to know the subject's progress, whether the analysis was proving effective, and what the future prospects might be as to outcome and prospective length of treatment. An understandable anxiety for superiors is whether the work of the analysis might contribute to undermining the patient's religious vocation, reflecting the typical mind-set described previously. I have found in treating religious that the issue of vocation is almost always in one or other form a salient aspect of the patient's difficulties. The resolution of ambivalence about vocation can go either way—as an analyst I would have no way to predict the course any patient would follow or what the ultimate fate of his or her vocation might be. Ultimately, such a decision lies with the patient himself. If the vocation is sincere and authentic, it will persevere; if it is not, it will not. All parties involved in the situation—the patient, the superiors, and the analyst himself—must be aware of and prepared to accept this possibility. If it cannot be accepted as one of the viable alternatives, the analysis will be frustrated, and is probably better not undertaken. But my experience has been that honest exploration of uncertainties, doubts, ambivalences, and motivations for the vocation are in the long run more beneficial than any attempts to avoid or circumvent them.

I regard these as legitimate and perfectly reasonable questions. At times they can be answered directly without jeopardy to the analysis, but never without full knowledge and acceptance by the patient himself. At other times, any answer would require an unacceptable degree of revealing of analytic material or communication that would be unfavorable or unacceptable to the patient. At such times, the analyst owes a prior obligation to his patient to protect his privacy and confidentiality, so that no information can be given to the superior and any communication in that regard must be left up to the patient. Under optimal circumstances, the pros and cons, ifs and ands, of this situation can be explored in detail with the patient and the further decisions of how he or she might wish to deal with the superior's questions left up to them. The focus on issues of the fee in this case were a displacement of Alan's more basic fears about favor-disfavor, dependence-independence, and vulnerability and indebtedness. We were not able to get to the point at which these concerns could be explored and discussed, and he was incapable of dealing with his superior in any more mature and effective negotiation—were that at all necessary.

My conclusion is that this case went awry not so much due to the level of pathology or the unsuitability of the patient for analysis, but from a combination of transference influences and special reality circumstances that conspired to frustrate and undermine the therapeutic alliance. The failure of the analyst to adequately appreciate the severity of the alliance disturbance and the misalliances it entailed, and his failure to take adequate steps to either effectively interpret the transference material or engage the patient in confronting and working through the alliance difficulties and misalliances, were also important contributing factors. Given the opportunity to engage these issues, the analysis might well have survived and proven effective—but the countervailing influences proved too powerful and the analysis was prematurely aborted.

References

Meissner, S.J., W. W. (1984), *Psychoanalysis and Religious Experience.* New Haven, CT: Yale University Press.
———— (1996), *The Therapeutic Alliance.* New Haven, CT: Yale University Press.
———— (1999), *To the Greater Glory—A Psychological Study of Ignatian Spirituality.* Milwaukee, WI: Marquette University Press.

9

Success or Failure: The Complexity of Assessment

ALAN Z. SKOLNIKOFF, M.D.

To judge the outcome of our work, we attempt to look at its results from different vantage points. I will describe my own analytic work with two patients. I will review my assessment and how it changed over time. To describe other perspectives, I will offer hypothetical assessments by evaluators of different persuasions. Throughout the complexity of assessment of outcome, particular measures such as success or failure will be emphasized.

Two case vignettes are presented. Either of my two cases could be seen as either successful or failed, depending on what is being measured, when, and by whom. These were patients whose professions were outside the mental health field, who were seen fifteen to twenty years ago. They were treated without any specific research or training considerations involved. I have described each of them in previous publications (Skolnikoff, 1984, 1993).

Case A

A. was a 38-year-old single man who was referred because of chronic depression. He had come to realize, particularly since the end of his last relationship, that although he wished to marry and have children, he found he couldn't sustain a sexual attraction to a woman who might be suitable for marriage. He was a businessman, but had a wide interest in civic affairs and philanthropy. He had an excellent academic background from a prominent Eastern college and graduate school, being interested in arts and theater, and appeared thoughtful about psychological matters. Even before he accepted the recommendation for analysis, he seemed to understand that what might undermine his intention to marry was his deeper awareness of a depressing situation within his own family: a domineering mother who was unhappy with his eccentric, uninvolved father. He never took his father seriously, turning to his mother for any advice or decisions. I recommended psychoanalysis after a few vis-à-vis sessions. I considered him engaging, thoughtful, psychologically minded, and motivated to change.

I was surprised with how he changed in the first analytic hours. Whatever subject he began with was drained of emotion. He spoke in a dull, monotonous voice, and whatever he described was boring to me and of little interest to him. Any comments I made were taken matter-of-factly, without evoking any emotional response. It felt as if he were speaking to himself. This continued for the first eighteen months of analysis. In a typical hour, he would begin with a list of business concerns; these concerns seemed ordinary. If there was a motive to recount them, it would be to describe how well his work was going. He was respected and his employees followed his direction. Toward the end of the hour, he might describe a situation in which some loneliness was implied. Such a situation might concern seeing a particular woman whom he wasn't enthusiastic about and felt alone with in her presence; a business trip that he had to go on that was tedious; or a social engagement with business or social friends that he wasn't looking forward to.

I commented on this sequence: his talking about a number of business and social situations he was handling well, with his then shifting to some situation in which he displayed a feeling of longing near the end of the hour. I wondered how he heard what he was saying? He would respond in a bored manner. "I don't know. I'm just telling you what's on my mind." I noted to myself that he spoke in a flowery language and frequently used words that I hardly understood. Either in empathic response or competition with him I would use more eloquent language than usual. On a few occasions, he didn't understand the meaning of my words. I explained them and wondered with him why he was using such eloquent language that I had trouble understanding. With more emotion than usual, he said he realized that this was the mode of conversation that his mother encouraged at the dinner table. His father would feel this kind of talk was affected and would speak in simpler language. A. had contempt for his father and wondered why he wouldn't speak more eloquently.

As we continued on one occasion, I questioned his pronunciation of a word that I didn't understand, wondering if he meant another word. He felt humiliated, feeling that I was criticizing his speech, the way his mother did. He then told me of situations in which his mother reprimanded him for not being precise in his written or spoken language.

In this first phase (18 months), there had been no change in any of his feelings about women he dated. He was no longer depressed and had no focused complaints about his life. In fact, his life seemed boringly predictable to both of us. I welcomed the exchange about our use of eloquent language, which appeared to reveal a conflict with his mother that was now experienced in our relationship. Despite this change, A.'s boring monologue continued. He kept recounting his usual business affairs and I said little. One day, as he talked about a major expansion of his business, he experienced a peculiar numb sensation around his mouth. He was aware that he had his hand placed right next to his mouth and remembered, in adolescence when his parents were fighting, he retreated to his room to avoid emotional turmoil. He would lie in bed and

contemplate his future. He'd have fantasies of becoming someone famous, perhaps the president of the United States. At
that point he'd feel sleepy, have his hand near his mouth, and
experience that same numb sensation. He felt alarmed experiencing this sensation now, something that he had been
ashamed of. He regained composure, thinking it part of the
analysis. He even felt intrigued, thinking this made his analysis
interesting. He began to expand his business, contemplating
opening branches in other parts of the country. At the same
time, he complained more about his lack of interest in developing a relationship with any woman, despite the fact that
many suitable women seemed interested in him.

The hours again became dull. He would take long business
trips, but arranged his schedule so that he hardly missed any
hours of his analysis. He did this perfunctorily, without expressing any longing for his appointments with me. His boring ren-
dition of business details took a different turn at this point.
On his trips, in the hotels he stayed in, he was served excellent
meals. On several occasions, he found himself staring at his
waiter, to whom he would feel a homosexual attraction. Over
a period of months, he gradually expressed his concern that
he might after all be latently homosexual. He said this in an
unemotional way, without revealing how deeply he might have
felt about this. It was as if he was talking about someone else.
These trips would also be isolated from his descriptions of his
life in San Francisco.

I tried to call this isolation to his attention and wondered if
he couldn't tell me what he felt about his homosexual fantasies.
It is difficult to describe his response to my interventions and
questions. Mostly he would rationalize these feelings by saying:

> I think it was just lonely on this trip, and I was just looking at
> this waiter, imagining that I would like to talk to him. Years ago
> when at college, I got drunk with this guy who was gay. I think
> he may have had sex with me when I was dead drunk. I'm not
> sure. I don't remember. I think, after dinner a week ago, this
> waiter who served me my meal, brought me some drinks late
> at night. I was drunk, and he may have had sex with me. I don't
> remember. Anyway, I don't think this is important because I
> don't think I'm homosexual.

I continued to focus on the vagueness and isolation of these events and how he wouldn't let himself be conscious of his own fears or desires. He listened respectfully to what I said, but this did not influence him to explore these feelings any more deeply. Instead, he shifted to talking about a series of relationships with women with whom he was becoming involved in an attempt to push himself to find the right one. He continued to be unenthusiastic about most women he met. One woman who was introduced to him by a couple he had known for many years became enthusiastic about him. He found their sexual relationship good enough, but didn't enjoy her excitement with him. He lost his enthusiasm for her, but was able to continue a sexual relationship because he thought it was what he should want. On one summer weekend, his friends invited them to spend the weekend at their country estate. He was happy to see them, but not enthusiastic to be with her. When they were shown to their guest cottage, she became very romantic, saying, "Let's make a baby." He felt numb and was afraid that he might be impotent. As he lay with her in bed, waiting to get excited to be able to perform intercourse with her, a disturbing fantasy entered his mind. He imagined a tall, thin man approaching him from the rear in order to have anal intercourse, saying "You can do it" (he is short and stocky and I am tall and thin). He was both frightened and despairing about this thought. For the first time, he seemed to be disturbed about the possibility that he might be homosexual. He was afraid he wasn't sufficiently heterosexual to sustain a relationship and marriage and have children. I was convinced of the transference connection to the homosexual fantasy, but was reluctant to directly interpret this for fear of humiliating him or having him massively defend against it. Out of tact, I interpreted his fear or desire of expressing his homosexual impulses. He wanted to deny the place they had in his feelings. He agreed and then was more forthcoming, not only about previous homosexual fantasies in college and later, but talked about current concerns about his appearance that led him to feel less masculine. He now began to talk more frankly about his body. He didn't like to wear a bathing suit for fear of being seen as fat and not handsome. He directly expressed envy of my thinness and imagined my being comfortable with my appearance. "You don't have to worry about being seen in a bathing suit. I'm sure you feel that you look good and that women are attracted to you directly because of how you look. I'm always trying to hide my body. I don't want to be seen by my girl friends when I'm naked." He had difficulty, however, in discussing the current homosexual fantasy that frequently reappeared in his relationship with his enthusiastic partner.

In discussing his despair about his body, he seemed to become less confident about his prospects for the future. He wondered if he could ever feel strong enough to be with any woman. He saw the connection between his mother's disdain for his father and his impaired masculinity. He developed an increasing degree of comfort to talk frankly about his fears. Now he eagerly looked forward to our sessions. Mixed with his enthusiasm was the fear that he'd never manage an adequate relationship with a woman. That's what he came to analysis for and he felt further from this than ever. He absolved me from responsibility for his feelings. He had wished I could do something magical to provide him with the enthusiasm he lacked. He was disturbed with the continuation of his homosexual fantasy that accompanied his sexual feelings toward his eager partner. He finally couldn't stand her any longer and abruptly ended their relationship.

As we continued, he expressed the fear that he would see me forever because he craved childish support. At this point, only three months after the initial appearance of the homosexual fantasy with his previous partner, he met a new, attractive, available woman to whom he felt strongly attracted. They quickly began a sexual relationship and he was astounded at how enthusiastic he was. What he previously labeled a constitutionally low sex drive now seemed to magically disappear. Within a week, he was convinced that he had solved his problem. He was deeply in love, sexually active, and emotionally involved and ready to marry. His homosexual fantasy had completely disappeared. He was very grateful to me and felt there would be no need to continue analysis for more than one or two more sessions.

At that time I had seen him for approximately three and a half years. I appealed to him to stay for a few months, to see if we could understand why things had gone so well so suddenly. I added that an understanding of the changes in him could make him more certain of his transformation. He was very skeptical of what I suggested. He couldn't imagine what the need for understanding was when he had overcome his difficulty so completely. Nevertheless, he agreed to continue for another three months because he trusted my analytic competence. He also wanted to leave without a strong disagreement with me.

The final three months of the analysis proceeded by his re-counting his sense of love for his fiancée, his enjoyment of his sexual activities with her, and his general pleasure for life, as well as his gratitude toward me. He never pursued understanding why things had changed or investigated the nature of his homosexual fantasy, despite my encouragement. During our final session he reported a dream. He was with his fianceé and this same tall, thin man was approaching him for anal intercourse with a supportive, "You can do it." In the dream, the patient felt that he didn't need this man, but enjoyed his presence anyway. I asked for his associations to the dream, and he thought somewhat vaguely that it must have something to do with the end of the analysis. He didn't think it was terribly important, however, since everything was going so well for him. He appeared to deny it having anything to do with his feelings toward me.

He married a few months later, after the end of the analysis, and I would periodically hear reports from the original referral source about superficial aspects of his life. In the first five years of his marriage, he had two children, and his wife complained a good deal about his being too involved in his business, although she said he was a very good father to his two daughters. About ten years after I saw him, he called, asking for a referral for a couples' therapist. Although he considered his relationship with his wife excellent, she complained that he wasn't deeply emotionally involved with her. Their sexual life was more than adequate so far as he was concerned, but she complained he didn't put much feeling into it. He thanked me once again for the help I had given him and was pleased with his life. Subsequent reports from the referral source reported that he continued to have a reasonable marriage and relationship with his children, and that he and his wife appeared close.

Success or failure? At termination, I felt that my work with A. represented a failure by psychoanalytic process measures. He was unable to understand or use the homosexual transference to overcome his homosexual fears. He was left with an isolated homosexual fantasy at the termination of analysis, which seemed to permit him, through denial and flight, to make what appeared to be a transiently successful heterosexual adjustment in marriage. Terms such as *flight into health* to avoid the homosexual transference seemed to describe this ending. At that time, I thought of the outcome as an instance where a patient can perceive the treatment to have had a positive effect, despite his defensive denial of his sexual conflicts. When this denial would break down, I would have predicted that his marriage would not last, nor would he continue to feel strong heterosexual impulses. Despite some emotional withdrawal from his wife that I described above, he seems to have sustained his marriage. The superficial reports that I have up to fifteen years after the end of the analysis suggest that he made an adequate adjustment and has benefited from his analysis. Would a follow-up by an outside researcher give a different picture? I believe such follow-up meetings, either with the original analyst or another analyst, can give interesting data, but would still have to be evaluated and compared with the analyst's and patient's perceptions of what took place at termination.

Case B

B. was a computer salesperson in his midtwenties, referred to me by his internist, who recognized as psychological B.'s main complaint of fearing that he had a body odor. Previously, he had an extensive physical workup at a major medical center, which did not determine any basis for his concerns. He had never had psychotherapy and readily accepted my invitation to explore the psychological nature of his symptoms. I decided to recommend a brief course of treatment to him for the following reasons: I feared that his symptoms might be protecting him from serious psychopathology, and I was interested in what could be accomplished in brief therapy focused on symptom reduction alone. He described situations in which he felt people thought he had a bad odor. These mostly centered around women who rejected him in casual encounters in bars. Occasionally he felt this symptom at work when a major business challenge occurred. Verbal presentations to his boss or a group of colleagues would leave him anxious about whether he could be seen in a favorable light. Here he was afraid that others thought he smelled. His symptom first appeared in college. After receiving a baseball scholarship, he injured his throwing arm his first year on the team. He wanted to continue with the team, but left because he feared the coach didn't like him because he smelled. He was depressed about the loss of his powerful throwing arm and developed other vague physical symptoms as well.

He described his mother affectionately. She was equally affectionate with him and always was concerned about his basic needs for food and comfort. She wanted him to relax in his work and not be so competitive. During his childhood, he remembered the father making fun of the mother, saying that she had bad breath and body odor. He praised her for being a giving and caring woman, but added she wasn't very smart. The father was proud of his son, B., whom he thought was tough, but would depreciate him if he seemed to lack courage, calling him a pussy. The father was a moderately successful salesman. He would often make derogatory remarks about how other more successful colleagues got ahead by "ass kissing." B. had a sister two years younger who was attractive but lacked confidence in her studies in college and in job pursuits. She continued to live at home, but was now threatening to move out to get away from father's criticisms. Father thought she was running around with too many boys and could be in danger of ruining her reputation, which would reflect on "the family."

The patient and I agreed on a formulation of his difficulties. Whenever he felt potentially criticized or humiliated, he would feel like a pussy and imagine himself smelling the way his mother did, who was the object of ridicule in his family. During our psychotherapy sessions on a once-a-week basis, he seemed to profit somewhat from the understanding of the dynamics of his symptoms, but this didn't lead to any significant change in his experience. To see if there was any transference element that could be linked to our work, I asked him to observe whether or not he thought that I would think that he smelled at any time during our sessions. He said that he didn't feel that I would think that about him. I seemed to be really paying careful attention to him and to respect him as a person, as well as his efforts to cure his symptom. I encouraged him, nevertheless, to notice this feeling if it should appear.

In the next hour, as he was talking in a repetitive way about his symptom and how it appeared in an encounter with a woman who rejected him at a bar, my attention lapsed. I took a deep breath or looked away from him as he was speaking, revealing some frustration with the repetitive story. He said, "Right now, Doc, I think you think that I smell." I perked up, admitting that, at that moment, my attention had lapsed. I hadn't been paying careful attention to what he was saying, feeling that what he had told me I had heard several times before. He wasn't aware of being hurt by my admission. He was surprised at how vulnerable he was to my not attending to him and how that might have produced the symptom. During the next sessions, his symptoms gradually disappeared. At first he thought that a particular individual might be thinking that he smelled, but then could see the humiliation inherent in the situation and the thought he smelled went away. He was happy, thinking how quickly his symptomatology had resolved, and pleased that I had accomplished this for him after such a brief period, considering how much money he had spent on previous medical workups. After a total of eight sessions, we agreed to stop, but I gave him three follow-up appointments at three months, six months, and a year. During these follow-ups, he continued without symptomatology. He had difficulty finding a woman he enjoyed and worried he quickly lost interest in them. He didn't want any treatment for that, assuming that he could get over this by trying to be friendly rather than just treating them as sexual objects. We agreed that he would call me in the future if there was any return of his symptom.

Two years later he came back with a different symptom. Now when in a bar looking for a woman or having a drink by himself, he thought other men or women were looking at him, thinking he was homosexual. When he had to make a presentation at work, he feared he appeared effeminate. He thought there might be a connection between his earlier fear of smelling bad and his current fear of thinking that others thought he was homosexual. He was anxious and wanted reassurance through understanding. Again, within eight sessions, he understood the fear of being viewed as homosexual was connected to his sense that he wasn't manly enough in his self presentation. This feeling appeared either in a bar as an eligible male to an attractive woman, or in his work setting as a knowledgeable salesperson to his colleagues. The symptom disappeared rapidly and we again arranged a follow-up visit in three months.

He then came without specific symptoms, but was generally depressed. He found his life less meaningful than before. Earlier he had enjoyed the competitiveness associated with getting large accounts. Now he lacked that enthusiasm necessary in sales. He also found it boring to look for women in bars. He would rather stay home and watch television. He realized he was retreating from his ambitions to marry and advance his career. He didn't know what was at the source of his difficulties, but thought psychoanalysis might be an appropriate treatment for him. His choice was also based on my having explained at the beginning of our work years before the forms of treatment that I might offer. After much self-reflection, he now decided that this was what he wanted. On my part, I was reluctant to start an analysis with him because of my apprehension of some underlying potentially disorganizing pathology. I was apprehensive that his underlying identification with his mother as the humiliated object would lead him to feel too weakened to sustain his livelihood in the competitive masculine field of sales. I was wary of his retreat from his earlier heterosexual pursuits, even though I had understood his engagement in casual relationships and sex as a defense against his fears of deeper intimacy or his underlying fears of homosexuality. With these misgivings, I decided to try. I considered him to be quite narcissistically vulnerable and decided to use some self psychological theory to apply to his treatment (Kohut, 1977).

I will describe the course of the analysis briefly. B. frequently became disturbingly regressed during the hours. He had fantasies of being a woman with rotting teeth, who disgusted everyone. Sometimes he saw himself as encountering a woman in a bar, going to be with her, and in the act of intercourse becoming a small child falling inside her vagina and being engulfed. This wasn't just a fantasy on the couch. On several occasions, he actually had that fantasy during sexual intercourse. This was very frightening, but he saw it as part of the work of analysis. He was comforted by the structure of analysis, which protected him from being overwhelmed. Earlier fears of being seen as a homosexual didn't clearly develop during the course of our work. He occasionally commented he was happy that I wasn't homosexual, although if he thought I were, then he might be afraid I'd want to have sex with him. This was said with anxious laughter.

My self psychological perspective changed my analytic stance in this case. As contrasted with many analyses I have conducted, I remained silent for long periods. My interventions were reflective rather than confrontative. I felt the patient was directing his own analysis, wanting me to remain on the sidelines as a witness to his thoughts and actions, with only occasional encouragement. As he continued the analysis, he made the decision to leave his work as a computer salesperson. Instead he became a computer consultant, a job that was less competitive, for which he received less than half his previous income. He stopped his habit of picking up women in bars, and instead sought out long-term friendships with women whom he would emotionally enjoy. He no longer had interest in quick sexual encounters. He became interested in transcendental meditation, men's groups, and other self-help groups. His whole way of being changed. Instead of displaying a blustery, aggressive attitude, he became soft spoken, thoughtful, and frequently silent and contemplative. As these changes became consolidated, he decided to terminate his analysis. Although I feared we had accomplished little in terms of materially improving his life situation, he had made changes which, although not positive in terms of maintaining his income or being able to get involved in a long-term intimate sexual relationship, nevertheless left him more at peace with himself and symptom free. When we ended analysis, I felt my work with him was questionable in terms of achieving his initial goals: improvement in his career and a deeper involvement with a woman. *He* was satisfied with the outcome. I thought he might be deceiving himself and using this satisfaction to defend against what might become an endless treatment, one in which he would become hopelessly dependent upon me.

Three years later, I had a chance encounter with him. He was on his way to a consultation appointment. He was happy to see me and we spent half an hour talking about what had happened to him since the end of his analysis. He had a long-term relationship with a woman that wasn't directly leading to marriage. This was the most profound relationship he had ever imagined. Sex was part of it, but not as important as his deep emotional tie. He felt as if they were soulmates. He also enjoyed his work and considered that he didn't have to compete with others doing consultations. Although his salary was half of what it had been, he felt the change in his feelings of well-being were worth it. He was very thankful for my help and thought that, without our work, he never would have been able to get over those symptoms of feeling that people thought he smelled or was homosexual.

In the next few years, his internist informed me that he continued to consult him occasionally for some minor physical injuries sustained in athletic activities. These were not serious, but the internist felt they served the purpose for B. to gain some covert reassurance about some underlying emotional issues. The internist noted that he seemed calmer and more confident than before, but still had the need to have him be reassuring, as many of his patients did. I imagined his relationship to his physician to be a milder displaced version of a regressed dependent transference to me. As with A., as time has gone by, I have reassessed in my own mind whether or not the result with B. represented a failed or successful analysis. I think the changes we were able to effect during the course of his

analysis were useful to him, despite their not representing success in our original conception of his goals.

Discussion

In reviewing my work with these two cases, I realized that I
formulated each of the cases in different clinical theoretical
frameworks. With A., I made the recommendation for psychoanalysis after the first few hours. I viewed his difficulties in
conflictual terms. He regressed from oedipal level conflicts,
became inhibited and depressed about not being able to engage in intimate relationships with appropriate women. Later,
his homosexual fantasies appeared to come in the form of a
regression from oedipal level heterosexual impulses. Ego psychological conflict theory dictated how I measured the outcome. He modified his conflicts sufficiently to achieve an
oedipal victory in behavioral terms. Nevertheless, in the process, he was unable to work with the homosexual transference,
but instead used his relationship with the analyst in a supportive manner. He used "flight into health" to avoid the dependent homosexual transference. If we use Brenner's concept of
compromise formation (1994), we could better conceptualize
the partial success. A. could achieve his oedipal triumph (intimate relationship plus children), but still had to maintain an
idealized transference to the analyst. This idealized transference would represent a compromise that would permit the
patient to avoid both the more competitive and regressed homosexual aspects of his masculinity.

With B., I did not believe that he was initially suitable for
psychoanalysis. In order to eventually accept him in analytic
treatment, I changed my clinical theoretical framework in the
direction of ideas derived from self psychology. This implied
more of a deficit model. There were things B. could not do.
His fear of his own conscious identifications with his mother
accompanied by a lack of solid support for his masculine strivings from either parent, made him narcissistically vulnerable
to a direct interpretation of his conflicts. A positive outcome
in self psychological terms would be that he would learn to

integrate his passive longings connected with a less aggressive masculine image. This type of outcome focuses on acceptance of the self structure as contrasted with an ego psychological conflict model where a positive outcome is associated with over-coming and mastering inhibitions toward the expression of oedipal level drive derivatives. Changes in technique involve more tact, less confrontation, to avoid causing further narcissis-tic injury. I remained more silent than usual, permitting him to follow his own free associative leads, with my interventions focusing on supporting him around his fears rather than con-fronting him with his defenses.

I will now list some alternate hypothetical hypotheses that might be made at the termination of the analyses of A. and B. from a variety of perspectives. First, some perspectives for case A.

1. Because the analyst and patient failed to engage in analyz-ing the homosexual transference, we might predict the patient would not be able to maintain a positive oedipal stance (inti-macy in marriage plus desire for children). On the other hand, instead of viewing the patient using "flight into health" to avoid the analysis of the dependent homosexual transference, we could view his result at termination as achieving a compro-mise formation (Brenner, 1994) that permitted him to have an oedipal victory while maintaining an unexplored idealized transference to the analyst.

2. From a cognitive behavioral perspective, where there would be a deemphasis of the working through of transference themes, one could point out that the patient developed consid-erable understanding of his family conflicts, his feared identi-fication with his eccentric father, and an awareness of his anger at the domineering nature of his mother to work through these difficulties and achieve his goals of an intimate relationship in marriage with children. One would add that he continued to receive the positive support of his analyst to achieve this lasting behavioral result.

3. From a self psychological perspective, one might have an-other view of the result at termination. We might question the unresolved passive needs of the patient. We could criticize the

analyst for focusing only on the patient's ambitions and oedipal goals, and failing to deal with his underlying defective self-concept. In this context, one could view his need for a homosexual connection as an attempt to repair his defective masculinity.

Some alternate hypotheses for case B:

1. From an ego psychological perspective, B. has had an analysis devoid of the interpretation of conflict. Was the analyst afraid of the potential aggression directed toward him or the regression in the homosexual transference? The analyst achieved a somewhat positive result through supportive measures alone. Although B. feels optimistic about the prospects for an intimate long-term heterosexual relationship, it is hard to imagine that he will be able to achieve this without the analyst's continued support afterwards. Perhaps he is attempting to leave the analysis because he is frightened of his continued attachment which he feels he can't resolve, or he doesn't wish to disappoint his analyst that he cannot accomplish more.

2. His behavior at termination indicates the possibility of a positive result in the area of his feeling that he might be able to engage in a long-term relationship. It is difficult to evaluate his professional development. Does his consultative work really permit him more satisfaction? His passivity and somewhat more somber mood have replaced his superficially active, exuberant stance at the beginning of treatment. It is true that he no longer suffers from troubling symptoms, but he has had to retreat from his initial professional goals.

3. From a self psychological perspective, B. has been able to explore aspects of his troubled self with the help of an empathic analyst, but he failed to develop, during the course of the analysis, a clear twinship or grandiose transference in the analytic setting. The results at termination appear superficial. There is little evidence of connection with the analyst, notwithstanding his expression of gratitude. If one assumes, however, that the changes in B. are more profound, one can describe the analytic process according to a more recent theory in self psychology (Shane, Shane, and Gales, 1997). We can theorize that B., in the analytic process, felt a new feeling of anxiety,

which permitted a consolidation of the self, which led to a capacity for intimate connectedness. This could develop without the working through of transferences.

In summary, I have offered these hypothetical constructs to show that different clinical theoretical frameworks offer different perceptions of outcome. We have to come to terms with a variety of psychoanalytic languages associated with these clinical theories that would be used to study evaluations of outcome. Since there are no studies that prove that one psychoanalytic clinical theory is better than any other, we try to study raw analytic data to assess outcome. No matter what our vantage point is, we are left with our differences as to what constitutes a successful result. Freud's maxim, "to be able to love and work," is still useful, but doesn't go far enough for most evaluations. His later work, "Analysis Terminable and Interminable" (Freud, 1937), gives us more of a sense of the difficulty in measuring outcome at any specific point in time.

In recent perspectives, there are several authors who describe sophisticated outcome measures that could be used to evaluate outcome. Dewitt, Hartley, Rosenberg, Zilberg, and Wallenstein (1991) have developed a series of ego capacity scales. These are measures of change in the ego that can be evaluated in simple atheoretical language at the beginning and end of treatment. Hoffman (1998) describes criteria for termination in terms of "good enough endings." Flax (1996) describes a patient's capacity at the end of an analysis to tolerate multiple and often contradictory stories and events, and to be able to live with them better than they had at the beginning of the analysis.

The evaluation of outcome has to do with when and by whom the success or failure of any analysis is judged. As analysts or patients, we acknowledge that at any point in analysis we might be unclear about what the eventual outcome might be. Even when we evaluate outcome at termination, we're not clear about what a follow-up evaluation might determine. The question arises: How might we get sufficient information at any given time to determine whether an analytic process, outcome, or follow-up has been successful for the patient? Shall we ask the patient, analyst, family, or researcher, or all of the above, to assess what the actual result might be?

With cases A. and B., I have presented patients who were not studied in depth by me or outside observers. I give them as examples of psychoanalysis conducted outside of a training setting where research or case study presentation was not contemplated, giving the advantage of its being uncontaminated by the needs of the analyst in that situation. The disadvantage is the lack of detail and the need to rely on the analyst's (and patient's) subjective reactions which can hide "actual" results. Schachter (Schachter, Martin, Gundle, and O'Neil, 1997) warns us to observe that conversations about success or failure of an analysis between patient and analyst can be self-serving, usually in the direction of falsely positive. The analyst and patient might be covertly saying, "Let's put the best spin on our work so as not to offend each other." The data collected are retrospective, without ongoing reports that structure what the analyst and patient were thinking at that time. Although I'm reporting cases A. and B. to the best of my recollection, with reference to sketchy notes at different intervals, I am mainly relying on my memories of termination and follow-ups. If these cases had been studied with prospective research protocols, different kinds of data (objective) would have been obtained and these results might be difficult to compare to my "subjective" report.

Earlier in my discussion, I presented hypothetical evaluations from different theoretical frameworks. Now for a summary of my views. With case A., my impression at termination was that he had a "flight into health" to avoid a frightening homosexual transference. I believed at that time that the analytic result was poor, even though the patient was satisfied. The sparse data from a ten-year follow-up suggest that some of the gains that were present at the end of the analysis were maintained. How do I understand that the patient did better than I thought he would? I speculate that there was sufficient unconscious identification with my heterosexual assertiveness which replaced the more impoverished identification with his eccentric weak father. I reconceptualized the ending in adaptive rather than defensive terms. This could be stated as follows: he used the sublimated form of the homosexual transference to gain strength in his heterosexual endeavors. My interpretations could have represented the helpful support that was represented in his final dream by the fear, threat, or wish of anal intercourse.

In case B., I was more skeptical of both the process and outcome of our work. At termination, I was convinced that he was mouthing psychological jargon as an intellectual defense. I doubted his feeling of comfort with his life. In my spontaneous follow-up three years later, I was impressed with his subjective sense of peace. Clearly he had changed the criteria for what he expected to achieve at the beginning of analysis. It changed my criteria for the evaluation of his outcome. It was still difficult for me to consider that his job as a consultant rather than computer sales executive represented a positive change. At the beginning, he solved his need to suppress his passive longings with pseudoassertive masculine behavior. A long-term relationship with a woman that had a predominantly emotional component replaced his previous focus on short-term sexual performance. This satisfied him, but left me questioning how he had achieved it. Again I changed my clinical theoretical orientation to reevaluate his impression of the positive outcome. Although I subscribe to self psychological theories concerning narcissistic problems, the experience with this patient convinced me how useful such formulations were in evaluating his treatment and outcome.

With both cases A. and B., as well as other experiences in my psychoanalytic practice, I have come to accept the difficulty at any given moment in knowing whether the work is going well or badly. The outcome of psychoanalysis is merely one point in the patient's life, rather than an end result ("Analysis Terminable and Interminable"). Likewise, every case an analyst treats represents a potential for learning and change in his capacity to evaluate and treat his patients as well as reformulating his clinical theoretical stance.

References

Brenner, C. (1994), The mind as conflict and compromise formation. *J. Clin. Psychoanal.*, 3:473–488.

Dewitt, K. N., Hartley, D. E., Rosenberg, S. E., Zilberg, N. J., & Wallerstein, R. S. (1991), Scales of psychological capacities: Development of an assessment approach. *Psychoanal. Contemp. Thought,* 14:343–361.

Flax, J. (1996), Taking multiplicity seriously: Some consequences for psychoanalytic theorizing and practice. *Contemp. Psychoanal.,* 32:577–593.

Freud, S. (1937), Analysis terminable and interminable. *Standard Edition,* 23:209–253. London: Hogarth Press, 1964.

Hoffman, I. (1998), Constructing good enough endings in psychoanalysis. In: *Ritual and Spontaneity in the Psychoanalytic Process.* Hillsdale, NJ: Analytic Press, pp. 245–274.

Kohut, H. (1977), *The Restoration of the Self.* New York: International Universities Press.

Schachter, J., Martin, G. C., Gundle, M. J., & O'Neil, M. K. (1997), Clinical experience with psychoanalytic post termination meetings. *Internat. J. PsychoAnal.,* 78:1183–1198.

Shane, M., Shane, E., & Gales, M. (1997), *Intimate Attachments: Towards a New Self Psychology.* New York: Guilford Press.

Skolnikoff, A. Z. (1984), Cures by psychotherapy: What effects change? In: *Configurational Analysis: A Method to Measure Change in Psychotherapy,* ed. J. M. Meyers. New York: Praeger, pp. 125–131.

——— (1993), The analyst's experience in a psychoanalytic situation: A continuum between objective and subjective reality. *Psychoanal. Inq.,* 13:296–309.

10

What We Can Learn from Failures: Using the Analyst and the Countertransference "Fit"

R. D. HINSHELWOOD, M.D.

> *Our business in this world is not to succeed, but to continue to fail, in good spirits [R. L. Stevenson, 1878].*

Of all Freud's major case histories, perhaps only the Rat Man was a success. Freud seems to have learned most from his failures. He fell foul of the negative transference with Dora; and learned from it. The Wolf Man is another example of a therapeutic impasse leading to theoretical developments. That patient remained passively in a chronic positive transference to the point of exasperating Freud: "The patient with whom I am here concerned remained for a long time unassailably entrenched behind an attitude of obliging apathy" (Freud, 1918, p. 11). Freud's language, "unassailably entrenched," "obliging apathy," conveys an affective response to the patient. He is not complimentary. Freud continued:

> His shrinking from a self-sufficient existence was so great as to outweigh all the vexations of his illness. Only one way was to be found of overcoming it. I was obliged to wait until his attachment to myself had become strong enough to counter-balance this shrinking, and then played off this one factor against the other [p. 11].

The Wolf Man was intractably passive, and clearly Freud's descriptions convey an irritation and impatience.[1] Moreover, Freud then reacted on the basis of his emotional state. He became correspondingly active. He set the termination date with some decisiveness. We know that subsequently he was still active on the Wolf Man's behalf by finding money for him (even begging from friends on the patient's behalf; Jones, 1955). The patient settled for a transference neurosis as a substitute for getting better (Freud, 1914).

Freud did not interpret that transference, nor use his own countertransference interpretatively. Indeed psychoanalytic technique had not advanced enough for him to understand these forms of enactment between patient and analyst. So, instead, he developed his theoretical formulations instead of his

---

[1] I am grateful to Ian Runnacles for the following comment regarding the Strachey translation into English of the emotional tone of Freud's descriptions:

The sentences you quote, as published in German read: "Der Patient, mit dem ich mich hier beschäftige, blieb lange Zeit hinter einer Einstellung von gefügiger Teilnahmslosigkeit unangreifbar verschanzt. . . . Seine Scheu vor einer selbständigen Existenz war so groß, daß sie alle Beschwerden des Krankseins aufwog. Es fand sich ein einziger Weg, um sie zu überwinden. Ich mußte warten, bis die Bindung an meine Person stark genug geworden war, um ihr das Gleichgewicht zu halten, dann spielte ich diesen einen Faktor gegen den anderen aus." I think I might translate "einer Einstellung von gefügiger Teinahmslosigkeit" as "a stance of compliant indifference." However it is translated, it confirms your feeling about Wolf Man's passivity as contrasted with Freud's own active emotionality. I do not sense there is any softening by translating "unangreifbar verschanzt" as "unassailably entrenched." "Angriefen" (the verb) means to attack and "Schanze" means a trench and has (and had in 1918) definite militaristic connotations.

Wolf Man's "Scheu" (related to the English "to shy away from") might be better rendered as "timidity" or perhaps stronger as "dread"—there is a definite affect-content of this word. "Ich mußte warten" is simply "I had to wait"—"was obliged to" does add a tone of impatience which the German can sometimes express, but if he wished to emphasize the compulsion he might have used other words such as *gezwungen*, which have more countertransference strength, if it can be so called (Personal communication, 1999).

technique.[2] He wrote about his patient's active and passive identifications in the primal scene. In a way, that theorizing could be seen as his own defense against his frustration with the patient's passivity.

Looking at the dynamics revealed in this brief summary we can see an analyst struggling with an analysis that is failing. He then reacts to the failure in a way that is specific to the dynamics of that case. However, his reaction feeds right back into the dynamic situation. Ultimately, that unresolved transference continued permanently after the end of the analysis—and so did the countertransference. The analyst's reaction fitted in with the patient's transference, although this "fit" occurred entirely unconsciously.[3]

Impasse and Failure

The numbers of euphemisms—resistance, negative therapeutic reaction, impasse, and so on—suggest the analyst's attempt to remove the responsibility from his own shoulders onto the patient. No doubt this helps the analyst, wishing as we do, to feel good at our job. This paper challenges the simple view that analysts can simply avoid failure. Rather it is an investigation into a curious gain in understanding that can come from a failing analysis.

Rosenfeld (1987) gave a comparable example of an enduring impasse. This was Eric who after eight years of analysis (prior to meeting Rosenfeld), had reacted badly when the analyst suggested they finish.

Shortly after [the analyst's suggestion], he was suddenly overcome by strong feelings of contempt for the audience to whom

---

[2]Freud was, however, formulating at this time a technical view on repetition in the transference in his 1914 paper "Remembering, Repeating and Working Through." He was writing this when he was bringing the Wolf Man case to a termination. But clearly this theory of the transference had advanced beyond his ability to put it properly into practice at this time.

[3]I could use the term *collusion*, or the more fashionable *enactment*. Later I will show how Brenman Pick (1985) uses the term *mate* in exactly the same way as I use *fit*. Sandler (1976) too has his own term, *role-responsiveness*, to indicate this mutual unconscious responsiveness.

he was at that moment lecturing. These feelings were so strong
that he was scarcely able to finish the lecture. . . . He was very
shocked by the incident because lecturing had been an activity
he always enjoyed. . . .

[This] experience at the lecture had an enormous impact on
him and made him feel a very much increased need for help
and understanding through his analysis. He . . . felt in a great
dilemma because [the analyst] seemed to be as shocked and at
a loss as he was about what had happened; and this may have
been true. . . . [H]e had not been able to detect any feeling of
understanding in her. This impression may perhaps have been
influenced by the fact that it appeared [the analyst] had concentrated her interpretations after the lecture incident almost entirely on the triumph and contempt, which she thought Eric
was expressing towards her. He reported, for example, that she
said that he wanted enviously to destroy the success of the analysis and make her look entirely incompetent. Interpretations of
this kind were felt by Eric as critical angry remarks which increased his hopelessness and isolation and made him feel unable to put anything in order. . . .

[H]e had felt very critical of [the analyst] at the time. He felt
she seemed to be unconcerned about the pain, depression, and
hopelessness he was feeling. He wanted to have a second opinion. . . . [However] he was too frightened. He . . . felt threatened by her hostile power if he did not completely obey her
[Rosenfeld, 1987, pp. 140–141].

Thus, an impasse developed over a number of years. The
analyst then reduced the number of sessions to once a week,
which Eric "experienced as a further threat and as an illustra-
tion of [the analyst's] cruelty" (p. 141). So Eric had become
increasingly sensitive to and suspicious of the analyst, and indeed interpreted her interpretations. Or rather the patient *mis-*
interpreted her. He believed the analyst was not impelled by
helpful intentions but by cruel and punitive wishes, delivered
with words meant to hurt.

Again we see an analyst struggling with a failing analysis. Like
Freud, the analyst decides to end the analysis, and this seems
to feed straight into the patient's difficulties. His disappointment at the prospect of losing his analyst who will help him
learn more about his problems, brings out a reaction which is
not just one of realistic disappointment. He was overwhelmed
by feelings of panic as well. That suggests an extreme emotional

reaction—one that implies that Eric is terrified of something. It is something in his working, learning situation that he links with the occurrence in his therapeutic learning. What the terrifying something is, remains unknown to Eric or to his analyst.

In fact, the analyst was shocked by Eric's reaction to her suggestion, and she could not retain the position of a listening analyst, and failed to take in properly what he was saying to her. She did not see Eric's reaction as disappointment, but as triumph. No doubt she was badly affected by failing with Eric and his unexpected catastrophic reaction, and like him she too could no longer conduct a learning situation.

Speculatively, the analyst had projected a cruel superego into Eric, which made her feel unduly incompetent; whilst he also saw a cruel superego that he had projected into her, which wanted to get rid of him. Whilst suffering the painful impact of these dynamics, both patient and analyst move from an epistemophilic enquiry to a cruel set of fantasies that are the antithesis of learning from each other. Interestingly, this static and torturing analysis continued "over a number of years," and we have to assume that quite unconsciously, both were engaging in some "solution" to the superego guilty about failing.

These are two examples of failed analyses that descend into continuing impasse that somehow "satisfies" both partners. My thesis in this paper is that most (but not all) failed analyses result from similar misunderstanding and defensiveness, which if understood could teach us about our patients. Moreover, if understood they could also promote the analyst's continuing self-analysis, by revealing just those dynamics in which he or she becomes entrapped. In addition, by providing that increment of understanding, there is the possibility of freeing the impasse. Failures could offer such benefits were they not so unconscious for both parties—especially, we might note, the analyst's predicament in needing to know what is happening unconsciously whilst being taken over by it but without insight.

The purpose in writing about this thesis is to give the analyst a resource—some assistance in inquiring into his own relating when he is consciously unaware. A consciousness of the possibilities offered by failing can function as a first step in processing untoward occurrences in an analysis. That first step is to consider, when confronted by a negative therapeutic reaction, impasse or failure, whether some dynamic, but unconscious, "fit" between transference and countertransference has taken a grip on both partners.

Money-Kyrle's Paradigm

Analysts who get stuck were considered by Roger Money-Kyrle (1956) in his classic paper on countertransference. He described the normal analytic process as repeated cycles of projection and introjection. The patient, as he reports his associations, projects into the analyst in the sense that the analyst has a set of emotional responses. He has as it were taken in something emotional from the patient. The analyst then processes these introjects within himself. He formulates them in words and returns them as articulated meanings back to the patient. This return to the patient is a reprojection in the form of an interpretation. The patient, in turn, introjects those meanings. Along with them he introjects an object capable of making sophisticated meaning out of emotional experiences.[4] This is what happens "when all goes well" as Money-Kyrle puts it; however, things can go wrong. He then described how the analyst can get stuck in one of two positions. One is the *introjective* phase, so that he gets loaded with the patient's emotional experiences, which for his own reasons he fails to process adequately. The other position is the *projective* phase, when he evacuates the experiences in an unarticulated form back into the patient. In either case the analyst must, as Money-Kyrle puts it, "do a small piece of self-analysis." He admits this may often have to be after the session. This is a useful paradigm. It helps us to ask what is going on when things seem stuck and it gives us a schema for thinking about our experience of being stuck.

It is also useful to recognize that often it is a positive transference that catches us in the introjective phase—the introjection

---

[1]Initially, self-understanding is, in this model, an internalized object. Clearly it is akin to superego formation, but at the same time, self-understanding as an internal object, when identified with, can give moments of self-reflection.

being invariably ego syntonic. I suggest the Wolf Man's positive but passive acquiescence to Freud's work projected something active into Freud who was willing to accept it and hang onto it. The negative transference can provoke being stuck in the projective phase, when noxious experiences from the patient have to be expelled back into him. And I chose the example of Eric to illustrate a mutual (and desperate) process of projection, as if a harsh superego guilt was passed back and forth like a shuttlecock in a badminton match.

Irma Brenman Pick (1985) also described this problem of mutual "fit." It is with the positive transference with a Mr. A. He had come to London having had a psychoanalysis in another country and he invited a collusive engagement that threatened to lead to impasse through an enduring positive contact with the analyst.

> He arrived for his session a few hours after having been involved in a car accident. . . . He was clearly still in a state of shock, yet he did not speak of shock or fear. Instead he explained with excessive care what had taken place, and the correct steps taken by him before and after the accident. He went on to say that by chance his mother phoned soon after the accident, and when told about it responded with "I wouldn't have phoned if I had known you'd have such awful news. I don't want to hear about it." He said that thanks to his previous analysis, he knew that he needed to understand that his mother could not do otherwise, and he accepted that [Brenman Pick, 1985, p. 37].

We are presented with a very cooperative sounding patient who knows how to deal with a shock. The patient is very aware of the impact of "bad news" on mother who does not want to listen to it. She needed his "understandingness." "He was however very angry with the other driver, and was belligerent in his contention that he would pursue, if necessary to court, his conviction that he would have to pay for the damage" (p. 37). Despite his understandingness he can also feel a litigious grievance.

The protectiveness of the patient toward his mother is clear enough; and that is why he is so understanding. But the patient talks so calmly to this analyst when actually he is distressed.

Therefore, he must believe the analyst, too, will not want to hear bad news and he is equally protective about disturbing her. The other, but unconscious, attitude—he will pursue his grievances to the bitter end—means he is splitting his object: one he must understand and protect (his mother); and another that unconsciously he will grievously accuse.

What happened to the actual object (the analyst in the transference)? The patient *did* make an impact on the analyst "in his 'competent' way of dealing with his feelings, yet he also conveyed a wish for there to be an analyst/mother who would take his fear and his rage" (p. 38). This impact was a projection; not of his shock, but of his loneliness. His stoical "understandingness" did affect her maternal feelings and sympathy. Now this supposes, she says, "the transference onto the analyst of a more understanding maternal figure" (p. 38)—a mother in the analyst who could be aroused by his loneliness. Her sympathy for his lonely suffering was a response to his wish for a perfectly understanding mother. As she puts it, his projection of his loneliness, " 'mates' with some part of the analyst that may wish to 'mother' the patient in such a situation."

She found herself comparing her sympathy with the mother's, and feeling superior to mother; that was the analyst's countertransference. In this way, the analyst had joined the patient in a pattern of interaction that seemed perfectly sensible to him; and indeed to her. He needs a better mother, one who can cope with bad news, and she finds herself drawn to do that. In this case there is a cosy mother and son together; they enjoy the benefits of splitting off the angry litigious son who is aggrieved by being rejected for disturbing a fragile mother. The link between the patient's projective defense and the analyst's mothering responses promises a stuck introjective phase. The failure is based on the analyst introjecting an unconscious and ego-syntonic "good mother," and keeping it.

Unconscious Misunderstanding

These failures which result from a "fit" between transference and countertransference occur when both parties happily find each other willing to engage in a very specific exchange of projections and introjections. Though this cannot cover all failures, it might be claimed that it covers most *preventable* ones.

Unconsciously, the patient retreats from his problems by engaging the analyst's wish to respond, although consciously both believe they are pursuing an analysis. Perhaps we might recall Bion's injunction to abandon memory and desire, so that when we find in ourselves a wish to move things on—as Freud did with the Wolf Man—we could then trigger in ourselves the recall of this kind of "mating." Then, at least, we can spot the moments to "do a little bit of self-analysis." When we feel an unsettling sense of repetition and stuckness, we need to recall consciously, the possibility that we are unwittingly fitting in with the patient's defensive structure. Joseph says something similar to my paradigm for recognizing this kind of failure. In considering the patient's need of the analyst, she says she starts with "the way in which patients use us—analysts—to help them with anxiety. After all, the reason which brings patients into analysis is fundamentally that they cannot manage anxiety" (Joseph, 1978, p. 223).

A patient manages his anxiety as best he can. His method has failed in the past (after all, that is precisely why he is in analysis), but his belief in those means remains undimmed, because he lacks alternative resources. He will inevitably use the analyst in accord with his past belief, however despairing. That defensiveness, and distortion of his objects, is, in fact, what we term *transference,* and therefore what he will repeat. It does mean, however, that we have to be alive to a use of ourselves that opposes, or is tangential to, what we expect—the patient's use of us to gain insight.

Melanie Klein similarly advised, "we must understand what in the patient's mind analysis unconsciously stands for at any particular moment" (1943, p. 637). This implies that analysis may not in fact stand for what it does in the analyst's mind, and does not necessarily or consistently stand for self-understanding. So, the patient may be seeking nonanalytic ends in his use of the analyst.[5]

---

⁵I refrain from using the term *resistance* here—though I am speaking of one form of resistance—because I want to convey that there is an entirely reasonable sense in

I suggest he may even regard the pursuit of analysis as a reckless and dangerous path taken by the analyst, if unconsciously it means abandoning his past methods of coping. Part of the analysis is therefore to bring to consciousness the patient's wish for the analyst's help to shore up his defenses, as much as his wish for awareness. To illustrate this I shall describe the case of Mr B., a psychologist, who was about 40.

He was senior in his particular branch of his field, and with a good knowledge of psychoanalysis. He had previously been in psychoanalysis for eight years, and came to me because he felt that he often lacked the feelings he should have, and that they must be inaccessibly bottled up.

He was always frank with me about himself, and gave no impression of concealing or resisting. For instance, he was quite willing to talk of a possible homosexual interest in a friend he had once worked with. He could talk as intelligently and with as much psychoanalytic sophistication about himself, as I could. He was not boring; in fact, his words revealed quite a creative way of expressing himself.

But he experienced himself as emotionally blocked, and so did I. When a family tragedy occurred to relatives, he knew it was a tragedy. In the ensuing rituals he played his part efficiently, but he did not know if he really felt how affected he was. He had no tears. In fact he had not had tears since he was a child.

He started a session, the first one after a break over Christmas, not long after he started with me, by talking about his father-in-law who had phoned one day very anxious and distressed because his elderly wife had collapsed. He was very troubled because the doctor had not arrived. The father-in-law felt abandoned with this crisis and did not know what to do. My patient went on to talk of a colleague who had left the country. That man had left his wife and children when he emigrated, but was due to return for a brief period to see the children. However, he missed the flight. My patient thought that the children would be distressed.

---

avoiding analytic understanding and in combating the wish for it, from the patient's point of view.

He was telling me of the abandoned feeling that both his father-in-law and his friend's children experienced. Commonly, after a break in analysis, patients talk of distressed and abandoned people, who usually represent the patient's feelings, which have been denied. When that is interpreted, a patient will either become thoughtful and appreciate something new in himself, or he will resist the interpretation strongly; but not so with my patient. He simply agreed that the abandoned people's distress might represent his own distress about the break. The problem with his agreement was that it seemed merely on the surface. My interpretation did nothing to put him in touch with any distress. Indeed it seemed as if those abandoned people he talked about were not *representations* of something in him at all. In other words, his distress was no longer in him, it was in *them*.

At this point, faced with his bland agreement, I decided to point out the difficulty of locating his distress. He agreed with this, too, in the same unruffled way. He talked then of something being locked up in him—he talked of a sealed "box" inside him. His appreciation of the problem was sophisticated, and he understood the unusual structure of his own mind. Curiously, I found myself engaged and interested in this division in his personality and how clearly he was describing it. I was responding to a strong move on his part to securely establish his professional self, one that could then be used by him to discuss *"about"* himself.

I was in a curious state. On the one hand, I felt my interest aroused by the problem that his case posed, and the fact that he could talk so eloquently about his problems. At the same time, I felt a strong frustration.

This man managed his distress by requiring everyone else around him to experience it—except for himself. As a psychologist, he knew enough intellectually to interest me, but as a personality, he could unconsciously use me to support his psychological sophistication with creative discussions. I thus assisted his habitual method of avoiding any depth of emotional knowledge of his experiences—and he endured a largely shallow or deadened experience of life and of himself. Sophisticated as he was, this patient was committed to a relationship with the analyst in which he would not feel the distress he knew he needed help with.

There was a deep sense of not meeting each other. The patient produced emotional-sounding material. The analyst gave what the patient was in need of—interpretations. The patient then used interpretations as interesting professional discussions. The analyst's professional interest was aroused—as a professional. But in so doing, both parties preserved a distance from distress. The analyst's aim of insight was received in such a way as to reinforce the patient's professional self. They are not meeting. This is clearly a failure of analysis that could produce an impasse.

As this analysis progressed, and awareness of the fear of abandoning the defensive posture increased, he eventually told me a dream:

> In the dream, he was in a house with some people. A Dr. X. was examining a wall and recommending that a hole or doorway be made in the wall. Through the hole a view would then be seen. That view would be a spit with meat cooking on it, there was some rusty old machinery which might be useful as a barbecue. Further away across a country valley were some houses, a village. But all the houses were leaning over. He realized that his own house was leaning too.
>
> He described Dr. X. as a practical person, a problem solver. Also he knows Dr. X.'s wife, in real life as well. She is a busy person who is always feeding people. Later he recalled that he knew Dr. X.'s wife is a work colleague of mine.

The relevance of this dream to my theme is twofold. First, it is clear that he has some thoughts about breaking out of his "sealed box"—the hole in his wall, and, in the dream, Dr. X., the problem solver, is clearly connected with myself, the analyst. But a second thought is that the result of Dr. X.'s—or my—efforts to expand the patient's view, would be to destabilize the world and the structure that Mr. B. lives in. So, success in the efforts to expand his analytic view threatens, he believes, to destabilize his mind; the psychic structure he inhabits will lean over. This is a stark warning from the patient—and is he wrong?

In my view he is appealing, unconsciously, for help in avoiding a calamity that will occur if I go on pushing him to break out of his confined walls. So, one use of the analyst would be to support his walls. By finding in me a willingness to discuss interpretations with the sophisticated psychologist in him, I am the kind of support that protects his psychic structure—his professional identity—against the calamity. The warning is that if I really help to see through to the hungry side of him (the cooking/barbecue), then he will be overwhelmed by a hungry perhaps greedy baby, and he will collapse.[6]

This complex situation is best understood by considering two motivations for continuing the analytic sessions. The patient wants to come because he has certain problems—of missing affects, and the analyst wants to conduct an analysis of these problems. The patient also wants something else—to escape from his fear that discovery of his feelings and opening up of the status quo will destabilize his mind. He expects, as he has always done, that he will erect a robust personal structure as a sophisticated psychologist ("internal" walls as it were against his wobbly stability) to ensure the affects remain out of sight. The analyst enjoyed joining a sophisticated discussion with the patient, thus fitting the patient's defensive need. The patient has "mated" successfully with a professional aspect of the analyst that seeks to make interpretations.

How can the analyst deal with this potential impasse, given that it is his unconscious that is powerfully involved? He might be aided by two things—first, a degree of frustration as a signal, and second, a recognition that such a frustration can indicate that he and his patient have formed a "fit" (or mating) between transference and countertransference. This can set the analyst thinking, consciously at least, that he is being used (in part) by a patient motivated against analytic understanding, and motivated for coping methods. Having achieved those steps, even mechanically, he has reached a position where he knows it will be worth considering the countertransference.

---

[6]This point of view insists that the motivation for treatment is a conflicted area; there is not a conflict-free autonomous therapeutic alliance.

Using the Analyst's Wish to Analyze

There is another interesting arrangement conveyed in the dream, which leads to a particularly tricky situation for the analyst. Although the patient is being host to the problem-solving Dr. X./analyst, the motivation to open up (motivation for a wider view) is absent from the patient. His own wish for analytic understanding is no longer part of himself. It resides as it were in the analyst and in the analyst's wish to give analytic advice. The patient's motivation to make progress (rather than retreat) has mated, as Brenman Pick would say, with the analyst's similar motivation, but then resides within the problem-solving analyst. In this way, the patient has *used* the analyst. That use is to afford an escape from the danger of a wider understanding. He needs his analyst to go on providing this escape for him. The patient is then left only with the wish to have an interesting sophisticated discussion *about* the dream. Whilst the analyst has introjected and represents the wish to learn, the patient retains *only* his defensive use of the analyst. In this case, the analysis is stuck in the analyst's introjective phase, containing in the analyst what the patient has projected into him, the patient's very motivation to understand himself.

This is perhaps a particularly obtuse problem—the patient's projection into the analyst's wish to analyze! This is difficult and entangled for the analyst; he receives an ego-syntonic projection. Every time the analyst's motivation leads to an interpretation to inform the patient of something that is not known, the patient thinks it is an opportunity to project his own motivation for treatment into the analyst.

It is my claim that the analysis is especially prone to fall victim to a transference–countertransference "mating" when this particular pattern of projections has become established. In other words, it is the patient's own wish to understand himself which is projected into the analyst; and it is a projection which is most likely to "mate" with the comparable part of the analyst and to remain stuck there, just because the analyst is motivated to understand the patient. This very specific use of the analyst ensures that when the analyst is doing his job of creating understanding, he is precisely at that moment also engaged in a collusive enactment with the patient.

When doing his job coincides with a defensive collusion, the analyst has the most difficulty finding his way out;[7] and in most need of the prompts to his thinking which I have suggested.

Discussion

I have concentrated on a particular experience of stuckness that leads to an enduring frustration from which analyst and patient find great difficulty escaping. It leads one or other, at least, to contemplate an arbitrary ending. It is, in my view, possible to trace this kind of potential impasse to a particularly close fit between transference and countertransference. I have illustrated one of the most difficult occurrences when the patient's motivation is itself projected into the analyst's.

I have not illustrated another tricky situation. Not uncommonly, the analyst gets a sharp experience of failure, an occurrence resulting from the patient's attempt to get across to the analyst his own intolerable feeling of failure. A projection of this kind is a little more easy for the analyst to identify as a countertransference experience. In this case, the patient has projected his sense of failure into the analyst's feeling of failing. For instance, inexperienced trainees have anxieties about learning the job which are potentially very available aspects of the analyst for the patient to project into.

I have chosen to exclude in this paper those patients who manifest particularly strong primary destructiveness. Those are patients who want to bring envy of such a degree that they are relentlessly compelled to prove that the analyst is not better able than they to cope with it. Envying the analyst renders the patient incapable of working with the analyst. Usually such patients do not stay long in treatment.

Related to this is another kind of patient, one which has received a lot of attention recently. Here, the negativity is dominant, but in addition such people seem to gain excitement

---

[7] It seems to me that this contorted problem is more common as societal knowledge of analysis and interpretations increases; as well, it might become more common as long analyses proceed and the patient gains more understanding of how to use his analyst's professional ambitions.

from their own negativity. They appear to erotize the defeat of the analyst in a sadomasochistic satisfaction. Perversely they *do* remain in treatment, simply because they gain satisfaction for cruel, erotic wishes. Their distress may then be worked with slowly (Joseph, 1989).

Sometimes less experienced analysts can easily miss technical problems. They attribute difficulties in the analysis to unbridled envy or unassailable resistance in the patient, when actually attention to the countertransference problems, as Money-Kyrle described, would reveal that the difficulty could well yield to a small piece of self-analysis instead.[8] And this therefore is a major reason to dwell on the impasses that arise from transference–countertransference "mating"; they can potentially be overcome.

These cases of transference–countertransference "fit" are very specific. Freud's patient, the Wolf Man, found an active side of Freud. For Eric it was a punitive superego; Brenman Pick's Mr. A. found her mothering wishes; and for Mr. B. it was the intellectual professional in me.

These occurrences might be gathered under Freud's term *transference neurosis* (Freud, 1914), but I have formulated this concept in terms of object relations. The impact of the patient's object search on the analyst's, affects both of them at all levels. The patient seeks out an aspect of the analyst that is comfortingly defensive for both (Hinshelwood, 1985). Because I am drawing attention to the unconscious level of defensiveness, the analyst is faced with the central problem of technique; how can he address his own unconscious defensiveness?

Intuitively, analysts have been attracted to the rule of abstinence. The analyst should not seek any affective gratification at all from the relationship. This in the past amounted to sustaining the steely posture of the blank screen. This nonreactive, satisfaction-eschewing role is no longer credible. It simply is not human. In object-relations terms the analyst cannot simply become a nonrelating person—he would then cease to be a

---

[8]These two forms of dominant negativity—envy, and the response to not feeling understood—may not be easy to distinguish. For instance Bion remarks of a patient who felt not listened to, that "His behaviour, isolated from the context of analysis, might have appeared to be an expression of primary aggression" (Bion, 1959, p. 103).

person. The analysand's perception of the analyst as a nonperson, a "mechanical brain" (Heimann, 1960, p. 152), has led to reactions against psychoanalysis all over the world. For half a century, psychoanalysis has been working out a new relationship with the reality of the analyst as a person (Hinshelwood, 1999). We have to accept the analyst's personality, warts and all.

A formulation of Bion's may help more than the rule of abstinence. He described L-, H-, and K-links between patient and analyst. The K-link is one in which the persons are linked in knowing and being known. Parallel there are two other links—L- and H-links. They mean, respectively, loving and being loved and hating and being hated. The purpose of an analysis is the production of new knowledge (K-link)—about the patient. However, as human beings, we cannot know the patient outside of his relations with others, and in particular his relationship with the analyst. Inevitably, the relationship consists of more than generating insight (K-link)—the specific ego-syntonic and ego-dystonic "fits" contribute to the L- and H-links.

Though an analytic setting consists of a K-link, a joining in knowledge production, both partners will automatically offer the potential for all three links. Therefore the structure of an analytic setting concentrates on a K-link devoted to knowing about those other links, L- and H-links. A kind of dominance in the analytic setting of the K-link over the other two is supposed. A rule of abstinence that outlaws L- and H-links, inevitably obstructs a K-link, which has to address the other two dimensions. Knowledge has to await the gathering of each partner into the transference in *all* dimensions.

Knowledge that is gained without a full and developing appreciation of these other dimensions is shallow and useless, as my patient, Mr. B., demonstrated—a minus-K-link, a form of the K-link that is devoted to not knowing. That kind of knowingness which Mr. B. illustrated well, does not produce knowledge. We can easily say in those circumstances that there is a problem with the K-link, and with epistemophilia, which must be reestablished. But my claim here is that focusing only on the degradation of K to minus-K misses the patient's actual diversion to L- or H-links. In other words, when K ceases, and knowledge production falls to zero, then it is worth checking if L- or H-links have gained dominance in the session. It is worth doing so as interpretations of that slippage to L or H is productively interpretable, and an impasse could be prevented.

In this sense of being engaged in all three dimensions, psychoanalysis is a practice that is set up to fail. Inevitably we fall from our aim of insight into the intensity of other emotional links. We fail at the rule of abstinence, as a matter of course. I have proposed a different rule of thumb, different from the harsh rule of abstinence, one that accepts the inevitability of our finding ourselves mated in collusions and learning from them.

The patient's need of analysis turns out to be only partly to gain understanding—to understand what, as Freud described, he already knows, unconsciously. We, as analysts, similarly are only partly in line with the patient's partial commitment. We find respite from the directive to learn, by solace in extraneous relationships the patient seeks and invites; those relationships that above all we aim to learn about.

That realization of mixed intentions on both sides has, curiously, opened a whole new field of understanding so that we can learn from technical failures as much as from successes. Psychoanalysis is oddly robust when it comes to the pitfalls of human relations. We not only learn about analytic theory (as in the Dora and Wolf Man cases) but also we learn specifically about each analysand. Psychoanalysis has something of the quality of a *via negativa*.

The psychoanalytic euphemisms for "failures"—*impasse, stuckness, negative therapeutic reaction*—are manifest in many instances as a joint slippage from the task of learning from being with each other. However, as analysts we have a particular method that can turn failures to advantage by understanding them. We have not an ideal model at which we fail sometimes, but a model which has failures at its core.

References

Bion, S. R. (1959), Attacks on linking. *Internat. J. Psycho-Anal.,* 40:308–315.

Brenman Pick, I. (1985), Working through in the countertransference. *Internat. J. Psycho-Anal.*, 66:157–166.

Freud, S. (1914), Remembering, repeating and working-through. *Standard Edition*, 12:145–156. London: Hogarth Press, 1958.

——— (1918), From the history of an infantile neurosis. *Standard Edition*, 17:1–122. London: Hogarth Press, 1955.

Heimann, P. (1960), Counter-transference. In: *About Children and Children-No-Longer.* London: Routledge, 1989, pp. 151–160.

Hinshelwood, R. D. (1985), The patient's defensive analyst. *Brit. J. Psychotherapy*, 2:30–41.

——— (1999), Countertransference. *Internat. J. Psycho-Anal.*, 80(4):797–818.

Jones, E. (1955), *Sigmund Freud: Life and Work*, Vol. 2. London: Hogarth Press.

Joseph, B. (1978), Different types of anxiety and their handling in the analytic situation. In: *Psychic Equilibrium and Psychic Change.* London: Routledge, 1989, pp. 106–115.

——— (1989), *Psychic Equilibrium and Psychic Change.* London: Routledge.

Klein, M. (1943), Memorandum on her technique. In: *The Freud-Klein Controversies 1941–1945*, ed. P. King & R. Steiner. London: Routledge, 1991, pp. 635–638).

Money-Kyrle, R. (1956), Normal counter-transference and some of its deviations. *Internat. J. Psycho-Anal.*, 37:360–366.

Rosenfeld, H. (1987), *Attention and Interpretation.* London: Routledge.

Sandler, J. (1976), Countertransference and role-responsiveness. *Internat. Rev. Psycho-Anal.*, 3:43–47.

11

Memory, Desire, and Understanding: Failures in Psychoanalytic Experiencing

JOSÉ AMÉRICO JUNQUEIRA DE MATTOS, M.D.

Introduction

The following example of a treatment *failure* comes from the third year of work with a four-times-a-week analytic patient. I wanted to take some notes during a session hoping that this would help me more clearly remember and provide a more *faithful* transcription of the session. My patient became aware of this, and the vignette that follows revolves around both the patient's and my own emotional experiences during the subsequent session. The vignette highlights the failure involved in both the desire to take notes as well as the attempt on my part to conceal this from my patient. My analysand, indeed, showed an awareness that my desire to take notes created a third object—the notes—that came between the patient and myself, thus weakening the link between us. This can be seen as reflective of Bion's ideas on the use of memory and desire during the session, where the development of the intersubjective emotional experiences of the analytic pair clearly shows the need for precise observation of what occurs during each session, the presentation of facts that are very often obvious, but nonetheless go unnoticed. In the following case I failed to see that the introduction of notes led to the presence of a foreign body in the dyad: the notes. I will also introduce theoretical speculations on the appropriateness or otherwise of using memory and desire, and conclude that if memory and desire are undesirable states during analytic work, then the most suitable state of mind for the analyst is that of having *faith*. This is a state of believing that there is an unconscious truth to be discovered or at least approached. This truth, however, is never attained, because as the analyst and analysand near it, new and renewed paths open out before them.

Clinical Material and Comments

I beeped my secretary over the intercom and asked her to send in my next patient. During the time it took my patient to walk down the hall to my consulting room, I took out a piece of paper from a pad, folded it, and placed it in my pocket as the patient entered the office. My patient lay on the couch but said nothing: a highly unusual experience. She then asked if I took notes during the sessions. I gave an evasive response that, as we shall see, satisfied neither of us. At this point I decided not to take notes, ending this issue, or so I thought.

The session that followed, a rare double session (100 minutes without a break) will be described. The patient entered the room, lay down on the couch, and remained silent for about ten minutes, which once again was unusual for her.

Analyst:	Why the silence?
Patient:	You seem to disapprove of something in me, or it's me who would like to be different. The other day you said that I was getting in the way of Dr. F.'s work. (Pause)
Patient:	The last session you didn't tell me whether you take notes or not. It's always been very important for me to tell the truth here, but you

gave me an evasive answer. Now I'd like to know directly if you take notes or not. I never felt that you wrote things down. In fact, I'd like to feel that you are with me while I'm here.

Comments: The patient clearly noticed my evasiveness. She apparently wants to know if I take notes or not in order to evaluate how I relate to her during the sessions. I now feel that it would have been better to have clearly admitted that I had intended to take notes and then discarded this idea. In being unable to freely admit this to the patient, I created two problems: she felt persecuted and imagined that she was hampering the work of analysis—alluded to in her reference to Dr. F. Second, on that occasion I felt that it was not my role to confess my mistakes and failures, burdening the analysand with my problems and difficulties. Although this is true in general, at that moment (and this opinion changed during the course of the session) my thinking was a rationalization that defended against my guilt feelings for not having been in a position to be sincere with my patient.

Analyst: You feel there is something between you and me and you call this *taking* notes.

Comments: In retrospect I might have said "You feel that I have placed something between us" having realized that I indeed placed a third object—the notes—between my patient and myself.

Patient: But you didn't answer me. I wanted a direct answer.

Analyst: I think that if you insist on something, on a direct answer, and keep on insisting, you create a difficulty. Your insisting keeps our work from moving ahead.

Comments: I see this as one more rationalization based on the mechanism of projective identification, in my thinking that her insistence in wanting a direct answer represented her desire to control me during the session. In fact, since I was unable to be sincere at that moment, I was the one who unconsciously wanted to control the patient.

Patient: I never lied here and I never felt that you were lying. I've always been free to say what I felt. Now, for the first time, I don't feel this here. I thought that what I felt here was direct, between you and me, with no interference. I always thought there was a situation of one person to another. Not saying what I felt would be to deny the obvious. I didn't like the feeling that I was in the position of a person being observed, a clinical case.

Comments: The patient realizes the need for the truth and relies upon my openness to the truth. She clearly feels that there is no knowledge in a lie and therefore no growth. If I take notes, she feels that she becomes a clinical case, an object to be studied. My attention would not be focused on her as a human being, but as an object for scientific purposes and an object of curiosity, rather than a state of concern for her feelings. The function of analysis would be displaced from the purposes for which she sought it out to an end that interested the analyst. By using projective identification, I was attempting to "take possession" of her mind in order to convince her that it was her insistence on knowing the truth that was creating the difficulties at that moment, and not the fact that I had been evasive. Additionally, when she sought analysis, she was hoping to understand her relationship with her husband in the hope of saving her marriage. She did not come to play the role of a clinical case, as an object of my curiosity and desire. This occurrence, even if only momentary, would characterize a parasitic link (Bion, 1970) that strips the analytic relationship of its vitality and creativity, making it persecutory and confusing for the analysand and a source of guilt and anxiety for the analyst.

Analyst: Is that how you feel now?

Patient: Yes. I never felt like that here before. I always felt there was something direct. I felt you with me, something that had never happened to me before. I felt that something very good was growing inside me, coming from a place a long way from me. I had the feeling of something closely related to me. And now this happens! This is the first time I've felt like this. When I was in that medical treatment, I had some tests taken that were sent to that doctor. I asked him if he had read the results. He didn't answer and said that I would have to remain in doubt. I didn't want to respond, but I didn't feel like saying anything else either. I thought that if he knew the results of the tests, he didn't need my participation any more. I asked him why he didn't answer, since it would be a simple matter, and it was important to me.

Comments: My patient talks about the experience she is having of a creative relationship in the analysis, characterized by: (1) not lying and (2) having no interference by a third object. The creative relationship evolves from the knowledge acquired in the direct relationship to the analyst in the here-and-now, the intersubjective emotional experiences in the analytic link. The important thing is what my patient says, not what is contained in any tests or notes. It is dynamic, created in the elusive flashing instance of the relationship between her and me. It therefore requires the concrete participation of both parties. The nonparticipation of one interferes with this dynamic and prevents movement in the session (Bion, 1967b), thereby preventing the appearance of the new, which constitutes the creativity of the link. Her anxiety is due to her fear that if I take notes, I will fail to open up a mental space for her within myself. The relationship would thus momentarily become impoverished and sterile. She also feels persecuted and afraid that a relationship that had been developing well for her may now be threatened by the introduction of a third object that is foreign to the dynamic between us—the notes.

Analyst: I think you feel that I already have everything "written down" and I won't need you to contribute any more. I would only have to consult my notes, my memory. We would then not be present together.

Patient: No, I don't feel that way. This thing of being present is only with me. You would need to take notes, to have something to know what went on. Where there is a real feeling, it doesn't depend on memorization (memory), it's there of itself. In the earlier treatment, I sometimes felt the need to write. I was afraid I couldn't contain things inside me. Here with you that only happened at the beginning, but not any more. I now feel that it's you who is in this position, not me. I don't feel the need to write because I feel you inside me. When I was in the other treatment I felt lost, distant, without the possibility of return. I would get home, see my kids, and feel that there was an insurmountable barrier. Sometimes I wrote down everything that happened and I was able to faithfully reproduce things. I often wanted to remember what had happened—this was after a certain time—but I couldn't. I had to read. I wasn't inside me, it was "written down." Today, I find you inside me. It doesn't depend on notes, you don't have me inside you.

Comments: I think she is here making a distinction between memory, on the one hand, which leads to a parasitic relationship, and on the other, a symbiotic relationship that is the product of her working through the development between container-contained (Bion, 1970). What is also implicit here is the distinction she makes between memory as a conscious attempt to recall and memory with dreamlike qualities that appears suddenly and atemporally. If the analysis serves the function of the development of a positive container–contained relationship, memory or notes can be completely done away with. She also realizes that a relationship that depends on memory or notes is weak and artificial. Bion (1967b, 1970) speaks of a type of "memory" that is essential in analytic work, one he called "dream memory." I shall return to this later.

Analyst: Did you read about this in some book on psychoanalysis?

Patient: No, it's how I feel. I didn't read about it in any book!

Comments: She referred so clearly to the model of the container–contained link in the analytic relationship (Bion, 1962b, 1970) that I felt forced to ask her if she had read about it, even though she did not work in any area remotely related to psychology. This once again shows us the importance of careful observation—as she was doing at this time—and how we as analysts can learn from our patients. What they bring us are not theories found in psychoanalytic texts, but a vivid understanding that unfolds before both of us, and is observable to both provided that the analyst "has the eyes to see" and is not "blinded" by his or her own needs, such as in my case, the taking of notes during the session.

Analyst: Do you imagine that I take notes during the session or afterwards?

Patient: During the session I feel like you're rejecting what I'm saying at the moment. Later it's different. You think, concentrate, get involved in it. Then I'm with you.

Analyst: Analysts occasionally write things down. I'm not saying whether I do or don't take notes. But this is done after the session. However, if this is so important to you, my way of working doesn't include taking notes during the session.

Comments: The climate of the session immediately changed and my patient was clearly relieved. It was as if I had said "I can contain you inside me. I now have room inside me for you." Understanding and exchange were reestablished, with the "failure in the analytic treatment" being amended. If we conceptualize in terms of internal object relations, we might say that the pair went from a schizoparanoid moment to a depressive one, where the analysand was depressed, she felt persecuted by the fear of losing both the analysis, and with it, the analyst, as a good internal object, while concurrently I felt anxious and persecuted by the guilt of not having been able to be sincere with her.

A few minutes of silence followed after my last intervention:

Patient: One of the things that has really improved since I started seeing you is the way I treat my children. You once said that there was no place inside me for my son D.; and this keeps him from getting closer to me. Now this has changed. This is why analysis is so important to me. This is the first time in my life that I have found some correspondence, that there's a place inside you for me. One difficulty I have with my husband is that he always answers in an oblique or diagonal way. So I was very afraid, because if you didn't answer me, something might break inside me. I might have come here and not been able to speak even if I wanted to.

Comments: She emphasizes that the analysis has been helpful in her developing the function of a container for both positive and negative capacities.

The son she is referring to is her youngest child. One of her complaints was that she wasn't able to be the mother she wanted to be with her older children. She hadn't been able to get close to them, but through the analysis she has been progressively developing the functions of container. She feels that it is essential that there is some correspondence, that is, that there be a space for both in the analytic relationship. She feels that her husband does not give her room. Her anxiety is that if I take notes then there will be no room for her inside me either, no correspondence in essence. That is, at the moment I am paying attention to what I am writing down, I am not psychically available to listen to her, and our relationship would move from a symbiotic to a parasitic one, if only for an instant. For her, correspondence is a dynamic container–contained relationship through intersubjective emotional experiences. She also has a clear understanding of unconscious phenomena and of unconscious defenses. Metaphorically, she was saying that while her feet could bring her to session her tongue might remain silent or even paralyzed. In other words, internal availability does not depend on conscious control or simple will.

Patient: My husband says I'm using some kind of Chinese torture on D.; repeating "Mommy missing in you," inside him. I think you have the feeling of having a mother inside you, but she is very distant. With analysis the feeling of having had a mother is beginning to come back again more intensely.

Comments: Even though aspects of my intervention came from my patient's associations, I think that I was at least partially betrayed here by the use of memory. Since early childhood my patient had serious difficulties with her mother to the point of saying that she had no notion of "mother." During the course of the treatment we discovered that this difficulty probably originated when she was an infant around the age of 4 months and was left with her grandmother as her parents traveled off to Europe. When they returned five months later, my patient no longer accepted her biological mother and was from then on regularly cared for by her grandmother. My patient claims that she was a "happy baby" having been breast-fed prior to the departure of her parents for Europe. After that incident she even refused the bottle and had to be spoon fed by the grandmother. My patient had the experience of having a generous mother in the sense of a "good breast." What she complains of is the absence, the separation, the loss of that mother and that "breast." She seems to have had the experience of something good that was subsequently lost, rather than of its never having been there. This is what she misses, what is longed for (Klein, 1957). I introduced this theoretical formulation into the session even though it was somewhat out of context. At that moment she seemed to be talking about something else, about her husband's feeling that the youngest son, in order to develop healthily, should introject not only the mother figure but also the masculine father image. If this did not happen, the fear was that something would be missing and the oedipal conflict would not come to a normal resolution.

Patient: Analysis has helped me a lot to get in touch with my children.

Analyst: Yes, you feel that you are learning to be a mother because you are starting to feel a mother inside you more clearly. Maybe you feel that I'm able to arouse this mother inside you, that before was someplace very far away.

Comments: I am basing my intervention on the idea that through the analytic process analogous to the primal relationship with the mother, and, even earlier with the mother's breast, the analysand can create an "apparatus for thinking" by creating the functions of a container and by internalizing the analyst's alpha function. This too I will return to in my discussion section.

Patient: Yes. I think so. But what I feel toward you is very complex and varied. I was invited to be the speaker of honor for a class of girls. I'm going to have to give a speech using a microphone. I don't think there will be any problem if I have to talk directly to the girls, but I have to use the microphone and that gives me the feeling of it being something too planned. I think I'll sound too distant and that this will cause me some difficulties.

Analyst: The microphone is like the notes. You'd have to remember in order to talk, and this sets up a barrier.

Comments: My patient returned to the subject of the third object, now the microphone, wedged between her and the audience. It is of interest to note that at the beginning of the previous session I had asked my secretary to send her into my office. In this kind of arrangement, the secretary can also often feel or act or be felt as a third object between the analyst and the analysand. Since unconscious factors are often operative, even when the employee has been well instructed, this aspect of the setting also affords possibilities for various types of acting out and manipulation by both the patient and the secretary. For this reason, I have since rearranged my office, having my secretary placed in a room to which my patients do not have access. I believe that this is an important point in regard

to technique and should be considered as crucial in maintaining the analytic frame.

Patient: That reminds me that my cousin also asked me
to write her graduation speech for her. She's
going to be the class valedictorian and she mentioned several possible topics for me to write
about. That was quite a while ago and I haven't
been able to put anything down on paper yet.
Yesterday she phoned me and I told her I
hadn't written anything and I started to talk to
her about the speech. She got going and we
were on the phone for over an hour. She said
that she wanted me to write about what we had
been talking about and all I had to do was write
down what we had just said. After I hung up I
felt that everything was so distant, as if it had
disappeared from my mind, as if it only existed
while I was talking to her, and that I might not
be able to reproduce what I had said. If I wrote
it down it would come out differently.

Comments: The session ended and there was no time for
any comments from me to her. It seemed, however, that what was artificial was that her cousin
wanted her to write something that only the
cousin herself could feel. In the same way, it is
artificial if the analyst brings in the past as memory related to some theory that he imagines the
patient is employing at that moment. The patient can direct the analyst's attention to the
complex and varied nature of what is happening
now, which does not of necessity fit within the
narrowing confines of any given theory. Even
though our theories are valuable, even indis-
pensable, they are incapable of containing and
explaining all phenomena that the analytic experience as well as life in general with all its
diversity affords us. As in the conversation with
my patient and her cousin, the analytic conversation is constructed by two people. If the analyst tries to write down everything the patient

> says he or she would fall for sure into the trap
> mentioned by Bion (1970): "The container can
> squeeze everything 'out of' the contained: or
> the 'pressure' may be exerted by the contained
> so that the container disintegrates. An illustra-
> tion would be the word used as a metaphor until
> the background is lost and the word loses its
> meaning" (p. 107).

If the analyst hears what the patient-contained says, he internally creates room for what the patient is expressing, and we
have what Bion called a "symbolic link." But if the analyst tries
to write down everything the patient says, he is running the
risk of stripping the patient's words of their meaning, because
what is being said is not being grasped, contained, or transformed by the analyst, but merely written down. Instead of
being assimilated, it would be like a foreign body inside the
analyst, and this characterizes a "parasitic link."

In this regard Bion (1970) states: "Thus an extremely greedy
patient may want to obtain as much as he can from his analysis
while giving as little as possible: we should expect this to show
itself by frequent events in which the container was denuding
the contained object, and vice-versa" (p. 109).

I would now state that the analyst who takes notes during a
session is in the position of this voracious patient, leading to
the impoverishment or destruction of the container–contained
relationship. I think my patient was saying this when she said:
"During the session (when notes are taken) I feel like you're
rejecting what I'm saying at the moment. Later, it's different.
You think, concentrate, get involved in it. Then I'm with you."

Theoretical Considerations

Bion's recommendation (1967b, 1970) that in every session
the analyst should work to avoid "memory, desire and understanding" is one of his most important contributions to psychoanalytic technique. If we as analysts insert ourselves in time,
which continuously "goes by," if we are preoccupied with what

our patient said fifteen minutes ago, half an hour ago, or even yesterday, the day before yesterday, last month, six months ago, or last year, our attention will be diverted from what is going on *now at this exact instant*. Likewise, if one tries to understand what the patient has just said, one will immediately stop hearing what the patient is saying at this exact moment, interfering with what one might be able to "hear" of what the patient is "creating" inside the analyst. I see (Junqueira de Mattos, 1997) this idea of Bion's as having both a theoretical as well as philosophical foundation in the following excerpt from St. Augustine:

> How is the future, that does not yet exist, reduced and consumed? And how does the past, that is no longer, grow, except because, in the soul, there are three things: the present, the past and the future? The soul in fact awaits, pays attention and recalls, so that what it waits for, enters the domain of memory through what it pays attention to. No one denies that the future does not yet exist; but the expectation of the future already exists in the soul. No one denies that the past no longer exists, but the memory of things past still exists in the soul. And no one denies that the present lacks duration, because it soon falls into the past: but attention lasts for what it is now and fades toward the past [*Confessions*, XI.28.1].

St. Augustine condensed this fundamental proposition into the statement that "Strictly speaking, there are not three times, the past, the present and the future, but only three presents: the present of the past, the present of the present and the present of the future" *(Confessions*, XI.20.1).

In other words, like all else, the analytic session takes place only in the present. Thus when an analysand refers to the past, which no longer exists, or to a future which does not yet exist, whatever the person is feeling, is being felt at that exact moment. Therefore, strictly speaking, one can say that it can neither be relived nor anticipated.

In a previous paper (in press), I elaborated on the idea that all analytic experience is transitory, with each analytic session having its own nonrepeatable history. Only the invariants in the transformation process remain (Bion, 1965), safeguarding the sense of identity. From this perspective, if the analyst strives to avoid using memory and desire in the analytic work, one can try to grasp what Bion calls *evolution*, that which evolves from the contact between the unconscious of analyst and patient, themselves generating shared intersubjective emotional experiences that present themselves through visual images and free associations. Such evolution presents what is new and has, until then, been unknown to both analyst and patient. Bion (1967b) stated that: "In any session, evolution takes place. Out of the darkness and formless something evolves. That evolution can bear a superficial resemblance to memory, but once it has been experienced it can never be confounded with memory. It shares with dreams the quality of being wholly present or unaccountably and suddenly absent. This evolution is what the psychoanalyst must be ready to interpret" (p. 272).

If this evolution is grasped and the analyst provides an interpretation, a change can occur in the analytic field whereby both participants arrive at new states of mind, new creative moments, new unknown paths: to something beyond. Since every session takes place in the fleeting and ephemeral present, that instance of time has no return and cannot be repeated. Here memory as a defense connects us to the past, while desire anticipates the future, giving the *illusion* of continuity for our experiences in time. While time is essential for using memory, for evolution, and for memory with its dreamlike qualities, time is irrelevant because this kind of memory is immediate and atemporal (Bion, 1970). In fact, all experiences in session, except for the invariants maintained during the process (Bion, 1965), consist of discontinuous moments that change in function constantly as a result of the intersubjective emotional experiences shared by the analytic pair, during the process of evolution of the session.

The use of memory and desire can be viewed as related to the pleasure principle; the avoidance of displeasure. We use memory and desire to flee from the frustrating experiences of facing the unknown (Bion, 1970). When we try to remember what a patient has said, the session nevertheless keeps moving and we become psychically absent, unable to hear the patient and grasp what is evolving at that moment. This seems clear from the clinical material I have presented. Additionally, both memory and desire are related to sensory experiences as well as the pleasure principle. Psychic reality, as Bion reminds us (1970), is not sensory. Anxiety has neither color, smell, nor taste. When the analyst tries to avoid memory and desire, even the desire to understand, a state of consciousness is entered—other than the usual state—where the pleasure principle *does not prevail*. This frequently leads to feelings of persecution, since one is oscillating through states of chaos, lack of understanding, and confrontation with the unknown, until something evolves and begins taking shape, something that gives consistency to what had hitherto been inconsistent and fragmentary. We then have the appearance of the *selected fact*, a term given by Poincaré to a mathematical formula, which, once devised, gives coherence, consistency, and integration to a series of mathematical elements that had hitherto been unrelated. Bion (1962b) states that "the only facts that are worth our attention are those that introduce order in the complexity, and therefore make the complexity accessible to us" (p. 72).

At this precise moment the analyst will have gone from an analogous state, one that as defined by Brugger (1957), is when there is both similarity and diversity between two things: to an oscillation between the schizoparanoid and depressive positions, from a state of "patience" to a state of "security" (Bion, 1970).

Memory and desire also avoid caesura (Bion, 1989), which is the discontinuity needed to grasp the new, the unknown. If we discipline ourselves to use neither memory nor desire, we live in the vortex of micromoments of catastrophic anxiety (Bion, 1970). Since we usually are in a state of mind regulated by the pleasure principle, there is a tendency to clutch onto what is already familiar, namely memory and desire, in the vain attempt to escape the fundamental anxiety that the unknown produces. The analysand unconsciously knows this, and this state of mind is uncomfortable to the patient and generates an attempt to induce the analyst through projective identification to entertain a state of mind saturated with memory and desire to avoid thought and its concomitants of suffering, development, and knowledge.

Thinking is a process that involves absence. We all dread the unknown, and when faced with it we feel fear and curiosity. In a few, curiosity prevails and we see in them the origins of the scientific state of mind. Eve, for example, challenged God's orders and ate from the tree of knowledge. In this mythical model, she believed, she had faith that there was something more in that beautiful tree of golden truth. Thanks to her curiosity and courage to transgress, we were humanized. This was the inauguration of the scientific spirit, that which helps us advance in the immense oceans of anxieties that the unknown holds in store for us.

According to Bion, thinking results from a process of mourning, which is related to absence, to lack, to frustration, and to the capacity to tolerate them. These are all states that must be faced when one disciplines oneself to give up memory and desire. Therefore we have to experience anxieties in every analytic session that are analogous to those that first arose in the infant with the formation of the "apparatus for dealing with thoughts." This also has analogies with the passage from the pleasure principle to the reality principle.

A hungry baby feels attacked internally by the hunger. Fearing annihilation, the infant tries to free itself from these feelings by projecting them, through projective identification, into the mother, or initially into the breast. The mother, if she can understand the infant's "language" and be in intimate consonance or psychic contact with the infant, what Bion calls "reverie," welcomes these feelings, removing from them their "excessiveness," and returns them, once again through projective identification, in a form which is now tolerable to the infant. The infant will now introject them with their new quality and new meaning. The projective identification thus used by the infant in its "sojourn" into the breast is once again introjected, and the infant identifies with it, a process Bion called "realistic projective identification" (Bion, 1959, 1962a, 1967a). When this occurs, the infant not only receives material comfort in the satisfying of hunger, but also experiences psychic and emotional comfort by feeling "loved" and "understood" by the mother who gives meaning and thus makes anguish bearable.

The projective identification with which the infant "makes" himself present "within" the mother is the most primitive and fundamental form of communication. The infant–mother dyad is therefore one of communication rather than one of drive discharge. The mother can respond or react in various ways. She can respond in a normal manner, one that Bion calls "realistic." Here she reacts to the infant's needs by transforming terror into safety, discomfort into rest, and longing into encounter. This is the beginnings of naming and of meaning, the origin of symbols, and this operation is what Bion terms the *alpha function*. By identifying with this containing mother, the infant opens up an internal space-content for the structuring of a dyad in intimate consonance (relation + container-contained), by internalizing the mother's alpha function, the emotional aspect of maternal love.

For this to be satisfactorily processed, both the infant's inborn capacity to tolerate frustration and the mother's receptivity (capacity for "reverie") must be harmonized in a state of resonance. Thus, when the mother, or to be more exact, the mother's breast, is not present, the "no-breast" or the "absent breast" is imaginatively created by the infant. We can view this as the painful presence of the absence or the absence painfully present. Here we have the initial matrix of thoughts and the beginning of the apparatus that will think them. When this is not processed adequately or realistically, one of the consequences is the premature formation of consciousness. This is consciousness too premature to bear the pressure from both external reality through the sense organs, and the emotional experiences that arise from the translation of feelings in the internal world. This can lead to an "attack" by the infant on the feeling of "twoness" and an attempt to "fuse" into the mother, seeking a primitive state of "fusion" or "oneness" with her, a defense against the anguish of the realization of separation and the feelings of solitude and loneliness that accompany it.

Bion (1962b) elaborated on the idea that thought processes and the development of the apparatus for thinking thoughts is born from the early use of projective identification mechanisms. Based on the concepts of the schizoparanoid and depressive positions, he elucidated another fundamental concept, the dynamic relationship between container-contained, which he expressed as (PS ↔ D) (♀ ♂). What we project is not projected into a void. There is a container or receptacle for these projective identifications. Based on these concepts, Bion concluded that there is a fundamental factor for the infant's growth and development, namely the notion of *reverie* in the mother, a transformer and moderator of the infant's anxieties identificatively projected into it. This is what Bion termed *realistic projective identification* (1959, 1962a, 1967a) and viewed as the most primitive form and the basis of communication.

Since the mother's *reverie* also includes the father and the link he has with the mother, we see here an addition of a triangular relationship (Bion, 1962b). This becomes an essential aspect of development, first in the father–mother–baby relationship, and later, in the analyst–analysand relationship when the analyst—through his alpha function—will perhaps be capable of transforming the beta elements from the analysand into alpha elements. Specifically, when the patient is unable to deal with feelings of pain, frustration, or envy and projects them into the analyst, the analyst through his or her *reverie* accepts them and divests them of their qualities of fear, hatred, and concreteness, returning them with a new quality, the symbolic, and making them tolerable to the patient. If the analysand, having become responsible for his or her psychic reality, is now able to tolerate feelings of pain, he or she will introject them in such a way that there is a growth of the analyst–analysand pair (a + (♀ ♂) (Bion, 1962b), in other words, a symbiotic relationship (Bion, 1970).

According to Bion, the alpha function integrates sensorial objects, sensations coming from the senses with the emotions stimulated by them. The alpha function, working on the one hand on the data of experience, links us to the outside world. On the other hand, the alpha function also deals with the data of emotional experience that arises from within, our internal world, and transforms them into alpha elements which unite to set up the "contact barrier" between the conscious and the unconscious. These alpha elements are used as pattern elements, or initial matrixes to furnish data for the structuring of thought, when we are asleep or awake. Due to deficiencies in the alpha function, however, the data from experience cannot be "*alphabetized*" (Grotstein, 1981) and the production of beta elements prevails, dispersing the contact barrier with the development and irruption of the psychotic part of the personality. Therefore, for Bion, there is no repression in the domain of the psychotic personality. We have an alpha function structuring alpha elements: these are a mental or psychic phenomenon. The beta elements, as concrete things and not a mental phenomenon, cannot be symbolized. This is the boundary between the normal and defective functioning (the reversal of the alpha function; Bion 1962b), which can also be seen as the frontier between what is thought and what is not thought, between the psychotic and nonpsychotic parts of the personality. Without intending a simplistic reification, I see the alpha function as analogous to the Disk Operating System (DOS) in data processing. It is the link between the computer, on the one hand, and the software program, on the other; without it the computer does not work. The alpha function is like this "interface," operating sensorial perception and emotional experience, giving coherence, consistency, and internal representation to, and later discrimination between internal and external reality.

In light of these formulations, let us look at the clinical vignette I have presented. At the moment when I was tempted to take notes, I introduced a third object between myself and my patient. At another moment I intrusively tried to convince the patient that it was her insistence on wanting an answer that created an impasse in the analysis. Speaking in microscopic terms, at that moment my alpha function was operating not in the service of the search for truth, but in order to create beta elements to be used in projective identification processes, aimed at "dominating" my patient's mind and trying to convince and control her. At this point, a hallucinatory state was created within me, what Bion termed *transformations in hallucinosis* (1965). If such transformations are often hard to grasp with the patient, they are even more so within the analyst, when he or she is involved in the process.

When the analyst works using memory and desire, including the taking of notes, he creates a state of hallucinosis, or possibly of dreaming while awake, which may have little to do with the patient and a good deal to do with the analyst. If, however, the analyst works with the discipline of avoiding memory and desire, and is in a state of reverie open to all the impressions impinging upon him from both the patient and his own internal world, he can become capable of "dreaming" through his alpha function (Bion, 1962b, 1992) what the patient, on his or her own, was unable to effect, and then to provide an interpretation.

Bion (1967a), however, points out a problem here: "How is one to explain the differences between a hallucination and an interpretation of an intuited psycho-analytic experience?" (p. 164). The answer to Bion's question can be sought in the emotional experience of what is taking place in the session. In the case presented, I started doubting my position after I argued that it was my patient's insistence on getting an answer that was hindering the progress of the session. My patient replied that she did not like being looked on as a clinical case, an object of study. It then began to dawn on me how anxious and guilty I was feeling. This became clearer when my patient said that she had not read any books on psychoanalysis and that her feeling resulted from her observations. The anxiety and guilt were therefore warning signs indicating to me that something was awry, leading me to an awareness of what was actually going on in the experience with my patient.

If memory and desire constitute undesirable states for the analyst, what then is the desirable state of mind? In regard to this, Bion (1970) had the following to say: "it may be wondered what state of mind is welcome if desires and memory are not. A term that would express approximately what I need to express is 'faith'—faith that there is an ultimate reality and truth—the unknown, unknowable, 'formless infinite' " (p. 31). He further goes on to say: "[a] thought has as its realizations a no-thing. An 'act of faith' has as its background realizations something that is unconscious and unknown because it has not happened" (p. 35).

In a previous paper (in press), I analyzed transference and countertransference as factors that are inherent to transience. I asserted that the use of memory and desire in the analytic session has the function of covering up the fact that all experience is transitory, that there is a discontinuity of experience in time, and that the function of transference and countertransference is to approximate a truth that is always out somewhere ahead of us. This is why it is crucial for the analyst to believe that there is something unconscious to be discovered, something like an antidote to entertaining memories or desires (Junquiere de Mattos, in press):

> In the final analysis, what is the function of transference and countertransference? In my opinion, they are factors of transience. That is, what we aim at with our search, with our transference and countertransference, with our curiosity for knowledge, our need to know, what Melanie Klein called the "epistophillic instinct" (Klein 1923, 1928, 1930) is, at the bottom line, knowledge of ourselves. Analysis is a privileged way of attaining, perhaps we should say, of nearing this unattainable end. . . . I would also say that, in order to work, the analyst must have faith; he must believe that there is a truth and an "ultimate reality" to be sought (Bion, 1970). Although it is unattainable, the patient is benefited, freed to the extent that he nears it, "You shall know the truth and the truth shall make you free" said Jesus (John 8:32). Caper (1997) takes an analogous position when he says that it is the love of psychoanalysis, as an internal object, that enables the analyst instead of identifying and becoming a prisoner embedded in the tangle of the patient's projective identifications, to have a mind of his own, and thus be able to analyze another. When I speak of faith, or belief, I am not referring to anything mythical or religious. On the contrary, I feel that this is a strictly scientific position related to the fact that truth is indispensable and that knowledge of the truth has, among other consequences, that of fostering greater integration of the self. If truth does not make us happier, at least it will make us feel more assured. Basically I am pre-supposing that there is a non-psychotic part functioning *pari passu* with a psychotic part of the mind (Bion, 1957, 1967a) and that it is these non-psychotic aspects related to the patient's "epistomophilic instinct" that comes for analysis, giving rise to transferential and countertransferential phenomena, both positive or negative. They are important and necessary but transitory accidents along the road, and they spur us on to take a further

step. . . . Encased in this mass of neurosis or psychosis, there is a mind. There is someone who is seeking the truth, who longs for freedom. . . .

I believe that Bion's position in regard to memory, desire and understanding and his having been the first to recognize in projective identification not only a mechanism to free the psyche of undesirable emotions and ideas, but also a form of communication, is among his most important contributions to psychoanalytic technique and has served as a basis for formulations of contemporary authors on intersubjectivity, in particular Ogden's concept of the "intersubjective analytic third" (1994).

As a coda I will quote from Bion's *Brazilian Lectures* (1990), which I feel synthesizes everything that I wished to convey in this paper:

> It becomes a serious matter if the analyst is present in mind but preoccupied with trying to remember. "Trying to remember" is, in my opinion, being "analytically" essentially absent. It is precisely during this short fifty minutes that one should not allow oneself either to "remember" or to "hope" or "wish for" or even to "understand" what the patient is talking about. Therefore, the analyst may not be able to make notes, but he should be able to "make the notes" essential for psycho-analysis. I cannot offer any suggestion as to where or how these notes are made, but in my experience, they are made ([p. 185].

References

Augustine, St. Confessions. *The Great Books*, Vol. 18. London: Encyclopedia Britannica, 1978.

Bion, W. R. (1957), Diffentiation of the psychotic from the non-psychotic personalities. *Internat. J. Psycho-Anal.*, 38:43–64.

———— (1959), Attacks on linking. *Internat. J. Psycho-Anal.*, 40:308–315.

———— (1962a), A theory of thinking. *Internat. J. Psycho-Anal.*, 43:306–314.

———— (1962b), Learning from experience. In: *Seven Servants*. New York: Jason Aronson, 1977, pp. 1–111.

———— (1965), Transformations. In: *Seven Servants*. New York: Jason Aronson, pp. 1–183.

———— (1967a), *Second Thoughts*. London: Heinemann Medical Books.

———— (1967b), Notes on memory and desire. *Psychoanal. Forum*, 2:271–280.

———— (1970), Attention and interpretation. In: *Seven Servants*. New York: Jason Aronson, 1977, pp. 1–136.

———— (1989), *The Grid and Caesura*. London: Karnac Books.

———— (1990), *Bion's Brazilian Lectures*. London: Karnac Books.

———— (1992), *Cogitations*. London: Karnac Books.

Brugger, W. (1957), *Dicionario de Filosofia*. San Paulo: FPU Editora Pedagogica e Univ.

Caper, R. (1997), A mind of one's own. *Internat. J. Psycho-Anal.*, 78:265–278.

Grotstein, J. (1981), Wilfred R. Bion: The man, the psychoanalyst, the mystic. A perspective on his life and work. In: *Do I Dare Disturb the Universe*. London: Karnac Books, pp. 1–35, 1993.

Junqueira de Mattos, J. A. (1997), Concentrated analysis: A three decade experience. In: *The Perverse Transferences and Other Matters*, ed. J. L. Ahumada, J. Olagaray, A. K. Richards, & A. D. Richards. Northvale, NJ: Jason Aronson, pp. 235–254.

———— (in press), Transference as transience. *Rev. Brasiliera de Psicoanalise*.

Klein, M. (1923), Early analysis. In: *Love, Guilt and Reparation and Other Works, 1921–1945*. London: Hogarth Press, 1975, pp. 77–105.

———— (1928), Early stages of the Oedipus conflict. In: *Love, Guilt and Reparation and Other Works, 1921–1945*. London: Hogarth Press, 1975, pp. 186–198.

———— (1930), The importance of symbol-formation in the development of the ego. In: *Love, Guilt and Reparation and Other Works, 1921–1945*. London: Hogarth Press, 1975, pp. 219–232.

———— (1957), Envy and gratitude. In: *Envy and Gratitude and Other Works, 1946–1963*. London: Hogarth Press, 1975, pp. 176–235.

Ogden, T. (1994), The analytic third: Working with intersubjective clinical facts. *Internat. J. Psycho-Anal.*, 75:3–18.

12

The Role of Fantasies of Cure in Psychoanalytic Failure

Augusto Escribens, Ph.D.

A First Appearance of Disruption

I was trying to listen to my patient, a young professional woman who had recently started her analysis, as she was talking about her disappointment with the man she was dating. She lay on the couch and played with one hand with the surface of her skirt, rubbing it as if she were caressing it. She had just told me how difficult it was for her to provide for her needs due to the cost of the analysis, and that she did not now have enough money to give herself the little pleasures she had become used to.

As I was listening to her I was laboriously trying to find my way through a complex of thoughts and feelings that centered around the idea that my patient was talking about her friend as an unconscious reference to me as someone who was disappointing and frustrating her, and that perhaps the soft caress to the surface of the skirt that covered her thigh was a subtle

seductive maneuver to induce me to provide her with the gratifications she felt deprived of. I was also thinking that this material appearing so early in her analysis indicated the possibility
that an eroticized transference might develop, but I knew that
it was too soon to interpret anything, because the working alliance was just being formed. I also was thinking that everything
was so evident that perhaps there was something more important being hidden and I would watch for its eventual emergence.

Then all of a sudden, it happened. I heard the outside door
being opened and I had to run out of the consulting room in
order to stop Nestor, a patient who was sitting in the waiting
room, from getting to the street. He had come to his session
so drunk that I had to tell him to wait for his girl friend to
come and pick him up and that he should not dare to leave.
Now I had to ask the watchman in the street not to allow him
out, to stop him by any and all means. When I returned to the
session I was thinking of the contrast between the very subtle
internal maneuvers I had to perform in order to be attuned to
the inner world of the patient who was lying on the couch, and
the gross protective measures that were necessary to stop a
drunken man from going outside where he could be hit by a
car. I was worried about having to leave a session for that reason, and I wondered how disruptive this would be for my patient. "Also disruptive for myself, to my peace of mind, and to
my relation to my analyzing instrument," I thought.

I asked myself what moved me to accept such a disturbed
patient, for this was but the most recent of an odd sequence
of actings out, including one in which I even had to go to his
apartment, ask the janitor to keep an eye on him until his girl
friend came, and page me if anything happened. At that time
I also had to confiscate a bottle of rum, telling him during the
next session that I was going to charge extra for merchandise
storage. That example of black humor on my part was, no
doubt, an expression of how heavy I felt the burden of his
pathology in my work space. Nestor was, undoubtedly, a therapeutic failure, and that was the session—the last one he showed
up for—that made it evident, after so much denial on my part.
At the time I did not review the case to try to understand what

had happened, I just wanted to be rid of this disappointing experience. I will, however, return to this case after some theoretical considerations.

The Elusive Ghost of Failure

The study of failures in psychoanalysis should be a priority because, as in any other discipline, the cases in which the instrument fails to met the needs of its task may provide evidence for its improvement. Nevertheless, it is infrequent in the analytic literature to find detailed information about failures. In a panel report on this topic, Dewald (Panel, 1993) mentions that, in spite of the importance for science of the lack of fit between theory and observable data, psychoanalytic literature tends to use clinical facts only to support hypotheses. Vignettes demonstrate success, never the need to modify a preset theory.

The analyst's subjectivity has a central role in both the generation of psychoanalytic failures and in the difficulty of studying them. It is the central technical issue that needs to be addressed by analysts and cuts across theoretical stances. If we think of psychoanalysis as a science or as a hermeneutic quest, or as a constructivist activity, it is clear that our discipline faces the special problem of having the analyst's mind as the instrument of clinical knowledge. Freud formulated the first entrée to the subjectivity of the analyst by his positing of countertransference as a disturbance of the analytic process. The emergence of affects in the analyst, concerning the analysand is from this perspective a product of unresolved neurotic conflicts within the analyst and the recommended remedial measure is analysis or reanalysis (Freud, 1910, 1912). In the 1950s, both Heimann (1950) and Racker (1953) presented an alternate vision of countertransference in which the affective reactions of the analyst did not come only from individual neurotic features, but was also a response to the conflicts and transference of the patient, thus becoming a useful element for analytic work. According to Kernberg (1965), these emotional reactions in the analyst are intimately fused, and even though the countertransference should be resolved, they are useful for understanding the patient. Bion (1962), King (1978), and Rosenfeld (1987) amongst others, have theorized about the role of the analyst's affect in clinical work, and others have highlighted it as a central issue, including Jacobs (1985, 1986, 1993) who elaborated on the analyst's use of his own personality in the psychoanalytic encounter. In two previous papers (1995, 1997) I have explored the presence of the analysand as a significant object for the analyst and have reflected on the effects of this on clinical work.

Stolorow, Brandchaft, and Atwood (1987) go further, defining psychoanalysis as the science of the intersubjective, and Renik (1993) has taken an even more radical stance, positing that intersubjectivity is irreducible to the point of determining each and every aspect of analytic understanding, thus rendering psychoanalysis as a mutually shared task of analysand and analyst. Renik also points out that the absolute proscription of the analyst's acting in cannot be maintained because it is based on a faulty theoretical supposition—the reflex arc theory put forward by Freud in 1900 in *The Interpretation of Dreams*, that opposes acting and thinking. For Renik, every thought by the analyst is permeated by his own subjectivity and he cannot do anything but act (even though he may think he is not acting while performing verbal acts) and he will only a posteriori know about his acting. All these contributions expand the field of exploration in the direction of the analyst's subjectivity and of interactional phenomena, even questioning the way in which speech has been traditionally conceptualized in psychoanalysis, and reminding us of the pragmatic aspects of language, as well as the importance of the other kinesic, proxemic, and paralinguistic channels of communication that go together with verbalizations. Regarding the issue of success or failure, we may be just arriving at a point where we have enough instruments to consistently approach our own subjectivities as both involved actors and biased evaluators of the psychoanalytic process.

Another problem in the attempt to understand psychoanalytic failures is the difficulty in defining both failure and successes. A failure in psychoanalysis would imply, *sensu stricto*, that a transference neurosis did not develop or was not resolved. Nevertheless, given the fact that a transference neurosis is not expected to develop in psychoanalytic psychotherapy, and the absence of a sharp delineation between psychoanalysis and psychotherapy (Bachrach and Leaff, 1978), it is not definitive to assign diagnostic value to the outcome of that specific process. When we turn to empirical research, we find that efficacy research in psychoanalysis has not always led to clear results. Kantrowitz's fifteen-year research project initially attempted to establish criteria for analyzability based on four variables: reality testing, affect availability and tolerance, level and quality of object relations, and motivation. At the end of the inquiry, none of these variables nor combinations of them predicted psychoanalytic outcome. Patients did get better by virtue of improvement in these areas, but it was impossible to assess any relation between therapeutic benefit and analytic result understood in terms of transference neurosis resolution. Nor was it possible to predict which patients would improve or maintain improvement (Kantrowitz, Singer, and Knapp, 1975; Kantrowitz, Katz, Paolitto, Sashin, and Solomon, 1986, 1987a, b; Kantrowitz, Katz, and Paolitto, 1990).

It is important to point out that, as a consequence of this disappointment with research results, Kantrowitz shifted to a hypothesis about patient–analyst match, and found more consistent results, providing evidence for the interactional character of psychoanalysis. Elements of patient–analyst match are features of individual histories, attitudes, values, and countertransference configurations (Kantrowitz, Katz, Greenman, Morris, Paolitto, Sashin, and Solomon, 1989). It takes us, once again, to the analyst's subjectivity as a source of outcome explanation.

It seems so difficult to pinpoint the meaning of outcome and analyzability, that only five of twenty-four studies surveyed in a study of efficacy of psychoanalysis (Bachrach and Leaff, 1978) clearly specify what is meant by a "favorable" or "successful" response to psychoanalytic treatment. Aarons (1962) defines successful outcome as "the resolution of unconscious conflict" distinguishing it from conformity, compliance, and "correct" behavior. Kernberg et al. (1972) based quantitative judgments on intrapsychic variables, such as ego strength and unconscious guilt. Sashin, Eldred, and Van Amerogen (1975) based their judgments on both supervisors' and analysts' opinions about global change and circumstances of termination. Klein (1960) and Weber, Bradlow, Moss, and Elinson (1974) used rating scales for certain areas of change and also follow-up criteria (cited in Bachrach and Leaff, 1978).

If we look at particulars, we may become astonished at how difficult it is for us to be certain about what we actually do with our patients, as compared with the relative certainty we have when we use concepts to describe and explain their inner processes. For example, when we survey the literature and look for contexts of the word *failure*, we may verify how certain psychoanalysts may be when writing about developmental failure, failure of the synthetic function of the ego, failure of earlier mirroring experiences, failure to achieve preoedipal and oedipal normative maturation, failure of differentiation, failure of appropriate internalization, failure of the libido to master the destructive impulses, and even object failure, failure of the holding environment, or parental failure. No definition of therapeutic failure is given, however, even in the paper by Dewald (Panel, 1993), which is about this very topic. It seems to me that the reason for this generalized difficulty comes from the fact that a psychoanalytic failure is a failure of the psychoanalytic dyad, and as such, it strongly involves the analyst's psyche.

I will not try to resolve the lack of definitional clarity here, and will simply approach the issue from a relative and intuitive point of view. We know when we have failed, and we also know that sometimes we fail more radically than at other times, and in that sense the subjective appreciation of the analyst involved in the failure is a very valuable criterion. Instead of attempting a definition, I will stick to that subjective, though ambiguous criterion, because I am more interested in describing a fantasy configuration that has proven useful to me for understanding those cases that would have to be considered as failures, as well as those in which this understanding came in time to turn them into successes.

Summing up, the study of failures should be a central issue in psychoanalysis, but it seems that it has not been so because it involves the psychoanalyst's subjectivity, which, being a central factor in the psychoanalytic process and cure, is also one that gives rise to the most important clinical and theoretical problems. It was not broached by psychoanalysis in its historical beginnings; however, there has been an evolution in conceptualization from the classical theory of countertransference to the current view of psychoanalysis as an interactive and intersubjective process. We may be at a time when we finally have the instruments to approach this complex issue of failures.

The Fantasies and *Folies* of Cure

Abend (1979) has pointed out that certain patients have a special interest as to how psychoanalysts cure, create personal theories about it, and these beliefs influence their attitudes and behavior in the course of treatment. He emphasized the importance of understanding and interpreting these fantasies of cure in order to untie transference elements hidden in them, and also clarify the meaning of many of the patient's behaviors. Goldberg (1991) introduced the notion of the patient's theories of pathogenesis, and related it to other entities such as autobiography, personal myth, fantasy of cure, and transference. For him, the theory of pathogenesis represents a gloss of autobiographical memories and reflects the patient's efforts at interpretation and synthesis, and being at a higher level of abstraction than autobiographical memories, it is used as a basis for selecting, editing, interpreting, and most of all distorting the biographical narrative to conceal certain aspects of it. "In its defensive deployment of the autobiography, the theory of pathogenesis serves a screen function" (p. 247). The concept of personal myth is closely related to theories of pathogenesis, and both serve screening functions in relation to unconscious memories and fantasies and are also subject to enactment in the transference.

The fantasy of cure is so closely related to the patient's theory of pathogenesis that it appears as if one is the beginning and the other the conclusion of a subnarrative in the patient's representation of his own life. Or, to put it in Goldberg's (1991) logical terms, they are closely related because "there is a complementary relationship between notions of causation

and notions of cure of illness, each one implying the other"
(p. 248). Regarding fantasies of cure, which is our subject here,
some of them appear to be unconscious productions that serve
defensive and wish-fulfilling purposes.

Both Abend and Goldberg restrict the exploration of fantasies of cure to those that may be inferred in the patient's psyche, even though both of them recognize the important
influence analysts may have on the development of the psychoanalytic process. They also mention that some psychoanalysts
may approach their clinical work with theories of pathogenesis
and cure that are rooted in the same matrixes as those in their
patients, having, beneath their appearance as theoretical constructs, defensive and wish-fulfilling functions (see also Arlow, 1981).

I would like to advance the hypothesis that unconscious fantasies of cure are always present in the psychoanalytic encounter, in both the analyst and the analysand, and that part of
the psychoanalytic process deals with the negotiation of these
fantasies toward a transaction that allows a common task to
develop. Most of the time, in normal clinical situations, with
patients who exhibit a mild form of pathology and in which
the analyst is not preoccupied with special circumstances that
affect his attitude toward his work, fantasies of cure on both
parts stay unconscious, and attention is not necessarily paid to
them, mainly because they coincide, or are highly compatible
with attitudes that allow the psychoanalytic process to develop.

To illustrate how this transaction between fantasies may occur, we may give as an example a case in which the analysand
may have a central pathological nucleus, an early maternal absence, and has the fantasy that his analyst is a new edition of
the mother, who is present to repair the early wounds. On the
other hand, we may have an analyst who understands this case
as one of deficit pathology, in which his main task will be to
accompany the patient to the completion of his arrested development. There may be, somewhere in the analyst's mind, the
fantasy that he is a generous mother whose main task in life is
to compensate for the failures of all those "mean" mothers
who abandon their children. In cases approximately similar to

this very schematic and oversimplified sketch, fantasies of cure probably never appear as an issue and need not be analyzed, because they are congruent to the establishment of a common goal.

We may posit, on the other hand, a case in which the same analyst—having the same underlying fantasy of cure—meets with a patient who has a predominantly hostile attitude toward the frustrating mother of his childhood and feels that he will only be cured when he can destroy that mother. This configuration of incompatible fantasies of cure may at best lead to an impasse in which the divergent fantasies may become visible, or in a worst case scenario, a slow build-up of aggression ends with the patient leaving analysis. In this context, it is important to keep in mind that we are speaking of distortions of the processing of meaning, which are concomitant to serious pathological configurations. Liberman (1962) conceptualizes this as a semantic distortion, presenting a disturbance in the axis of significance of the analysis and Grinberg describes it as presenting a predominance of pathological desire of cure (Prego-Silva, 1978).

We have considered fantasies of cure in both the analyst and the analysand and the possible relations between them. There is a third element, however, to be considered in relation to the two previous ones, an element we can call *reality;* even though this term points to one of the most equivocal, troublesome, poorly defined aspects with which psychoanalysts have to deal. Nevertheless, even though we will not try to define it here, we may easily imagine some variants of *folie à deux* an analyst and analysand may live—including different brands of perversification of the analytic relationship—if they share a fantasy of cure but also share the lack of a minimum adjustment to the reality principle. Perhaps for less severe cases, in which the sense of reality is not acutely distorted but nevertheless does not completely fit conventional definitions of the analytic process, we can understand from this those cases where the outcome is an improvement in some areas of the patient's life without the concomitant analytic results.

Nestor, a Reappearance

Nestor was an Argentinian economist working in Peru on community development projects related to nongovernmental organizations of a moderately leftist orientation. He had fled his homeland because of political persecution, but being a member of a legal party, the extent of the difficulties he got into made me think that his personality disturbances had more to do with these problems than his political views. He first came for a consultation, being referred by a former patient, and because I am not a physician and he was on a very tight budget, I referred him to a colleague who could both prescribe medication and conduct a psychoanalytic psychotherapy. He reappeared in my office two years later and told me that while things went fairly well with my colleague, he felt that I had understood him better in the two interviews we had than my colleague had in several months of treatment. He also told me that he now had severe interpersonal problems and he wanted to face them once and for all. He was certain that I was the one who could help him.

I was very suspicious about his certainty in choosing me because I knew he was appealing to my narcissism and flattering me in order to get me to take him on as a patient. However, I thought I could start seeing him on a trial basis and try to work out the problems affecting the setting and the therapeutic process. I knew that there was a danger of the therapeutic alliance becoming distorted, knowing that he was, constantly in a subtle way, appealing to a residue of the radical leftist ideas I cherished twenty years earlier, an aspect of my life he had easily found out about in the gossipy Lima milieu. I arranged for a psychiatrist to provide him with medication and began psychoanalytic psychotherapy on a three times a week basis. I must add that I label it "psychotherapy" because of International Psychoanalytic Association standards of frequency; however, it was a three times a week psychoanalysis with the sole exception of those parameters necessitated by the severity of his pathology.

What emerged is that Nestor had an underlying borderline personality with severe ego fragility and very poor impulse control. His very pronounced dependent and masochistic submissive tendencies derived from the relationship with an internal mother who tried to control and dominate him as a provider of narcissistic supplies, but was also a chronically depressed and masochistic personality. On the other hand, he despised his father, who was a militant of a leftist party in Argentina but had become corrupt, as evidence by the fact that he did not have a difficult time while others were persecuted for their ideas. Nestor's internal representation of his father was as a devalued object with whom he could not identify.

Currently, besides being a heavy drinker who frequently got into trouble because of aggressive outbursts during alcoholic episodes, he had a conflictual relationship with the director of the institute where he worked, in what seemed to be a submissive–rebellious dynamic alternating with a deeply ambivalent attitude. At the time of entering treatment he also had an equally ambivalent love relationship with a woman twenty years younger than he, to whom he delegated the administration of his life and against whom he recurrently rebelled. These rebellious moods, toward both his boss and his girl friend, often marked the inception of alcoholic episodes.

Why do I consider this case a failure? Nestor improved in some ways as a result of the therapy. He stopped fighting with the director of the institute, developed better relations with colleagues and other professionals in related areas, and became more productive in his work. Despite these changes in his behavior, I know that some specific and critical areas of his inner world escaped elaboration in the therapy because, for some reason that only became clear to me recently, I got too involved in both trying to stop him from drinking heavily and in aiding his recovery of control over his daily affairs. I have asked myself if things could have gone differently. It seems clear to me now that the reason for this therapeutic failure is not that his pathology made him unanalyzable, but that from the very beginning there were some unconscious movements on both our parts that made the treatment bound to fail.

A Tango, a Lamppost, and a Sunset

I was back in Buenos Aires after twenty-six years. Of course I went to that small plaza near the docks, and sat alone in the café next to it, drinking a beer. It was cold outside and the place was nearly empty except for a couple sitting at a nearby table. I was so taken by nostalgia that I felt just short of crying. But then, the worst of what could have happened, occurred: the radio began playing a tango, an old one that Carlos Gardel used to sing and that I had listened to since childhood. Now, it was sung by a woman with a young and tender voice. Its words spoke of remembrance and the irreparable nature of time goneby: "I am afraid of an encounter/with the past coming back/to stand up against my life." I had to go outside. Embracing a lamppost, I started crying there in the empty street with a magnificent but sad sunset as my only accomplice. It was the same café that I had been sitting in one Sunday, twenty-six years earlier, when I was 21.

My memories took me back some three hours before that long ago café sojourn when I was at the Carrasco Airport in Montevideo, watching in despair the heavy storm that made it impossible for propeller planes to land and take off. Technically, the airport was closed for all flights. I had recently met someone in Montevideo and I had plans to meet her again at the café in Buenos Aires three hours from then. I did not have an address in that city where I could meet her, so if I failed to show up at the café nothing could be done. Then I heard a radio on a Brazilian airline counter. A few men were gathered there listening to the conversation between the tower controller and the pilot of a plane that was unsuccessfully trying to land. The pilot sounded cool and unflustered as he described the fifth time he had failed to enter the approximation cone, but the men listening to the broadcast were tense. The pilot asked for an ambulance because most of the passengers were in a state of panic and had vomited. "These Brazilians, these madmen" a man at the counter said, "I bet even after this he'll take off again and make it to Buenos Aires." I was on a scholarship in Montevideo and could not change my ticket to another airline. While I was counting the few dollars I had left, the small one-eleven airplane landed. While I handed the remains of my money to the ticket clerk at the counter, I could see the passengers coming out of the gate, looking as if they were coming from a war zone.

The plane took off again, bound for Buenos Aires, including me amongst its passengers. The short and bumpy flight over the La Plata river was at the same time the most frightening and the most cherished air trip of my life. A few hours later as scheduled I got to meet an unforgettable woman in that café. Twenty-six years later, while visiting, I was pained by the memories of that encounter, and the magic times that followed. The city had remained the same scenario for a piece of my personal history, and which became a personal myth in which I felt myself as the hero I never got to be again.

The visit to Buenos Aires occurred at a time when I was treating Nestor, but I never made any connection except for acknowledging the idea, at the beginning of the treatment, that I was taking on such a difficult patient in part because he came from a country and a city to which I was indebted for an important and intense personal experience. "Okay, I'll do it out of gratitude for Buenos Aires," I remember telling myself.

At a later time, after Nestor's analysis had ended, both things, the failure of the treatment and the memories of that mythical time in Buenos Aires, came together. I had already realized that Nestor had the underlying fantasy that my role as therapist would be to become an omnipotent father, a real hero to replace the antihero his father was. I knew he wanted me to become that type of person instead of analyzing him, and I had interpreted this fantasy to him many times. What I had never before realized was that I had the secret fantasy of embracing the heroic identity with which love had invested me twenty-six years before, and that I would rather be a paternal hero who would take him, my son, away from the mother he was submissive to, and from his alcoholism, which made him feel unworthy. The problem was that my fantasies, not being conscious, were acted upon, leading me into a competition with his girl friend who closely controlled his life and his behavior. I also took direct action in some of his acting out; for example, by seizing the bottle of rum. There was, then, an important part of my relationship with him that had become a blind spot I had never overcome.

Lorena, a Prevented Failure

Lorena, an economist in her thirties, came to treatment because she had difficulties in establishing and maintaining relationships. She had been married for two years to a man who seemed to be a narcissistic personality strongly tied to his mother. She had a 10-year-old son with him and had become the sole caretaker since he lived in a province far from Lima. After her divorce she had a few relationships with men who seemed to want something serious, but something always happened that made these relationships fall apart. The most lasting relationship—and apparently the best one she had—was a covert one with a married man who let her know that he had no intention of divorcing his wife. My patient was a very efficient professional, doing well economically, and it appeared as if she could dispense with others to fulfill her needs. But she also at times felt depressed, with no obvious precipitant for her mood, and at those times it became very difficult for her to even get out of bed in the morning.

This analysis seemed to be a very successful one, because the patient presented material that was at once increasingly complex but easy to understand. She was also doing better at work and socialized more, overcoming a mild phobia reported at the beginning of treatment. Nevertheless, the depressive moments became more intense, and she started to develop an increasingly hostile transference. At a time when I thought the analysis might be interrupted with her running away, I discovered that she had the hidden fantasy that I would cure her by providing her with a penis, and she felt that I was being successful, which in turn made her more hostile toward me, because now she could feel free to despise men given the fact that she did not need them. I, however, did not have a concurrent fantasy, so I always felt uncomfortable with that side of the analytic relationship until I could get to uncover it.

Delia: A Prevented Folie à Deux

Delia is a 45-year-old professional woman married to a contractor who builds recreational facilities, and the mother of three children. Due to the nature of her husband's work, which is tied to large recreational projects, the family has periods of economic affluence followed by long stretches when there is no income. The last few years have been problematic in this respect. Even though she is a professional, she has only started working just recently, because it seems that child rearing had been a burdensome task for her. As a matter of fact, at the beginning of her analysis, many aspects of her life appeared to be burdensome, and she frequently recounted stories in which many circumstances emotionally overwhelmed her. When she did start working it was clear to me that she was doing so only to patch the holes that were left in their budget due to her husband's lack of business. There were many other memories of her having to hold people in her family, which were replayings of her relationship with a mother she had to emotionally support from very early in her life. She could be diagnosed as having a precocious ego, except for the fact that this defensive structure always kept crumbling, revealing an underlying depression.

I had never envisioned this case as a possible failure, even though Delia was about to leave treatment on two separate occasions, feeling both times that I was not paying real attention to her. Both times, the interpretation of her complaint as a resistance was effective in stopping her from fleeing the analysis. As a matter of fact, analysis had been effective in helping her manage the projective identifications that she frequently employed. For the last two years I had often felt that all that had been achieved in this treatment was to make her suffering milder and, even worse than that, to make her defensive maneuvers more effective.

In a session about six months ago, she was talking about her feelings regarding her brother's severe economic problems, which had invaded the psychic space of the entire family. "I think my mother is the one responsible for that, I think she allows this to happen, all the time she is talking about him and his problems. Yesterday I had to tell her not to speak about it." While my patient was talking, a series of images and thoughts appeared to me. First it was a piece of pine wood, with its characteristic design of darker (harder) and lighter (softer) parts. It just happened that the lighter parts were lacking, as if eaten by moths, and it looked like a baroque openwork embroidery. I then remembered the title *Raise High the Roof Beam Carpenter* by Salinger and at last the image came to me of a beam I saw at a demolition site, which had just that pattern. I found myself bothered by thinking about these things while I had a patient in session, as if I were seriously neglecting her, and as if something terrible could result from that.

Synthesizing these images I managed to say to her that she probably had two conflicting feelings: on the one hand she felt that she had to be strong enough to support everyone, but that made her feel that no one was taking care of her, which she badly needed. On the other hand, she felt very weak, but that feeling made her afraid that everything would fall apart. So, she felt like a perforated beam that had to support a roof near its breaking point. I told her that she must feel trapped by the feeling that the better she felt, the more she experienced the neglect inflicted on her.

While she associated to her early relationship with her mother, I realized that my discomfort about her analysis had to do with the fact that I had been trying to support her and avoid an inferred but never explicitly admitted breakdown. I also managed to interpret to her the latent expectancy of my acting as someone who supported her the same way she had to support her mother. What was at work here, I discovered, was the shared unconscious fantasy of cure in which my role was to bolster her against a breakdown as she did with her mother, and by the way, her mother with my patient's grandmother. After I realized this, and interpreted it to her, she began to work through a long-standing complex of depressive feelings and contents centered around her early relationship with a mother who was apparently constantly concerned with everything and everyone, but who was in reality unconcerned with my patient's emotional needs, and also pushed my patient into the supportive position. I could also trace my own fantasy of cure to similar childhood experiences.

The problem of a prevented failure is that one cannot tell how it would have evolved. I think this case would have had the most dire outcome: an endless stagnation in an unfinishable and unproductive analysis which, nevertheless, would have appeared as a discretely therapeutic process; one of those analyses that have the salutary effect of making us realize the limitations of our clinical instrument and invite us to be mature enough to renounce omnipotent fantasies.

On Failures and Fantasies: Final Comments

The idea of fantasy of cure, as developed in this paper, has proven to be a valuable construct to detect the possible distortion of the meaning that the psychoanalytic process may have for both analyst and analysand. Since these distortions affect the whole process, due to their being predicated on both members of the analytic dyad, and their relationship, they may be instrumental in producing either stagnation or even the collapse of the treatment. Of the three cases discussed, the first one, Nestor, shows the convergence of two different but complementary underlying fantasies of cure in both members of the dyad, which led to the failure of the analysis. In the second case, Lorena, we see how being free of any concurrent fantasy of cure allows the analyst to discover the patient's relatively early in the treatment and prevent its corrosive effects. In the third case, Delia, unrest about something that seemed to be missing in the analysis set in motion a process in the analyst which led to the discovery of a convergence of fantasies in both parties, which gave a reciprocal feedback to avoid a feared breakdown. This, in turn, prevented the working through of important conflicts and depressive feelings. In Nestor's and Delia's cases, the situations were similar, but Nestor's fantasy was somehow different from my corresponding one. Delia's fantasy and mine were very similar to each other and had similar historical and dynamic origins. Of course the other difference consists in my discovery of Delia's fantasy and its interpretation.

References

Aarons, Z. A. (1962), Indications for analysis and problems of analyzability. *Psychoanal. Quart.*, 31:514–531.
Abend, S. M. (1979), Unconscious fantasy and theories of cure, *J. Amer. Psychoanal. Assn.*, 27:579–596.
Arlow, J. (1981), Theories of pathogenesis. *Psychoanal. Quart.*, 50:488–514.
Bachrach, H. M., & Leaff, L. A. (1978), "Analyzability": A systematic review of the clinical and quantitative literature. *J. Amer. Psychoanal. Assn.*, 26:881–920.
Bion, W. R. (1962), Symposium: The psycho-analytic study of thinking: II. A theory of thinking. *Internat. J. Psycho-Anal.*, 43:306–310.
Escribens, A. (1995), The patient who inhabits us: Some clinical effects of the analysand's representation in the analyst's mind. In: *Psychoanalysis in Latin America*, ed. A. Alcorta. Monterrey, Mexico: FEPAL (Latin American Federation of Psychoanalysis).
——— (1997), Psychoanalysis and its discontents: Interminable self analysis. In: *The Perverse Transference and Other Matters. Essays in Honor of Horacio Etchegoyen*, ed. J. Ahumada. Northvale, NJ: Jason Aronson, pp. 217–221.
Freud, S. (1900), The Interpretation of Dreams. *Standard Edition*, 4 & 5. London: Hogarth Press, 1953.
——— (1910), The future prospects of psycho-analytic therapy. *Standard Edition*, 11:139–151. London: Hogarth Press, 1957.
——— (1912), Recommendations to physicians practising psychoanalysis. *Standard Edition*, 12:89–96. London: Hogarth Press, 1958.
Goldberg, S. (1991), Patients' theories of pathogenesis. *Psychoanal. Quart.*, 60:245–275.
Heimann, P. (1950), On counter-transference. *Internat. J. Psycho-Anal.*, 31:81–84.
Jacobs, T. J. (1985), The use of the self: The analyst and the analytic instrument in the clinical situation. In: *Analysts at Work: Practice, Principles and Techniques*, ed. J. Reppen. Hillsdale, NJ: Analytic Press, pp. 43–57.

—————— (1986), On countertransference enactments. *J. Amer. Psychoanal. Assn.*, 34:289–308.

—————— (1993), The inner experiences of the analyst: Their contribution to the analytic process. *Internat. J. Psycho-Anal.*, 74:7–14.

Kantrowitz, J. L., Katz, A. L., Greenman, D., Morris, H., Paolitto, F., Sashin, J., & Solomon, L. (1989), The patient–analyst match and the outcome of psychoanalysis: A pilot study. *J. Amer. Psychoanal. Assn.*, 37:893–919.

—————— —————— Paolitto, F. (1990), Follow-up of psychoanalysis five to ten years after termination: I. Stability of change. *J. Amer. Psychoanal. Assn.*, 38:471–496.

—————— —————— —————— Sashin, I., & Solomon, L. (1986), Affect availability, tolerance, complexity, and modulation in psychoanalysis: Follow-up of a longitudinal study. *J. Amer. Psychoanal. Assn.*, 34:529–560.

—————— —————— —————— —————— —————— (1987a), Changes in the level and quality of object relations in psychoanalysis: Follow-up of a longitudinal prospect study. *J. Amer. Psychoanal. Assn.*, 35:23–46.

—————— —————— —————— —————— —————— (1987b), The role of reality testing in the outcome of psychoanalysis: Follow-up of 22 cases. *J. Amer. Psychoanal. Assn.*, 35:367–386.

—————— Singer, J., & Knapp, P. (1975), Methodology for a prospective study of psychoanalysis: The role of psychological tests. *Psychoanal. Quart.*, 44:371–391.

Kernberg, O. (1965), Notes on countertransference. *J. Amer. Psychoanal. Assn.*, 13:38–56.

—————— Burstein, E., Coyne, L., Appelbaum, A., Horwitz, L., & Voth, H. (1972), Psychotherapy and psychoanalysis: Final report of the Menninger Foundation's Psychotherapy Research Project. *Bull. Menninger Clinic*, 36:1–275.

King, P. (1978), Affective response of the analyst to the patient's communications. *Internat. J. Psycho-Anal.*, 59:329–334.

Klein, H. (1960), A study of changes occurring in patients during and after psychoanalytic treatment. In: *Current Approaches to Psychoanalysis*, ed. P. Hoch & J. Zubin. New York: Grune & Stratton, pp. 151–175.

Liberman, D. (1962), *La Comunicación en Terapéutica Psicoanalítica.* Buenos Aires: Eudeba.

Panel (1993), Learning from our unsuccessful cases. Reporter: E. J. Nuetzel. *J. Amer. Psychoanal. Assn.*, 41:743–754.

Prego-Silva, L. E. (1978), Dialogue on "Depression and other painful affects." *Internat. J. Psycho-Anal.*, 59:517–532.

Racker, H. (1953), A contribution to the problem of countertransference. *Internat J. Psycho-Anal.*, 34:313–324.

Renik, O. (1993), Analytic interaction: Conceptualizing technique in light of the analyst's irreducible subjectivity. *Psychoanal. Quart.*, 62:553–571.

Rosenfeld, H. (1987), *Impasse and Interpretation*. London: Routledge/ Institute of Psycho-Analysis.

Sashin, J. I., Eldred, S. H., & Van Amerogen, S. T. (1975), A search for predictive factors in institute supervised cases: A retrospective study of 183 cases from 1959–1966 at the Boston Psychoanalytic Society and Institute. *Internat. J. Psycho-Anal.*, 56:343–359.

Stolorow, R., Brandchaft, B., and Atwood, G. (1987). *Psychoanalytic Treatment: An Intersubjective Approach*. Hillsdale, NJ: Analytic Press.

Weber, J., Bradlow, P., Moss, L., & Elinson, J. (1974), Predictions of outcome in psychoanalysis and analytic psychotherapy. *Psychiat. Quart.*, 40:1–33.

13

Others' Failures—And One's Own

EMANUEL BERMAN, PH.D.

There are two possibly related biases that exist in the psychoanalytic clinical literature: one is the proclivity to write more
about successes than about failures; the other is that while analysts freely describe their work with their patients, they rarely
describe their own experiences as analysands.

The discussion of therapeutic failures, so it seems, is ban-
ished from the central ("high") professional discourse, and is
relegated to marginal discourse channels. One such channel
consists of informal oral discussions (common amongst therapists) about their own experiences as patients (Berman, 1995).
This form of discussion, which can be called "the reverse case
conference" (a professional version of the witches "sabbath"?)
is rarely public and seldom published (for notable exceptions
see Guntrip [1975]; Simon [1993]; Little [1990]; Lichtenberg, [1998]).

A second channel through which failures are explored are
the discussions by analysts of failures of *other* analysts and therapists, notably the former analysts of their patients. This discourse often becomes an exercise in scapegoating. As
evidenced by our professional rescue fantasies (Berman, 1993a,

1997), we are often prone to imagine ourselves as better parents than the patient's actual parents, and when we accept a patient into treatment who is unhappy with a former analysis, this naturally activates our competitiveness, and a determination to do better.

From my quite extensive experience of being the second (or third) analyst of patients, I have observed that my own transferential feelings toward their former analysts and therapists vary tremendously, irrespective of whether or not I personally know them. With some I experience an *imaginary alliance,* gratitude for helping my patient in the past, or identification vis-à-vis repeated difficulties; with some, *distance* (as their focuses appear so different from mine); and with others, *anger* because I feel that they were apparently destructive, and the present treatment has to deal with the posttraumatic impact of their work.

Naturally, I ask myself: How will future analysts of some of my patients experience me and my work? In this chapter I hope to overcome this tendency to externalize, and while I begin with the failures of others, I will conclude with an example of my own clinical failure.

When I took it upon myself to write this chapter, I was eager to start from the analysand's point of view. I published an announcement in Israeli professional journals and newsletters, asking colleagues to send me brief anonymous accounts of analyses or analytic therapies they went through, and which they experienced as failures. I deliberately chose a subjective definition of failure, not wishing to broach the complex issue of how we can operationally define a failure. I received only a few responses, which I will briefly summarize.

Several responses dealt with ethical transgressions and boundary violations. This, I am sure, is a major source of analytic failures. My interest for this chapter, however, is rather in those less sharply identifiable cases in which ethical rules are maintained and where the apparent failure had more subtle dynamics. Two respondents described experiences of feeling disliked by their analysts, of being seen as enormously disturbed, or of feeling harshly criticized ("No, you are wrong, I am not disappointed with you—I have known all along who I am dealing with"). One of them who couldn't tolerate being constantly told that she was being resistant, decided to leave, and was warned that discontinuation of the analysis would have dire consequences. "In retrospect," this colleague writes, "fleeing that analysis was the healthiest step I took in my life."

Another respondent described an analysis that fostered regression but did not equip her to function in life, leaving her deeply depressed and in need of antidepressive medication for the first time in her life. Two other respondents emphasized issues of rigidity. One wrote of a painful analysis with a candidate, who apparently felt very restricted by the expectations of the Institute, "needed a very particular analysand, not like me," and "saw any emotional support as an undesirable parameter." The other respondent described an analysis he underwent in his youth with an older senior analyst. He found out by chance that his analyst's wife was having an affair and brought this burdensome knowledge into the analysis. The analyst—who was apparently unable to deal with the analysand's experience—maintained a blank screen, and became "loudly silent" for some time. "Luckily, in later therapies . . . I was able or enabled to break out of these deathlike hours on the couch."

Freud appears to be one of those rare analysts who attempted to openly explore their own failures. I particularly think of his case study of "Dora," the pseudonym he gave his adolescent patient Ida Bauer (Freud, 1905). Freud's own exploration, in his Postscript, is interesting (discussing his inattention to Dora's transference) but appears very partial. For some years now, ever since I edited the Hebrew translation of the case, and surveyed the literature on it for my introduction (Berman, 1993b), I contemplated these questions: Why did Dora terminate her analysis so abruptly and one-sidedly? Why, when two years later she asked Freud to accept her back in treatment, did he turn her down, disbelieving her motives?

I find it striking to notice the extent that earlier generations of analysts revere this case, which today is painful for me to read. I am also fascinated by the turnabout, starting with the critical comments of Lacan (1952) and Wolstein (1954), and gaining momentum following Erikson's (1962) critique and emphasis on Freud's misunderstanding of Dora's adolescent quest for truth. During the past few decades, scores of analysts, historians, and feminist and literary scholars have tried, in fantasy, to undo Freud's failure and assume the position of Dora's next, more effective analyst. They have offered her the empathic understanding and mirroring (Ornstein, 1993), which her family never gave her, and which Freud appeared unable to mobilize.

Among the reasons that have been posited for Freud's inability to provide this have been his theoretical–polemical agenda (Mahony, 1996), and his conception of analytic technique at that time ("interpret at all costs"). Freud realized that Dora might have remained in treatment if he had shown a warm personal interest in her, but he rejects this option, calling it "acting a part." Finally, there existed countertransferential issues, which we can explore more fully with Freud than any other analyst, because biographical knowledge is now so extensive (Berman, in press).

I have come to view Dora and Freud as partners in a complex intersubjective encounter, in which Freud's countertransference is omnipresent. This countertransference, in the broadest sense of the term, includes sociocultural aspects such as conventional views of femininity typical of the period; that is, the male as the bearer of knowledge, having the sole power to penetrate women and to penetrate the text (Moi, 1981); and individual aspects such as the impact of Freud's childhood relationships with his mother and his nursemaid (Glenn, 1986). There were conscious levels, such as Freud's ambition to find support for his controversial theoretical views, and *unconscious levels,* such as his struggle with feminine identifications and homosexual urges (Hertz, 1983). There were permanent character traits, such as his tendency to come to authoritative conclusions (described by Marcus, 1975, as hubris, or chutzpah). There were specific reactions like his anger at Dora for depriving him of a full success, which may have later led to a vindictive rejection when she wanted to return. There were "concordant" identifications (Racker, 1968), which led to some of the more empathic interpretations (supporting Dora's view that she was being used as a trade-off to allow her father's affair with Frau K.), and "complimentary" identifications with the older men in her life, her father and Herr K. (Lacan, 1952), which eventually appear to have taken the upper hand. There were affective manifestations, such as Freud's open annoyance with Dora for turning down "attractive" Herr K., and cognitive manifestations such as Freud's consistent errors regarding the time of the analysis (reported as 1899, not 1900) and regarding Dora's age (making her older, making the sexual abuse by Herr K. appear less significant). There was direct countertransference to young and attractive Dora and "indirect" countertransference (Racker, 1968) influenced by Freud's relationship with Breuer (whose daughter was named Dora) and Fliess (to whom Freud reports—proudly at first—his progress with his young patient).

Was Dora's analysis a failure? While many authors are confident that it was, Decker (1991) reminds us that Freud at least listened to Dora, more than other physicians did, and was the first person to believe her stories, although he remained unempathic to her plight. Though truncated and faulty, the brief analysis helped her confront Herr and Frau K. with the truth of the deceptive reality created by them in conjunction with her parents, and subsequently allowed her to separate from her parents, get married, and become a mother.

Moreover, while Freud presents Dora through his own prism, he appears to allow her personality and voice enough presence, as a subtext (Mahony, 1996), to enable contemporary readers to form an identification with her, formulate their own original interpretations, and script alternative ways of treating her, thus fulfilling the powerful rescue fantasies her drama appears to arouse. Therefore we can conclude that with this case as with others, the definition of analytic failure cannot be too absolute.

I shall now turn to a more contemporary case: Betty Joseph's (1993) eight-year analysis of Dr. B. which she describes as ineffective. Before I discuss my critical observations, I must first say that I deeply respect Joseph's work. She has helped me contemplate and improve my work with "patients who are difficult to reach," and allowed me better contact with Kleinian theory, which was also in some older versions difficult to reach.

I have found enormously helpful her way of transforming general Kleinian insights into minute observations of the here-and-now of the transference, into rich descriptions of how the patient experiences him- or herself at a particular moment in the session, as well as the patient's experience of the analyst and the analytic relationship. I fully share her emphasis on striving to understand the total transferential situation, including its nonverbal layers and its impact on the analyst's emotions and actions, and her belief that only full experiencing can promote analytic progress.

And yet, when I was asked in 1994 to serve as a discussant of her paper on "nonresonance," I found myself quite concerned about a central aspect of it. Viewing resistance as a property of the patient alone may stop us from seeing how it may result from an interactive dyadic difficulty. Conceptualizing the negative therapeutic reaction as a result of the patient's ingrained problems may also cloud its possible sources in an intersubjective disjunction (Stolorow and Atwood, 1992). While Joseph's title refers to "nonresonance," her paper focused exclusively on the pathology of the nonresonating patient.

This focus may imply taking our own role and technique for granted, thus avoiding the possibility that the patient's nonresonance in some way reflects a difficulty we as analysts have in fully resonating with a patient, or a mismatch in our mutual expectations of the treatment. If we approach each patient with deeply held beliefs as to what constitutes effective analysis, what is real psychic change, and what are useful analytic interventions (the kind of confidence Freud felt while working with Dora), we run the risk of not taking seriously enough the signals from our patient that he or she needs something else, and finds our analytic style or interventions unhelpful.

Joseph suggests that nonresonance "can be approached from two angles, that are, of course, connected: that of technique (are we failing to reach our patients because of faulty handling of the case) or that of pathology (of the patient)" (1993, p. 311). This implies that the part played by the analyst can be differentiated into either "proper technique" or else "faulty handling." While the analyst's role is mentioned, the rest of the paper discusses the patient's pathology.

I find Racker's view (1968) more helpful:

The first distortion of truth in the "myth of the analytic situation" is that analysis is an interaction between a sick person and a healthy one. The truth is that it is an interaction between two personalities, in both of which the ego is under pressure from the Id, the Superego and the external world; each personality has its internal and external dependencies, anxieties and pathological defenses; each is also a child with his internal parents; and each of these whole personalities—that of the analysand and that of the analyst—responds to every event of the analytic situation [p. 132].

This perspective leads to the belief that technique is molded anew by each analyst with every patient, and its actual expressions, unavoidably colored by the analyst's personality and countertransference, keep fluctuating between being helpful, being destructive, and innumerable points in between. This applies to all kinds of interventions, supportive or interpretive, verbal or silent. Rather than striving to crystallize a "correct technique," we may be more effective if we keep listening to the indications of the actual impact of each intervention, and are free to consider our own possible contribution to its failure, if it indeed fails.

The equation unavoidably includes countertransference, which is not only influenced by the patient, but also influences him or her (transference as countercountertransference; Racker [1968]). When all manifestations of countertransference are interpreted as reactions to the patient's pathology, as they sometimes are in the Kleinian literature, it may signify that part of the puzzle is in sharp focus, while other parts remain more cloudy. Of course, I cannot discuss Joseph's specific countertransference toward Dr. B., respecting her privacy, and (unlike with Freud) having no biographical sources, but I take it for granted that it played a role in molding their joint intersubjective field, which evolved into a nonresonant field.

In discussing Dr. B., Joseph states: "something always prevented any real deep contact between my interpretations and my patient's mind" (1993, p. 317). She appears confident that this "something" resides solely in the patient, and would therefore appear in any analysis or analytic therapy with Dr. B. This may be so, but I find it questionable to take this for granted. If the kind of interpreting, undoubtedly helpful to other of Joseph's patients makes Dr. B. feel her "to be extremely insensitive, crude and forceful" (p. 318), I do not see this as necessarily either a pure projection or an "objective" and accurate assessment. It may be a complex amalgam of perceptions and projections, a partial and very subjective truth, which nevertheless testifies to the fact that the analytic style of this particular analyst "rubs" this particular patient "the wrong way."

When Joseph shows Dr. B. how he expects to be treated badly by her, he responds "as if [she] had said something disturbing or had not realized what [she] had done, and he would need to defend himself further" (p. 318). I am convinced that this reaction reflects his inner object world, but I am suggesting that it may additionally be influenced by his realistic awareness that his analyst considers his defensiveness as totally determined by his pathology, not giving any credence to the possibility that she may have inadvertently contributed to strengthening his "fears of being humiliated, criticized, made to feel guilty" (p. 318). This vicious circle may play a role in his tendency to have a "minor explosion of anger, irritation or some other feeling" (p. 318) in response to interpretations.

This viewpoint leads to a possible additional interpretation of a dream of Dr. B.'s. The analysand, while working as a doctor, pushed a man out of the door and down the stairs, then realized that the man was a cripple. He felt awful. While Dr. B. directly refers to himself, I wonder whether this could also be a reproach against the analyst, as the "doctor" who treats him roughly without the compassion he feels entitled to as an emotional cripple. This interpretation can be seen as an example of transference expressed in a disguised way through identification with the experienced attributes of the analyst (Gill, 1982).

This line of thought is indeed pursued by Joseph when she discusses the image of the owl in Dr. B.'s second dream, where an owl squirted liquid at the dreamer, and then sucked bubbles of air into the water in a tank. "Is it partly myself seen not really as a wise person, but seen in a narcissistic light? Is this partly a me with whom he is identified?'' Discussing the squirting of a liquid, which could be either milk or urine, she wonders, "Can this also be understood as an identification with an analyst who is felt to squirt analytic theories at him, in place of real understanding?'' (p. 322).

This courageous thought could perhaps be extended to the final part of the dream when "the owl seemed to suck bubbles of air into the water, and take them down, bubble by bubble, to its home, a kind of cardboard box at the bottom of the tank, so it had an independent place and supplied itself with air'' (p. 321). This might be viewed as a cruel caricature of the analyst's meticulous interpretations, gradually accumulated, and used to fortify a self-contained and isolated world of meanings, enjoyed by the analyst but depriving the patient of the fresh air he yearns for.

We do not know whether this aspect of the dream's possible meaning appeared in session. I need to emphasize, however, that mentioning it may still be seen as accusatory; that is, experienced as if the analyst is protesting a gross and unfounded distortion, proving the patient's pathology. "I give you good milk, and you spoil it and turn it into urine.'' In my view, a direct acknowledgment that the patient's complaints may have a grain of truth is needed at times to enable the analytic dyad to move out of an impasse. Such an acknowledgment may need to be expressed in active terms as well; for example, an attempt by the analyst to avoid the kinds of interventions that irritate the patient, to try a different style or focus of interpretations, and maybe even refrain from giving interpretations altogether, thus maintaining a patient and empathic atmosphere, awaiting the time when the patient could make their own interpretations.

Undoubtedly, Dr. B. was a very difficult patient, and I have no guarantee that my style of analysis would have been more effective. Possibly my way would have solved some of the difficulties described by Joseph, but created other equal or more serious ones. There are obviously potential risks in any analytic model, particularly if we take its accuracy and usefulness for granted.

I shall now consider a case where my own model of analytic practice may have backfired. I worked with my analysand for more than a year until she decided to discontinue the analysis. I was drawn to call her "Alice" here, consciously not knowing why, and only later recalled how she spoke eloquently of *Alice in Wonderland* where all the doors open up when Alice follows the rabbit. For reasons of confidentiality, I will omit biographical details, skipping many of the issues that came up in the analysis regarding her history and present life. Instead, I will focus here (chronologically, most of the time) on our evolving relationship: and I will add thoughts I had at the time of writing, which I will summarize toward the end of this paper.

In reviewing my notes, I recall how in the first session Alice was eager to move onto the couch, expressing a fantasy of a penetrating laser beam, which will save the need for a gradual peeling, layer by layer. She also spoke of her fear that my interpretations might be aggressive, and related this to a fear of her own aggression, which she tended to hide, letting it accumulate until it burst out (an early warning to which I did not sufficiently attend). She described a previous therapy in which her relationship with her therapist was not explored, leading to a sense of falseness; and she wondered why it is so easy for people to try to convince her that she is actually fine, and that her pain and anxieties were insignificant. I experienced her, during this first session, as likable and interesting and felt optimistic about the analysis.

In the second session she lay on the couch, telling me how conflicted she was about it. I had mentioned that it was customary to start with a few sessions face to face, and although I left her the choice, she was afraid that I would be angry at her if she lay down too soon. I commented that she was not sure I was honest with her about my feelings, and she said that if it was simply my personal wish, it did not belong here (I now realize how early she expressed the need to keep my personal feelings out of the analysis). Her associations went to her mother's violent outbursts, which used to subside instantly if an outsider rang the doorbell, since facades were very important for the family. I mentioned how little space for freedom and inner balance was left in between the outbursts and the facades.

(What I better understand in retrospect is her wish for an impersonal analyst, related to how frightening her mother was when she was "being personal.")

One session she entered the room running, and spoke of how she hates being late, feeling out of control, and leaving a crack through which I could see things that she doesn't see. She hates it when people come over unexpectedly, she added. I commented on the tension between her need to be taken care of, often frustrated in her childhood, and her need for control, one of her major survival strategies as a child. Soon afterwards she expressed her fear of "all the runners who started running inside her once she entered analysis," but also trust at my supplying a security net. With friends, she mentioned, she always maintains some distance, so as not to be swallowed up.

Recountings of various relationships, past and present, led me to say that she fluctuates between rage and total identification with the other, with difficulty in integrating these phases. She opened the following session by saying that I had spoken too much and had left her confused. When I responded by saying that apparently my pace had been too fast for her, she was surprised, being sure that I would tell her she was resisting the analysis. I noted her expectation that I would require an adjustment to my pace and style rather than striving to adjust to her. She then spoke of her fear of insulting me, as she insults her mother by constantly telling her that all she gives—including her customary makeup gifts—never fit. (In retrospect, was I busy subtly reassuring her I was not insulted, and missed the ominous signs that eventually she will tell me too that all I give doesn't fit her?) Subsequently, she connected her unease about my taking responsibility for confusing her, with her need for me to be perfect; she also expressed concern that she was becoming too intense, starting to unbearably analyze every word I uttered.

Meeting another of my analysands, whom she knew, outside my office, was experienced by her as painful. She spoke of a protective envelope that broke down when foreign experiences were introduced, a fear of boring me and a need to impress me. I raised the question as to whether these new elements were really foreign, or perhaps were present all along but cast aside. My question aroused shame and sadness: How could she be so dumb, denying these feelings? I commented that first she perfectionistically attempted to avoid "dirty" and petty feelings, and when they came to the surface she perfectionistically scolded herself for daring to deny them.

Her associations led to a memory from childhood: she was noisy and a neighbor threatened to tell her parents; she said she didn't mind, they would not punish her. Her mother then came out and contradicted her. She felt horribly shamed, "caught with her panties down." When I said she chose a metaphor of sexual humiliation, she was taken aback, but then agreed. (I now wonder: Was I too pushy and threatening with this sexual interpretation, the way Freud often was with Dora?) I emphasized her pain in her mother spoiling her confidence that her parents were on her side. She said that with many people she is not sure, and agreed with me when I added that there is a side of her that is not on her side, and I had a feeling that if I'll be too much on her side, she may turn against me.

Shortly afterwards she started a session by announcing that she had several complaints: I don't focus on her resistance and I let things go. Was I weak like her father? I noted that she appeared to assume that she was only trying to evade things, and only I could make her look at them. Perhaps, I wondered, she was conflicted between wishing to see and wishing to avoid? She responded by saying she needs me to be up, and herself to be down; I must be in a tall watchtower from which everything can be observed, even if this implies that the territory is fenced in. (In retrospect, once again, this was a clear expression of a value conflict between us. I have always been critical of hierarchical structures [Berman, 1998, 2000]. It should have alerted me to the danger that I might have been trying to make her accept my egalitarian values; lacking empathy for her deep need for a powerful guardian.)

Other themes that emerged during this period were her fear of being flooded if she knew too much about me, her turning me into a severe judge rather than an ally when describing her professional plans; the way in which analysis quickly shifted from a choice to a chore; and associations to her father as disconnected, confused, and untrustworthy as a protector. Still, before I left for my first vacation since I had been seeing her, she listed me as one of the good fathers she was able to find in her life.

After the vacation, however, she expressed humiliation at "having to buy empathy from me." When she brought up intense feelings of envy, and I wondered about their reference to us, she said that she did not envy me, because all I had could contribute to her development, but envy may still appear later in the treatment. She was hurt that I didn't congratulate her on a professional achievement, but had a difficult time expressing her disappointment, fearful that I would experience it as burdensome demandingness. In the following session she said she was reluctant to come, because my acceptance of her disappointment made her feel close to me. Exposing her neediness, she said, was so embarrassing. Soon afterwards she again criticized: she needs every session to be whole and perfect in itself. (I brought up her perfectionism, a reaction that in hindsight appears to me as defensive.)

She wanted someone who could meet her needs accurately, Alice continued in the next session; explanations or subsequent corrections were no good. Later on, she mentioned her fear that I accepted her exaggerated reactions to her parents too easily, and maybe others helped her more by telling her not to take things to heart. She was afraid of being swallowed up by the world of analysis, which signified seriousness and dedication, but also being spoiled, endlessly discussing every emotional nuance.

When I noted, earlier on, that she had not reported any dreams, it turned out that she was writing them down meticulously, but did not feel secure enough to bring up material she did not fully understand. She mentioned at a later time, in passing, that after I brought up the question (prematurely, I now feel), she stopped remembering her dreams.

The first dream she did report, several months into the analysis, involved someone she knew being a sect member and committing suicide by making cuts along his body. In addition to her associations related to this person and his relationship to her family, which I shall skip, I raised my association of her tendency "to cut herself." She asked me if the dream, then, was about self-castration, and when I commented to her wish for a definitive bottom line, she said that this wish is in itself a form of castration. In the next session she voiced her disappointment with the incomplete interpretation, experienced as either her failure or mine, even if cognitively she knew better. Due to her intense anxiety about opening up, expressed by her either suppressing or repressing her dreams, bringing this dream into analysis was a courageous step, perhaps an acknowledgment of her terror that the "cuts" required by the analytic "sect" could kill her. (I wonder how I could have prevented this step from "turning sour" for her. Was talking of her need for a definitive bottom line too hurtful?)

Once again Alice met my other analysand, the one she knew, this time at my door, because I uncharacteristically failed to notice that the other patient's session went beyond its scheduled time. (The slip, I believe, was related to the dynamics of the other analysis, but it made me feel guilty toward Alice.) When, toward the end of the session, I mentioned her avoidance of discussing this encounter, she angrily said that she didn't feel like discussing the event just because it was expected of her. There was a power struggle between us, she added, as to who would raise it first. In the next session, she expressed anger at me for not protecting her, a fear that I favored the other analysand, and a feeling that an immediate reaction would have allowed me to sidetrack her hurt by working on the event's significance. She wasn't sure I could do anything to make the situation better; apologizing could also be a defense against her anger. She later said that this meeting led her to be anxious that she was marginal for me, and aroused a concern that if she fell silent, which she never did, my thoughts would float away from her.

On one occasion, she requested a shift for a particular session to an earlier hour, but then failed to show up. It crossed my mind that she might have forgotten the change, and might show up at her regular hour, which I had already filled. So I called her, and it turned out that she had indeed forgotten. A week later, she brought up my call as a confusing boundary violation, "bursting the bubble," as equivalent to allowing her to meet the other analysand at my door, or to my still being on the phone when she came in on another occasion. She would have preferred to have come at the usual hour and be sent away, she said; my call strengthened her guilt for forgetting. She needs the analysis to be conducted in sterile conditions, she added. (I made an effort to be empathic with her needs, but thinking about it now, I see that her reaction irritated me. Having to send her away would have been most unpleasant for me, and I experienced her preference as both masochistic and coercive; trying to turn me into a rigid formal person, which I never was and do not wish to become.) She later said that it was a relief that I wasn't intimidated by her anger, and did not surrender to her pressure.

When I spoke of times when I had inadvertently hurt her, and my need to know about them so as to better understand her experience and take it into account, she heard me as saying that she is problematic and in need of special consideration. She would prefer an analyst who could foresee her sensitivities, see them as universal, and not unique to her. I interpreted her repeated fear of being scolded for her sensitivity and neediness. Alice started weeping, saying that it was so difficult to cry while lying down, so painful to consider that being humiliated may have been her fantasy (and not my intention). (I felt very warmly toward her during that session, after a period of relative distance.)

The following time she said that it was difficult for her to come. We became close, and my empathy aroused erotic feelings in her. In general she found sexual themes quite embarrassing to discuss with me. Her ambivalent attitude toward male sexuality came up very hesitantly, later on, and she laughed and agreed when I said she responds to my encouragement to discuss sexuality as a threatening masculine penetration in itself, or as a form of voyeurism. She associated to her father's insistence on washing her hair until she had to ask him to stop during her early adolescence.

Alice reported a dream, in which she found a stone or a rock in a house similar to her childhood home; I appeared in the dream and said that I also wanted a stone, but then called her by the name of her friend rather than her name. When I discussed the fluctuations of closeness and distance between us, and pointed to a possible feeling that I needed something from her, she brought up her fear of taking too much from me and losing her separate identity. Later, she described the domineering aspect of her mother's needs, and I related her suspiciousness toward her mother to the way she experiences me.

Once more, Alice expressed disappointment: the benefits of analysis are not clear, she hasn't changed much. She again brought up fears of boring me, relating them to her parents' impatience, their self-absorbed difficulty in listening to her. She also mentioned things she had to discover for herself as a child due to the negligence of her parents; for example, she learned from reading a book that it is advisable to wash every day. I related this to her difficulty in internalizing anything from relationships, including the one with me. I mentioned her preference to come at the wrong hour and discover on her own that she had forgotten the change, rather than get a phone call from me. Alice added that at times her parents were also intrusive. (While I consciously felt empathic with her, in retrospect I notice an aggressive element in my interpretation, as if I were telling her, "You see, it's your problem after all"; and her response can be understood in this context to mean "You may not be neglectful like my parents were, but you do remind me of them in your intrusiveness.")

In the following session she said that she had felt remote when we had discussed her self-sufficiency. I suggested that she is quite conflicted about achieving greater intimacy with people and she emphatically responded that she doesn't want to be helpless and dependent. (Again I now notice how fearful she was about some goals that I consider central to analysis, such as a better capacity for intimacy.)

After another break in the treatment due to my vacation, Alice again recalled times when she had felt hurt or misunderstood by me. My repeated emphasis on analysis as a continuous process of disappointments and reparations is difficult for her, she added, because of her wish for a perfect, omniscient analyst, and due to her doubt that I could even care about her.

(Here she literally disarmed me. I feel that caring and a capacity for reparation are among my best qualities as an analyst, while various shortcomings I am aware of stop me from making any claim of perfection.) Later on I brought up her constant fear of the analysis unsettling her long-established survival strategies, which she had experienced as vital while growing up; she felt that this was indeed so.

I also pointed out passive–aggressive elements in her manner of dealing with me, the combination of feeling weak, "playing dumb" at times, watching to see if I'll notice things—coming late and testing me, will I respond, for example—while inwardly knowing exactly what I should have done. (This interpretation, I now see, also expressed my frustration and anger at her growing criticisms; I described the pattern accurately, but I was not empathic to its possible sources, such as distrust that I would really take care of her, leading her to secretly take control, in spite of her yearning to be childlike and passive and allow me to "parent" her.)

Issues of envy and competition, of loaded triangles, came up in many contexts, as well as her mentioning the complaints of many people about her angry outbursts. She spoke of her wish to have everything inside her, and of her despair when she realized this was not so.

At that point the analysis had to be conducted erratically due to an emergency situation in Alice's family. Our few sessions were devoted to her experience of that emergency and all its vicissitudes. From my point of view, I was quite empathically involved. At a fateful point in that process, I became aware of a sadness that she didn't phone me to bring me up to date on the situation, which I had mentioned was an option. I was identified with her anxiety and felt that she had rejected that identification. Later, she mentioned that she had no need to call me at the time, and calling because of my need appeared to her as too submissive.

When the crisis was over, the issue of payment for missed sessions came up. Our agreement all along was that she would pay 50 percent for sessions canceled in advance. After much hesitation I decided to apply this principle to the period in question, though a bit more liberally. (I charged 50 percent also for sessions canceled at the last moment or missed, which usually would have required a full payment.) Alice, however, felt I was being rigid. She was disappointed that I wasn't more generous, that I didn't tell her that she need not pay at all for sessions missed during that difficult period, a desire that part of me could identify with.

After much hesitation, and a fear of being petty, she brought up her disappointment that when she goes to the bathroom before her session starts, I do not wait for her in the consulting room, but wait in my adjoining study (this has been a habit of mine for years, and prior to her complaint I never gave it much thought). Is it a proof of my lack of investment in her, reminiscent of her mother's forgetfulness of her friends' names? Is the need to bring up such things a bad sign in itself, she wondered? I again spoke of her wish for a smooth fit without words, of her impatience, evident outside the analysis as well, with the process of building up a better relationship by identifying and verbalizing the unavoidable points of poor fit.

Subsequently, I decided to wait for her in the consulting room. When it first happened, she smiled; later on, however, she returned to the inevitable: whether my changing my habit for her was a sign of weakness. She would have felt better if I had waited for her in the consulting room for my own reasons, not out of consideration for her.

There were numerous tensions with her parents, and Alice insisted that her refusal to contain their madness is what allowed her to maintain her own sanity. She mentioned her feeling that her parents drove her crazy by denying things that she perceived. A session in which she complained bitterly about various family members left me relatively silent, and in the following session she bitterly complained about me, not responding to my attempts to figure out better what had happened between us.

Alice needed to take a leave from analysis for a while, and once more she protested that paying 50 percent for those hours was unfair, unreasonable, enslaving rather than liberating. Still, she said, she knew I wouldn't budge. Recalling my guilt on the previous occasion when this became an issue (and probably also trying to fight her projection onto me of her rigid super-ego), I said I was willing to discuss the matter anew. (I wrote in my notebook that she sounded relieved, which with hindsight I now find ironic; was it my projection, or part of her fluctuations, a result of her unresolved conflict?)

She brought up the topic again in the first session after her leave, while announcing that she wished to end the analysis, and preferred to pay me in full as compensation. Anyhow, she added, she never asked for a change in the financial arrangement between us, it was my need to reconsider it. She said that I have a tendency for concrete solutions (e.g., calling her when she forgot the session, waiting for her in the consulting room when she felt hurt by my waiting in my study), which narrowed down her space.

I shared with Alice my feeling that my own needs might indeed have influenced me in ways that became confusing for her, but I might also have been responding to unresolved conflicts of hers—her rage at my rigidity, her fear and guilt vis-à-vis my flexibility/weakness—which combine to create a situation of "damned if you do and damned if you don't." Understanding this cycle, I suggested, may be a crucial part of our analytic work. To this she reacted by saying that she didn't wish to treat me so that I could treat her.

Alice added that I seemed enamored with my flexibility, and that she was afraid that I was more invested in my ideological "baby" than in her needs as a baby. This was damaging to her basic needs, so the issue was not individual fine tuning, as I believed. The session ended with a heaviness that filled the room.

We continued the dialogue, with her elaborating her fear that I was working with her as a parent-friend dealing with an adolescent, while she experienced herself as much younger. I suggested that she was afraid that I would reject her if she failed in the role I offered her and expressed her more infantile needs. When I pointed out that her way of portraying me was quite bleak, she felt accused, and associated to her mother's accusations. I suggested that we had reached the most crucial stage in the analysis, in which the rage and bitterness she used to describe in other relationships actually was being experienced in the room, and while this was enormously painful, it could also become a springboard for deeper work and eventually for change. She said she was happy that we finally saw things eye to eye, but soon expressed annoyance that I offered hope while she was still enraged, and said that a new beginning was more appealing to her. (Maybe she was also unhappy with my—defensive?—implication that the issue was *her* rage and bitterness?)

Shortly afterwards, Alice decided to terminate, and suggested we meet one more time. I interpreted that she was afraid to stay in the room with me after being aggressive toward me, and she confirmed this.

After some discussion, she accepted my preference to meet for two more months. We decided that she would pay fully the agreed-upon 50 percent for the period of her leave, and she said that this was a relief, as my trying to meet her halfway always made it hard for her, blocking her aggression. In childhood, she recalled, her father's "rigid" compulsive rules saved her from chaos. In this context, she experienced my insistence on a termination period as helpful. Still, she feared I would seduce her to stay, or she would regret her decision, but felt relieved that I didn't sound vindictive.

Among the themes that appeared during the termination phase were her tendency to devalue others and to disconnect inwardly, to enable her to separate; her need to depart triumphantly, while actually feeling small inside; her realization that her protests about our financial arrangement expressed a pretense of adulthood, and my willingness to discuss it "between adults" meant for her that I fell into a trap; her reluctance to acknowledge her mother's craziness because this meant giving mother "allowances," and her fear that when I tried to show her how she often provoked her mother to retraumatize her, this implied justifying mother, or else once more asking her to be grown up, as daddy always did, and "understand" that mom was so vulnerable.

In one of the more moving sessions, Alice spoke of her mother, who for years had been practically absent from family life, due to her professional aspirations, until she suddenly "returned home" as a result of a physical and emotional breakdown. Mother then wanted to become close to Alice, but Alice couldn't meet this need, having given up on her, unable to forgive her betrayal, and being by then more invested in her peers. I related her pain during her mother's absence with her fear that I was more committed to my professional values than to her "baby needs"; and her reluctance to become newly involved with mother, to her disbelief in reparation between us, possibly colored by a suspicion that I was still motivated by my own needs, such as protecting my self-image and reputation.

Following that session, Alice said that I had touched her the way she needed and paradoxically this made it easier to leave, knowing that she did get something here, and better understanding what went wrong. Toward the end she became quite remote, saying that she experienced no sadness. She felt more invested in a potential new analysis in the future; reparation, she commented, carries with it the rupture. I spoke of her fantasy wish for a relationship without ruptures. We parted in a guardedly friendly manner.

Writing up this analysis has been a painful experience for me. Overall, I experience it as a failure, even though I believe it still may prove to have some value for Alice. It is indeed easier to explore the failures of others. Again and again I have felt annoyed with myself for not doing better with this patient.

I can well imagine analyzing this failure with an emphasis on Alice's pathology. It would not be wrong. Her fear of intimacy, her castrating attitude toward me, her clinging to defensive structures ("character armor"), her punitive superego, her fluctuation between seemingly submissive passive-aggression and rageful outbursts, her need to control me and make me fit exactly her expectations, her fantasy of a seamless, perfect relationship, her impatience with having to negotiate her needs with the other (Mitchell, 1991), her distrust of reparation, her impulse to abandon me triumphantly—all these were present.

And yet, I believe she may be more successful with another analyst, not only because she will benefit from the lessons of this first analysis (toward the end we talked of it as having been a "dress rehearsal"), but because the fit with another character style and another analytic style may work better for her.

I could also well imagine analyzing this failure in terms of the shortcomings of my analytic technique. I am sure a more classical analyst could easily find fault with many of my interventions, and agree with Alice fully that my attempts to accommodate her were often counterproductive, not leaving enough room for fuller intrapsychic exploration. As a matter of fact, with hindsight I think so myself when I review some episodes. But a polemical emphasis on the universal advantages of a different analytic technique, would miss three points;

1. Some more classical analysts fail due to their refusal to make any accommodations to frame and rules. I personally know colleagues who angrily left analysis due to disputes about paying for canceled sessions, for example; my query to colleagues cited at the beginning of this chapter, elicited similar responses.
2. With some other analysands, interventions similar to those that backfired with Alice have been very effective. For example, my insistence "to remain myself" not yielding to pressure to be rigidly rule-bound, was effective in achieving a softening of persecutory superego forces with some analysands, while it was ineffective (and possibly destructive) with Alice.
3. Some of my reactions (e.g., interpretations sharply focusing on her pathology) were unique to my work with Alice, and must therefore be related to specific transference–countertransference patterns.

In other words, I view the failure of my work with Alice neither as her personal failure, nor as my own (personal or theoretical) failure; but as *a failure of the two of us as a team, based on a transference–countertransference entanglement which we did not manage to disentangle early enough.* In this respect, I want to think of it along the same lines as Freud's failure with Dora, and Joseph's failure with Dr. B.

What was my countertransference in this analysis? I was quite fond of Alice all along, even though at times I felt hurt by her

or mad at her (or, as a colleague suggested, mad by her . . .).
Yet, from early on, I experienced us as enormously different.
Contemplating this experience now, I have reached the conclusion that I must discuss some details of my own childhood,
something that I did not plan to do when I started writing
this chapter.

The gist of the matter is this: I had reasons to identify with
some of Alice's biographical background, but our solutions to
our childhood traumas were almost entirely opposite. I suspect
this variance took its toll on my ability to be empathically attuned to her.

For example, like Alice, I also grew up with a very disturbed
parent, my stepmother. My father also frequently begged of
me to understand her vulnerability and forgive her excesses.
However, unlike Alice, what helped me keep my sanity was
accepting his wish, rarely confronting my stepmother, disiden-
tifying with her by fully acknowledging her craziness, and learning to avoid painful clashes by understanding and predicting
her behavior. I assume this was easier for me because she was
not my biological mother, and I had an internalized sane
mother to hold onto.

Another major difference between Alice's childhood and my
own was that in my family, unlike hers, the compulsive parent—in terms of demands toward me for "law and order"—was
also the crazier one, while my father was generally quite permis-
sive. It is not surprising that Alice identifies strict authority with
sanity, while for me it is usually something negative. My father
did treat me as a grown-up from early on, and unlike Alice I
liked this attitude and it undoubtedly contributed to my rebel-
liousness whenever I felt infantilized (in high school, in the
army, or during my analytic training; Berman [1998, 2000]).

Two other differences between my history and Alice's need
mentioning. The early death of my mother mobilized within
me an early need to be grown-up, and while my own two analyses were helpful in many ways, I was never too regressed in
either of them. In spite of my awareness that for some people
regression in analysis is quite crucial, and my conscious eagerness to make it possible when needed, I realize that this does
not "come naturally" for me. The risk of not allowing enough

regression to develop due to my relational emphasis on mutual influences has come up with some other analysands as well. Fortunately, in these other analyses it has been worked through more effectively.

As a child I was not too social. Establishing intimate ties with others was a major achievement of my adolescence, and has been paramount for me ever since. With this history, I found it difficult to identify with Alice's struggle not to become open and intimate and her seeing this as a potential source of humiliation and loss of control.

I was not sufficiently aware of the impact of these issues in the earlier phases of my work with Alice, and I now regret not seeking consultation at the time. I now realize that when I offered her "adult to adult" contact, for me it brought up a supportive respectful father, while for her it was a disappointing father, not allowing her to remain a child, and trying to get her to forgive her destructive mother with whom he was aligned. (My father, I always knew, was more deeply aligned with me than with his wife.) On the other hand, my expression of personal feelings led her to identify me with her mother's lack of boundaries. In sum, both of these transferential aspects were negative for her.

Alice was correct in sensing my commitment to certain values, to my "ideological babies." Being involved in the development of relational and intersubjective models in psychoanalysis during the past decade has been a source of excitement for me. Nevertheless, she was mistaken in her fear that I therefore cared less about her personally. A more accurate formulation would be that my commitment to egalitarian models of treatment (which, as must be evident, is rooted in my life history), as well as my own excitement about openness and intimacy, may have led me to be too confident that my caring for her would be best expressed through helping her reduce her rigidity and need for control, become less dominated by her punitive superego, and allow her a freer personal and intimate involvement with myself and others.

In this respect, I may have tried to mold *our* analytic goals in *my* own direction, not sufficiently taking to heart her protests that these were not *her* goals. A power struggle evolved with each of us forcefully attempting to bring the other to a particular emotional position. Alice, in some ways, "became the crazy mother" in the transference, but I couldn't stay with her in that regressive "crazy" world patiently enough, and found myself clawing my way out, offering her my solutions, which she couldn't use. Not "going mad" together, we could not survive together.

Alice correctly perceived my reluctance to assume the role of a perfectly containing guardian, an ideal father-mother for whom she yearned. It is also true that she often undermined and sabotaged my authority, but I may have overreacted to these aggressive sides of her, losing contact in turn with the desperately needy regressive wishes clouded by them. We locked each other out.

I feel considerable responsibility for the development of this process, though the way Alice expressed her distrust of interpersonal negotiations and of reparation also played an important role in our inability to eventually put our budding awareness of this transference–countertransference entanglement to constructive use, and to reach a different phase in our joint endeavor.

References

Berman, E. (1993a), Psychoanalysis, rescue and utopia. *Utopian Studies*, 4:44–56.

———— (1993b), Dora and Freud: Another reading. Introduction. In: *Freud and Dora*, ed. E. Berman. Tel Aviv: Am Oved, pp. 7–30.

———— (1995), On analyzing colleagues. *Contemp. Psychoanal.*, 31:521–539.

———— (1997), Hitchcock's *Vertigo:* The collapse of a rescue fantasy. *Internat. J. Psycho-Anal.*, 78:975–996.

———— (1998), Structure and individuality in psychoanalytic training. The Israeli controversial discussions. *Amer. J. Psychoanal.*, 58:117–133.

———— (2000), The utopian fantasy of a New Person and the danger of a false analytic self. *Psychoanal. Psych.*, 17(1):38–60.

———— (in press), Dora. In: *The Freud Encyclopedia*, ed. E. Erwin. New York: Garland.

Decker, H. (1991), *Freud, Dora and Vienna 1900*. New York: Free Press.

Erikson, E. H. (1962), Reality and actuality: An address. *J. Amer. Psychoanal. Assn.*, 10:451–474.

Freud, S. (1905), Fragment of an analysis of a case of hysteria. *Standard Edition*, 7:1–122. London: Hogarth Press, 1953.

Gill, M. M. (1982), *Analysis of Transference*. New York: International Universities Press.

Glenn, J. (1986), Freud, Dora and the maid: A study of countertransference. *J. Amer. Psychoanal. Assn.*, 34:591–606.

Guntrip, H. (1975), My experience of analysis with Fairbairn and Winnicott. *Internat. Rev. Psycho-Anal.*, 2:145–156.

Hertz, N. (1983), Dora's secrets, Freud's techniques. *Diacritics*, Spring:65–76.

Joseph, B. (1993), A factor militating against psychic change. Nonresonance. In: *Psychic Structure and Psychic Change*, ed. M. J. Horowitz, O. F. Kernberg, & E. M. Weinschel. Madison, CT: International Universities Press, pp. 311–325.

Lacan, J. (1952), Intervention on transference. In: *Feminine Sexuality*, ed. J. Mitchell & J. Rose. New York: W. W. Norton, 1983.

Lichtenberg, J. D. (1998), Experience as a guide to psychoanalytic theory and practice. *J. Amer. Psychoanal. Assn.*, 46:17–36.

Little, M. (1990), *Psychotic Anxieties and Containment*. Northvale, NJ: Jason Aronson.

Mahony, P. J. (1996), *Freud's Dora*. New Haven, CT: Yale University Press.

Marcus, S. (1975), Freud and Dora: Story, history, case history. In: *In Dora's Case*, ed. G. Bernheimer & C. Kahane. New York: Columbia University Press, 1985, pp. 56–91.

Mitchell, S. A. (1991), Wishes, needs, and interpersonal negotiations. *Psychoanal. Inq.*, 11:147–170.

Moi, T. (1981), Representation of patriarchy: Sexuality and epistemology in Freud's Dora. *Feminist Rev.*, 9:60–73.

Ornstein, P. H. (1993), Did Freud understand Dora? In: *Freud's Case Studies: Self-Psychological Perspectives*, ed. B. Magid. Hillsdale, NJ: Analytic Press, pp. 31–85.

Racker, H. (1968), *Transference and Countertransference*. London: Maresfield, 1982.

Simon, B. (1993), In search of psychoanalytic technique: Perspectives from the couch and from behind the couch. *J. Amer. Psychoanal. Assn.*, 41:1051–1082.

Stolorow, R. D., & Atwood, G. E. (1992), *Contexts of Being*. Hillsdale, NJ: Analytic Press.

Wolstein, B. (1954), *Transference: Its Meaning and Formation in Psychoanalytic Therapy*. New York: Grune & Stratton.

Name Index

Subject Index

www.ingramcontent.com/pod-product-compliance
Lightning Source LLC
Chambersburg PA
CBHW051712020426
42333CB00014B/947